Praise for previous editions of

North Carolina
Off the Beaten Path®

"Includes tips on best places to eat and sleep, little-known gems, and how to bypass the tourist traps."

— *The Salisbury Post* (NC)

"Fascinating reading . . . a melange of sites, restaurants, lodgings, and directions leading to the author['s] personal choices. Lovingly written . . . enthusiastically testif[ies] to the old notion about seeing America first."

— *Booklist,* American Library Association

"Reveals features [that] will attract even those who had not planned on ever visiting the state. When they do, this will be the handbook to choose."

— *Midwest Book Review*

"The off-the-beaten-path traveler is assured of enjoying these discoveries as much as the author did."

— *Bookpage*

"Ms. Pitzer writes with enthusiasm and knowledge. When she says someplace is worth visiting, you can count on it."

— *The State* (Columbia, SC)

"When you're accompanied by *North Carolina: Off the Beaten Path,* it's like having your own personal tour guide."

— *Southern Living*

Help Us Keep This Guide Up-to-Date

Every effort has been made by the author and editors to make this guide as accurate and useful as possible. However, many things can change after a guide is published—establishments close, phone numbers change, hiking trails are rerouted, facilities come under new management, etc.

We would love to hear from you concerning your experiences with this guide and how you feel it could be made better and be kept up-to-date. While we may not be able to respond to all comments and suggestions, we'll take them to heart, and we'll also make certain to share them with the author. Please send your comments and suggestions to the following address:

The Globe Pequot Press
Reader Response/Editorial Department
P.O. Box 480
Guilford, CT 06437

Or you may e-mail us at:
editorial@globe-pequot.com

Thanks for your input, and happy travels!

OFF THE BEATEN PATH® SERIES

North Carolina

FIFTH EDITION

by Sara Pitzer

The Globe Pequot Press

Guilford, Connecticut

Off the Beaten Path is a registered trademark of The Globe Pequot Press.

Cover and text design: Laura Augustine
Cover photo: Randy Taylor/Index Stock
Maps created by Equator Graphics © The Globe Pequot Press
Illustrations by Carole Drong

Library of Congress Cataloging-in-Publication Data

Pitzer, Sara.
        North Carolina : off the beaten path / Sara Pitzer.—5th ed.
          p. cm. — (Off the beaten path series)
        Includes index.
        ISBN 0-7627-0818-2
        1. North Carolina—Guidebooks.   I. Title.   II. Series.

  F252.3 .P58 2000
  917.5604'44—dc21   00-061040

Manufactured in the United States of America
Fifth Edition/First Printing

This is for Judy.
She gave me a house, so I'm giving her a book.
I really needed a house.
I don't think Judy needs a book,
but it's the best I can do.

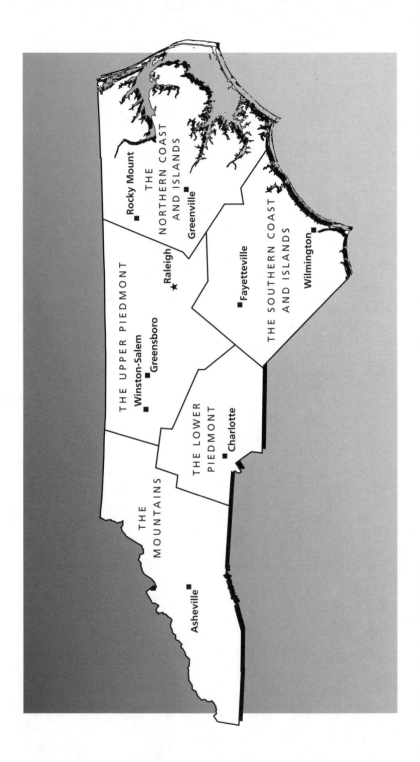

Contents

Acknowledgments

Many of the photographs from which the drawings in this book were made were provided by the North Carolina Division of Travel and Tourism.

Introduction

I was lost—again—somewhere around Raleigh, but nowhere near the place I wanted to be. I'd already pulled into the entrance of a large industrial park, where an executive stopped on his way out to ask if he could help me. I'd already walked along the sidewalk in front of North Carolina State University, where a professor leaving campus gave me detailed instructions on getting out of the city in the direction I wanted to go. And I was pretty sure I was going to get it right, if I could just find the beltway. Seeing that the car in the next lane had both windows down as we waited for a light to turn, I called across to the driver, "Is this road going to take me to the beltway?"

"Where do you want to go?" he yelled back. I told him. "Follow me," he shouted, and when the light changed, took off in a cloud of exhaust. I followed him nearly 10 miles. At the proper entrance onto the beltway, he blinked his turn signal and also pointed emphatically with his left hand, just in case I missed the signal. I turned. He was already gone, leaving me with a grin and a wave.

And that's how people in North Carolina are.

For me, living in North Carolina is no accident of birth or whim of corporate transfer; it's a studied choice. When my husband and I decided that we should both work freelance, it meant that we could live pretty much wherever we wanted to. We spent the better part of a year looking for a place where the topography was appealing, the climate was sunny and temperate, the economy was thriving, and the people were nice. We found North Carolina.

In the years since we moved here in 1983, life has been one joyful discovery about the state after another. Indeed, sometimes it seems too good to believe. Many mornings I wake up thinking: Today's the day I'm going to be disappointed. But I never am.

In 1993 my husband Croy died of ALS (Lou Gehrig's Disease). In a way it was the happiest year of his life. Although his body deteriorated, his mind did not, so he knew and understood every day the remarkable friendship and love that our North Carolina friends, neighbors, and business associates showered upon him without restraint. The last photograph ever taken of Croy, a week before he died, shows him sitting by our pool in the sun at the edge of the woods, surrounded by his friends. The sky was Carolina blue, the people were joking, and everybody, including Croy, was laughing. He often said, "This is the most wonderful place on earth." And that day, after sharing a decade of discoveries in North Carolina, we knew it was true more than ever.

I'm making the discoveries on my own now. It tells you a lot about North Carolina that there are still lots of laughing friends around and that the experience continues to delight me. I know you'll enjoy my discoveries, too.

Take the barbecue, for instance. Two authors writing an article on southern barbecue for *Cook's* magazine traveled through several states looking for the best barbecue restaurants, but they were not able to get to North Carolina. They apologized in their article, because, they said, in comparison, nothing else is barbecue at all. (North Carolina barbecue is always pork cooked over a wood fire, never prepared in a sauce, and usually served with slaw and hush puppies.)

Then there's the pottery. This state has scores and scores of potters, working in the historic old production styles and in contemporary studio modes, producing such a variety of work that a collection could easily crowd everything else from a room.

As for topography, North Carolina has some of the oldest mountains in the world, the largest natural sand dune on the East Coast, and some of the most unspoiled beaches and islands in the country. The rich soil of the Piedmont and foothills grows apples, vegetables, Christmas trees, cotton, and tobacco, a problematic crop with much historic significance.

Also historically important, North Carolina, one of the thirteen original colonies, played key roles in the Revolutionary War, the Civil War, and World Wars I and II. The area is rich in Indian history; blacks made many early significant advances here; and the Moravians created a historic settlement at Old Salem. The Wright brothers first accomplished powered flight in North Carolina, on a site that is popular today with hang gliders more interested in playing than in setting records.

Each of the three major geographic areas of the state—the coastal plain, the Piedmont, and the mountains—differs radically from the others. It's almost like traveling through three smaller states. The nature of each region influenced the kinds of commerce that flourished historically and continue to flourish, and also left a mark on the people. As you travel you'll hear fascinating changes in the music of the accents of people native to each region.

The coastal plain accounts for almost two-fifths of the state's area. The North Carolina coast has been considered dangerous since the first settlers tried to cope with its ever-changing beaches, currents, and waterways. There was no guarantee that just because you had safely sailed into a particular port once, you would find it safe, or even open, the next time you tried. That's at least one reason why English colonization shifted up toward the Chesapeake and why North Carolina was settled more sparsely and slowly than some other colonies were. Even today you'll find areas that are remarkably sparsely settled compared to most states' coastal regions. For vacationers the main activities and sightseeing highlights are related to the same activities that have long supported the area economically—fishing, boating, and beachgoing.

In the Piedmont, which makes up about another two-fifths of the state, you'll find mostly rolling hills and red clay. Although the clay is harder to work than the sandy soil of the coast, it seems to have held its fertility better against some pretty bad early farming habits. (Wherever they are grown, cotton and tobacco are notorious for wearing out the soil.) Since the Piedmont doesn't have many large stretches of flat land, it didn't invite the huge plantations that had to be worked with many slaves. Smaller family farms were often worked by the people who owned them, perhaps with some hired help. The historians Hugh Talmage Lefler and Albert Ray Newsome point out in their classic *The History of a State: North Carolina* that the narrow, swift streams of the Piedmont, which weren't worth much for transportation, were great for generating power. And that, along with the presence of hardwoods and other resources, accounts for the great number of manufacturing activities that flourish in the Piedmont. Here you find lots of attractions related to manufacturing—tobacco museums, furniture showrooms, and more outlet stores than you can count. Probably because of the past concentration of moneyed manufacturers and merchants, you'll also find rich lodes of cultural attractions and arts here.

The mountains make up the smallest part of the state, but they compensate in interest and beauty for what they lack in area. Some of the highest mountains in the Appalachians are here. As anyone who drives in the mountains knows, transportation is difficult. In earlier times it was nearly impossible; hence the development of small pockets of civilization separated by stretches of wilderness, creating those tough, independent, resourceful, self-sufficient folks—mountain people. This kind of early self-sufficiency and distance from major metropolitan areas made the growth of all kinds of crafts almost inevitable. The mountains are still the richest source of handcrafts in the state.

Although tourism and technology have homogenized somewhat the state's regional populations, you can still find lots of those tall, thin, rangy people. It remains a pretty good joke in the Piedmont for a young woman marrying outside the area to claim she's found herself a mountain man.

Of course, today the immigration of Yankees from "up north" and considerable growth mean that every region has its share of developers, builders, and real estate people. These activities, however, tend to be clustered mostly around the major cities and a few popular mountain and beach resort areas. There are still lots of places off the beaten path to go for fun.

As a place to play, the state offers hiking and white-water rafting, waterskiing and snow skiing, freshwater and saltwater fishing and boating, athletics, auto racing, horseback riding, and golf on some of the most famous courses in the country.

Face it, you're not going to be able to do it all or see it all in one trip, or even in ten trips. Don't try to squeeze too much into a single trip, or you'll end up driving a lot and not doing much else. But the driving you do shouldn't be unpleasant if you avoid the interstates around major cities at rush hour and accept the fact that the two-lane roads tend to be well maintained but slow, since there are few good places for passing slow drivers and tractors. To understand the roads and decide when to travel on a major highway and when to get onto secondary roads, you'll definitely need a state map. The best one is the North Carolina transportation map, issued by the North Carolina Department of Transportation and the Division of Travel and Tourism (800–847–4862). You may pick one up free at a welcome center or receive it by writing North Carolina Division of Travel and Tourism, 430 North Salisbury Street, Raleigh 27611.

If you or those traveling with you are in any way physically challenged, you should also request a copy of the book *Access, North Carolina*. This is a remarkably good book published by the North Carolina Department of Human Resources, the Division of Vocational Rehabilitation Services, and the Division of Travel and Tourism. It briefly describes historic sites, state and national parks and forests, and general-interest attractions, focusing on their accessibility of parking, entrance, interior rooms, exterior areas, and rest rooms. The book is free. Call the aforementioned tourism number or check the Web site: www.ncnatural.com/access-nc/.

A state with so many resources inevitably becomes the subject of many books. Depending on your interests, you may find several of them interesting to use along with this guide. The University of North Carolina Press publishes *Turners and Burners: The Folk Potters of North Carolina,* by Charles G. Zug III, the most complete explication of the subject available. The press also publishes many books about North Carolina history. For further information, write University of North Carolina Press, P.O. Box 2288, Chapel Hill 27514.

If you are a devotee of back roads, you may enjoy Earl Thollander's *Back Roads of the Carolinas,* devoted entirely to "nonhighway" drives along roads that often aren't on regular maps. Thollander designed the book, lettered the text in calligraphy, and drew the maps and wash illustrations himself.

North Carolina General Web Sites

North Carolina Division of Tourism
www.visitnc.com

Bed-and-Breakfasts and Inns
www.bbonline.com/nc/ncbbi

Carolina NetDiner
www.ncra.org/

Often Thollander suggests a dirt road or other obscure route from one historic point to another, which you could use as a much, much slower alternative to the routes I suggest. It is published by Clarkson N. Potter, Inc., One Park Avenue, New York, NY 10016. Finally, the North Carolina publisher John F. Blair (1406 Plaza Drive, Winston-Salem, 27103–1485) offers several books about the history and ecology of the North Carolina coast, plus an appealing book of photographs and native comment, *Ocracoke Portrait,* by Ann Ehringhaus, whose bed-and-breakfast inn on Ocracoke appears in this guidebook. It's especially fun to read such books ahead of time and then carry them with you to consult, because the material comes alive as you see the subject matter firsthand.

With or without the books, though, North Carolina comes alive when you travel here because of its people. Significant history, appealing countryside, even good food can be part of any well-planned trip. Adding helpful, friendly, almost uniformly cheerful people changes the mix from plain cake to an angel food celebration. In the years I've been traveling almost continuously about the state, I've not had a single unpleasant experience with a North Carolinian. Unless you carry a chip the size of one of Mount Mitchell's ancient trees on your shoulder, you won't either. And if you're in that bad a mood, don't come. If you can't have fun in North Carolina, you can't enjoy yourself anywhere. Might as well stay home.

The Southern Coast and Islands

Along the Grand Strand

ike most of this country's coastal areas, the beaches of North Carolina attract plenty of tourists, but some have so far managed to avoid the near honky-tonk atmosphere of the better-known places such as Myrtle Beach, just below the North Carolina–South Carolina border.

Close enough to that border to confuse anyone who misses the North Carolina welcome center on Highway 17, the little community of *Calabash* comes as a surprise to all but the people who visit beaches in the area regularly. The sign proclaiming Calabash the seafood capital of the world seems bigger than the town, which covers only a couple of miles and has only a few hundred permanent residents. But you'll find more than thirty restaurants, all specializing in seafood. Mostly they're owned and run by local fishing families, are casual, and feature fresh "Calabash-style" deep-fried seafood.

Two families, the Becks and the Colemans, claim ownership of the

Talkin' the Talk

*I*n North Carolina what we say is sometimes just the opposite of what we mean, but other North Carolinians get the point. For instance, when a comment that begins, "Bless his heart," or "Bless her heart," it sounds as if you're about to say something nice, but it's actually a signal that what's coming next is critical; "Bless his heart, his elevator doesn't go all the way to the top." Or "Bless her heart, she can't even boil water in a microwave."

On the other hand, we show affection with the seemingly negative statement, "She's a mess." Or, even more affectionately, "She's a real mess."

And when someone says something with which we agree, we don't say so. Instead we say, "You got that right."

It all makes perfect sense. You just have to know the code.

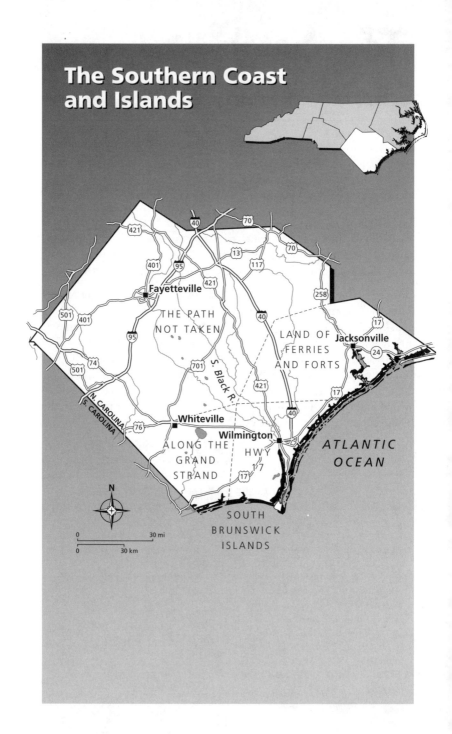

The Southern Coast and Islands

THE PATH NOT TAKEN

LAND OF FERRIES AND FORTS

Jacksonville

ATLANTIC OCEAN

Fayetteville

Whiteville

Wilmington

ALONG THE GRAND STRAND

HWY 17

SOUTH BRUNSWICK ISLANDS

N. CAROLINA
S. CAROLINA

S. Black R.

N

0   30 mi
0   30 km

original Calabash restaurant. Both families started by holding outdoor oyster roasts in the 1930s. When they moved to indoor restaurants, they added fried seafood, which is what most people think of now when they think of Calabash, although the oyster roast is still popular with diners who don't mind a little mess.

"Calabash-style" means the seafood has a light, almost tempuralike, coating. Of course it's always served with hush puppies; it's easier to separate income and tax than it is to get seafood in Calabash without hush puppies.

When you order an oyster roast, you're presented with a huge kettle full of oysters steamed just until they opened, a shucking knife to prod the oysters out of their shells, a dish of melted butter, a roll of paper towels, and a wastebasket to catch the oyster shells as you open them.

Don't expect the kind of oyster you get when you order oysters on the half shell—neatly arranged on a bed of ice, usually a dozen to a plate. Rock oysters come in big stuck-together clumps, large, medium, and small.

ANNUAL EVENTS IN THE SOUTHERN COAST AND ISLANDS

Holden Beach
Day at the Docks
(late March)
(910) 842–6888

Shalotte
Annual N.C. Oyster Festival
(mid October)
(800) 426–6644

Wilmington
Annual Holiday Lighting of the Battleship
(most of December)
(910) 251–5797

Chili Cook–Off
(late October)
(910) 763–6216

N.C. Azalea Festival
(early March)
(910) 754–7177

Wrightsville Beach
N.C. Holiday Flotilla
(late November)
(910) 291–4122

The restaurants in Calabash sit along both sides of NC–179, just off Highway 17. They also run down a couple of side streets toward the water. Only a few years ago, the restaurants were the only thing there, but as the area continues to develop, such unlikely businesses as a New York–style deli and bakery and several clusters of specialty shops have sprung up. Somehow the restaurants just keep on serving fish and don't seem to pay much attention to the other establishments. And lots of local people from the Myrtle Beach area still drive to Calabash for a weekly outing.

One of the largest restaurants is *Captain Nance's Seafood Restaurant,* on the Calabash River (which is still full of shrimp, crabs, and flounder). The restaurant is open from 11:00 A.M. to 9:00 P.M. seven days a week, year-round (910–579–2574).

Becks and *Coleman's Original Calabash* are still operated by the founding families. Becks is open from 11:00 A.M. to 9:00 P.M., seven days a week, year-round, (910–579–6776). Coleman's hours vary. Call (910) 579–6875.

Heads Up! Heads On!

*I*f you've never seen shrimp with their heads and legs on, you're in for a surprise, because they look like squirmy, swimming critters, not the neat, pink C-shaped bits surrounding a cup of cocktail sauce.

Local shrimpers sell some of their catch by the sides of most of the roads in the coastal area. They may set up in a crude shelter or off the back of a truck or simply sit there in lawn chairs. They keep the shrimp iced down in coolers.

When you buy shrimp this way, the price per pound is lower than in markets because the shrimp still have their heads on. They seem so loosely attached you can't help but marvel that they haven't come off during some underwater activity! You can pop the heads off easily.

If you have any worries about the freshness of the shrimp, just ask to smell them. If they smell briny, they're fine. If you catch a whiff of ammonia (which has never happened to me at a roadside stand), don't buy them.

Ella's of Calabash is another small restaurant, with a southern family feel, that is popular with local folks looking for a low-key atmosphere in which to enjoy seafood and a beer or soft drink. This place has been around since the 1950s and has a comfortable, well-established feel. Ella's presumably has fed its full share of rainy-day customers, judging by the following legend displayed near the front: COIL UP YOUR ROPES AND ANCHOR HERE/TILL BETTER WEATHER DOTH APPEAR. You can seek food or shelter here from 11:00 A.M. to 9:00 P.M., seven days a week, year-round except from November 23 through December 25.

In summer Calabash is busy, attracting tourists from Myrtle Beach as well as from the beaches to the north, so the best time to visit is in the slower seasons.

Nearby, also on the Calabash River, ***Captain Jim's Marina*** charters boats at reasonable rates for full- and half-day fishing. If you enjoy the sport but hate the mess that follows, you'll appreciate the free fish-cleaning service. And if you find the whole fishing thing just too gory for words, you're a likely customer for an evening riding cruise. Charters leave from the marina every day. If you're seriously interested in boating, you should call ahead (910–579–3660), as weather, special charters, and slow seasons can affect the regular schedule.

The South Brunswick Islands

Driving north on Highway 17 just over 10 miles takes you to the beginning of the South Brunswick Islands. Sunset Beach, Ocean Isle Beach, and Holden Beach differ from one another as much as the siblings in most families. Part of the chain of barrier islands off the coast that stretches both north and south, the South Brunswick Islands have no boardwalks and relatively little commercial development except for beach houses and a few small grocery stores.

In the fall of 1989, Hurricane Hugo accentuated an interesting phenomenon along Holden Beach, Ocean Isle, and Sunset Beach. The hurricane didn't do any more damage than any good storm does, breaking up some docks, flooding some first-floor rooms in cabins, and lifting off a piece of roof here and there. But it changed the beaches, hastening an erosion process that was already obvious, moving sand and dunes from the east and depositing them farther west. This means that beachfront at Holden Beach grows noticeably more

Spanish Moss

Not Spanish and not moss. This gray-green epiphite thrives almost anywhere in the South where warm air and high humidity are present.

Legend has it that an Indian princess cut her hair on her wedding day, as was traditional, and hung it over an oak tree. But the newlyweds were killed the day they married and buried under the same oak. The princess' hair turned gray, started to grow, and has been spreading among the trees ever since.

Southerners have been trying to figure out a use for Spanish moss for generations. In Louisiana it was used to stuff mattresses in the 1800s. Those that survive are decidedly stiff and crinkly. More recently it's been bagged as a decorative item for florists, but it's only pretty as long as it's exposed to moisture in the air. Take it inland and it turns gray and brittle and crumbles.

My college roommate, back in my Pennsylvania days, kept a bunch, tied with pink ribbon, hanging on a nozzle in the shower room. It did very well there until somebody stole it.

If you want to take Spanish moss home with you, keep it damp as you travel. At home, hang it in a steamy place, such as a shower stall.

narrow with each storm, as does the east end of Ocean Isle's beach-front, leading to such black-humor jokes as the one suggesting that the way to get an oceanfront property here is to buy third row and wait. Meanwhile the beaches on the west end of Ocean Isle and those on Sunset Beach are growing visibly broader. It takes regular dredging to keep the waterway between Ocean Isle and Sunset Beach open because the currents continue to dump sand there. Beaches have broadened so much at Sunset Beach that when you stand at water's edge, you can't see the first-row cottages behind the dunes. It sounds like good, forward-thinking planning; actually, it's nature.

This shifting creates some problems for developers and homeowners but does not in any way spoil the pleasure of visiting any of the islands. Indeed, if you're interested in the ecology of coastlines, try to find a copy of *The Beaches are Moving,* by Wallace Kaufman and Orrin H. Pilkey, Jr., published by Duke University Press in 1979. The book describes, explains, and predicts such activity, though it focuses on beaches along both the east and west coasts and doesn't talk specifically about the South Brunswick Islands. Browsing through the book, which is rich in historical data and information about how tides, storms, and

Beach Memory

*W*hen we first visited Ocean Isle Beach, my husband and I stayed in one of the units of the Pirates' Den, an inexpensive beachfront accommodation with one bedroom, a pretty decent kitchen, a toilet that rocked a little on its base, a slightly musty smell, and an outstanding view of the ocean. It remained a favorite place for a long time. Once I spent a couple of weeks there finishing a manuscript while Himself went back to work. Being without a car, I walked across the causeway to Williamson Realty to mail the manuscript. This was scary because the sides of the bridge came only about to my knees. To get away from the feeling of falling over the edge, I crossed the causeway, walking on the yellow line.

When the people at Williamson heard my story, they mailed my manuscript and then drove me back across the causeway.

In later years, when we had a little more money and wanted to include kids and friends in our vacations, we stayed in larger, nicer homes on the canals. But recently, in the off-season, when I wanted to go back alone for a week to read and listen to jazz, I returned to the Pirates' Den. It stands as stable as ever, one of the sturdiest buildings on the beach. The toilet still rocks a little on its base, the place still smells musty, and it still has an outstanding view of the ocean.

I'll go again.

so on work, while you stay in the South Brunswick Islands is like having your very own little nature model to study as you read. It's great fun and genuinely instructive.

Access to **Sunset Beach** still depends on a one-lane swing bridge across the Intracoastal Waterway. A swing bridge differs from a drawbridge in that the movable part of the bridge swings to the side rather than lifting up to allow tall ships to pass under. It's unique in these times. It's also threatened. Developers have plans to replace it with a higher, modern bridge that would accommodate more and faster traffic. At the moment, people who like the sleepy, undeveloped atmosphere of Sunset Beach are fighting to stop the new bridge. They'll probably lose. But at least for the immediate future, this is a place with only a few paved roads and side-walks, no high-rise condos, and no pink giraffes, water slides, or beach-front grills. What the island does have is glorious, wide, flat beaches and clean white sand. From most of the beach area, you can't see any build-ings at all. The beach homes, most of which are available for rent, sit hid-den behind the dunes. The best way to enjoy Sunset Beach is to rent one of these houses. They are handled by three rental agents. The newest of these, which may therefore be trying harder, is the Odom Company, which does everything from letting you go directly to your rental home instead of stopping to check in at the office to lending you crab traps and charcoal grills. The office (910–579–3515 or 800– 446–3435) is open seven days a week, year-round, from 9:00 A.M. to 5:00 P.M. During the summer season cottage rentals are usually by the week, Saturday to Sat-urday. At other times terms are more flexible. Other agencies are Sunset Vacations (910–579–5400 or 800–331–6428) and Sunset Properties (910–579–9900 or 800–525–0182). Web site: www.sunsetbeachnc.com.

Also, near where the bridge comes onto the island, you can rent rooms at Sunset Beach Motel on Main Street (910–579–7093). Web site: www.northst.com/sunsetbe.htm.

Whether you stay awhile or just pass through, a nice place to stop for din-ner is the **Italian Fisherman,** on the mainland right next to the bridge that crosses the waterway to the island. The restaurant is one of the thor-oughly established operations in the area that attracts customers year-round. In addition to seafood prepared with Italian seasonings, you can order several fine veal dishes, a variety of pasta dishes, and wonderful fried calamari. This is the kind of place where the same people work year after year and remember those visitors who return. Although there is a complete bar, and drinks are served in the dining rooms as well, the atmosphere is holiday casual, and entire families, including babies in high chairs, can eat comfortably here. The guests tend to be as friendly as the staff, often striking up conversations from one table to another. One summer evening an eighteen-month-old in a high chair was doing a standard smear job on her face, head, and hair with spaghetti. A diner at the next table snapped a picture of the scene and later sent it to the child's parents. The Italian Fisherman (910–579–2929) is open seven days a week during the summer season, from 5:00 to 9:00 P.M. In the off-season the restaurant is open only Wednesday through Sunday. In November the days are Thursday through Sunday. They are usually busy, so reservations are a very good idea.

Just south of Sunset Beach, by water, not by road, lies **Bird Island.** It is one of the last undeveloped, privately owned barrier islands on the East Coast. It is a popular place for birding and just spending time in a spot that people have not managed to change. The only sure way to get there is by boat. If you don't own one, try visiting a marina. Some people wade across from Sunset Beach at low tide, but a few of them have come close to having to spend the night there when the tide came in again faster than they realized.

The next island north is **Ocean Isle Beach.** To get there, drive north on Highway 17 about 5 miles and turn right onto Route 179 South, which takes you directly to the Odell Williamson Bridge, across the Intracoastal Waterway. The fact that the island was originally settled in 1954 by Odell and his family, who rowed across the waterway after Hurricane Hazel to get to the island, tells you something about the island. The Williamson family still runs a lively rental, sales, and building business on the island. Although there is a water slide, you'll find little other commercial development here. A few convenience shops and gift shops sell beachwear, suntan lotion, and other items tourists buy. This island is more settled, with sidewalks, all-paved roads, some cluster homes and condos on the west end, and more traditional beach homes on the east end. Also on the east end, a series of paved and natural canals, where the homes have docks, can accommodate boats or just provide pleasant off-ocean outdoor lounging space. A few hundred permanent residents live on the island. Their homes are mingled among those used strictly for vacation and rental. It's a nice mix, and especially if you do not stay in beachfront properties, you can learn a lot about the island from these people and form friendships that continue past your visit. In recent years the relatively new **Museum of Coastal Carolina,** 21 East Second Street, Ocean Isle Beach 28469 (910–579–1016), has attracted vacationing children and school groups. The museum of natural history concentrates on the Carolina's coast, with dioramas and Civil War artifacts, as well as Native American artifacts and a fine collection of seashells and fossils. The

A Birdie at the Beach

*S*and makes great beaches. It also makes devilish sand traps. It takes another golfing enthusiast to understand why you'd go to the beach and spend the time playing golf, but if you do, you'll be in good company. New golf courses spring up faster than dandelions.

North Carolina has more than 500 golf courses dotted across the state, designed by such masters as Donald Ross, Tom Fazio, *Arnold Palmer, Rees Jones, and Jack Nicklaus.*

North Carolina golf courses have hosted the Ryder Cup, the US Open, the US Senior Open, the US Women's Open, and regular PGA tour events.

For a free copy of the North Carolina Golf Guide, *a comprehensive listing of courses in the state, call (800) VISIT–NC or check the web site:* www.visitnc.com.

museum is open from 9:00 A.M. to 5:00 P.M. Friday and Saturday, 1:00 P.M. to 5:00 P.M. Sunday. The hours are shorter in the off-season. **Williamson Realty,** one of several realtors that handle island homes, is pleasant to deal with if you want to rent a cottage or condo. Their Saturday-to-Saturday rental schedule during the season, with more flexibility at other times, operates much the same as on Sunset Beach. The office (910–579–2373 or 800–727–9222) is open from 9:00 A.M. to 5:00 P.M., Monday through Saturday, and Sunday from noon to 4:00 P.M. (closed on Sundays during December, January, and February) Web site: www.williamsonrealty.com. **Sloan Realty** (800– 843–6044) is another well-established, friendly rental agency. Their offices are open six days a week from 9:00 A.M. to 5:00 P.M., Sundays from 10:00 A.M. to 4:00 P.M., except June 2 to September 1, when hours are 12:30 to 5:00 PM. Web site: www.sloanerealty.com.

Ocean Isle Inn (800–352–5988) rents nice waterfront motel rooms by the night. Web site: www.oceanisleinn.com.

Or try **The Islander Inn** (888–325–4753). Web site: www.islanderinn. com. Whatever you do while you're at Ocean Isle Beach, spend some time at **Scheffield's.** It has a boat dock in back, automobile gas pumps in front, groceries, fishing supplies, and beer inside, and the nicest people imaginable everywhere. You can buy just-caught shrimp and fish, newly dug clams, all the fixin's to go with them, and in the process, trade recipes with the proprietors for preparing whatever you bought. Scheffield's (910–579–2574) is open from 7:30 A.M. to 9:00 P.M. (10:00 P.M. on weekends) seven days a week, year-round.

Standing on the west end of Ocean Isle Beach, you can see Sunset Beach. It looks close enough to wade over, which old-timers remember doing before erosion and currents changed the shape of the islands. Standing on the east end of Ocean Isle Beach, you see **Holden Beach,** also seeming almost close enough to wade across. Without a boat, though, getting to Holden Beach requires a drive of about fifteen minutes. Richard Mubel, the news editor for the *State Port Pilot,* once wrote for the *Brunswick Magazine* that Holden is a place where "old meets new, where tradition bisects progress and where history intersects the path of the future." He's talking about the contrasts between the back side of the island, along the Atlantic Intracoastal Waterway and the Lockwood Folly River Inlet, and the oceanfront. Shrimpers and anglers descended from families who settled the area still work along the waterway and inlet, as well as in the open sea, but the oceanfront is strictly a vacationland of white beaches and summer cottages. You'll find more shopping in this area, but compared to major coastal resort areas, it's still quiet and appeals to people who like a little more activity than can be found at Sunset or Ocean Isle without getting into plastic, chrome, and glass. Half a dozen rental agents renting cottages and condos, a campground, and a motel serve the area. **Alan Holden Realty** (800–720–2200) has the most properties and friendly people to answer the phone. They're open from 9:00 A.M. to 5:00 P.M., seven days a week, year-round. Web site: www.holden-beach.com. **Coastal Vacation Resorts** rents nearly 200 cottages and a few condos. Call (800) 252–7000. Web site: www.atlantic-vacation.com. **The Gray Gull Motel** (910–842–6775), an older but clean establishment, rents individual rooms. They, too, operate year-round. This small motel is located between the light and the bridge where you first drive onto the island.

If you enjoy local festivals and if you lo-o-o-o-ve seafood, try to schedule your Brunswick Island trip for the third weekend in October, during the annual **North Carolina Oyster Festival.** This festival began as a small oyster roast in the late 1970s. Every year the party got a little better and in three years got itself proclaimed the official oyster festival of North Carolina. It takes a couple hundred community volunteers to run the event, which now includes a beach run, a bullshooting (tall-tale-telling) contest, and the North Carolina Oyster Shucking Championship. This contest is no small potatoes. It has produced not only a national oyster shucking champion but also the top female oyster shucker in the world. With all that shucking going on, it stands to reason somebody's got to be doing some eating. That's where you come in. Steamed oysters, fried oysters, oysters on the half shell, boiled shrimp,

BETTER KNOWN ATTRACTIONS IN THE
SOUTHERN COAST AND ISLANDS

WILMINGTON
Battleship *North Carolina*
(910) 251–5797

Cape Fear Museum
(910) 341–4350

CAPE FEAR COASTAL BEACHES
Wrightsville, Carolina, Kure
(800) 222–4757;
www.capefear.nc.us

fried flounder, and of course the ubiquitous hush puppies are available in abundance. Food is served from noon to 7:00 P.M. on Saturday and, on a more limited scale, from 1:00 to 5:00 P.M. on Sunday. In addition to the food and contests, the festival features two days of live music that include beach music (shag), top forty, country and western, and gospel. Also artists and craftspeople display their wares for sale. For fuller details and firm dates in any year, call *North Carolina's Brunswick Islands,* (800) 795–SAND. Web site: www.ncbrunswick.com.

Highway 17

The Brunswick Isles are served by businesses in the town of *Shalotte,* a few miles inland on Highway 17. This is the place to stop when you need to do laundry or pick up a bicycle pump from the hardware store or get a prescription filled in a good-sized pharmacy. From Shalotte, driving north on Highway 17 for a little less than an hour brings you to Wilmington. On the way you should take a little side trip to *Southport,* on the western bank of the *Cape Fear River* where the river joins the Atlantic Ocean. The harbor accommodates yachts, charter boats, and fishing piers. The town, rich in military and maritime history, was first called Smithville after Benjamin Smith, who became governor of North Carolina, but in 1887 the name was changed to Southport. To get into town from Highway 17, turn right onto State Highway 211. Shortly you'll be driving into what is obviously still a real fishing village with stores and gas stations and marinas that look functional rather than prettily gentrified. Many of the homes in Southport are listed on the National Register of Historic Places. Although the word "quaint" is overused, it pertains here. For instance the old twelve-bed *Fort Johnston Hospital,* dating back to about 1852, has been moved and turned into a private residence; the *Old Brunswick Jail,* dating back to the early 1900s, now houses the Southport Historical Society. In the *Keziah Memorial Park* you find a tree that the Cape Fear Indians bent over as a marker when it was just a sapling. It may be more than 800 years old. Half a century ago children could crawl under its arch. And the *A. E. Stevens House,* circa 1894, is noted as the home built for Mr. Stevens and his betrothed. She changed her mind and married his best friend. They built a house across from Mr. Stevens, who remained a

Some Kinder, Gentler Prose

*T*he author Robert Ruark was born in Southport. He wrote novels that made people angry, especially Something of Value, *about Africa. (After it was published, the government of Kenya wouldn't let him back in the country.)*

He was rough, tough, rude, and crude, and he died in London from internal bleeding before he was fifty.

But he had a softer side, too. Ruark wrote The Old Man and the Boy, *a memoir about spending time as a boy with his grandfather, E. H. Adkins, a Southport river pilot. He often stayed in his grandfather's house at 119 North Lord Street. The house, still a private residence, is now 110 years old. It is not open to visitors, but the book is easy to find because of its local interest.*

bachelor the rest of his life. There's lots more, equally human and interesting, all mapped out on a 1-mile, self-guided walking tour called **Southport Trail.** You'll find a nice assortment of restaurants, antiques shops, and specialty stores in the area, too. Their names and sometimes their proprietors may change from year to year, but they're always fun. A shopping guide with a map as well as the free self-guided walking-tour brochure of Southport's historic sites is available at the visitors center, 4841 Long Beach Road, Southport 28461. The center is open from 8:30 A.M. to 5:00 P.M. Monday through Friday, 9:00 A.M. to 400 P.M. Saturday. Closed on Saturday from March through December. Call (800) 457–6964. Web site: www.southport.net.

Southport used to be the special province of people with boats and people who fish. Even those who docked their boats in Southport and lived inland didn't expect much in the way of elaborate accommodations or shopping. This is all changing—that's the good news *and* the bad news. As specialty shops and antiques shops open, more tourists come in, making the place not quite so off-the-beaten-path as it used to be. But the good news is that you can find more places to stay and eat.

Cape Fear Inn, at 317 West Bay Street, Southport, 28461, straddles both eras. The inn has twelve rooms on the waterfront and a fishing pier, and it provides bicycles for guests who want to explore without driving. It's close to several eating places and the *Blues Tavern,* which books various kinds of music for dancing. The inn serves a light continental breakfast and snacks. The owner is John Barbee, but Pamela Huff, the manager, is the voice you'll hear when you call and the person you'll see when you visit. "I do everything," she says. The inn's schedule depends on the weather. Sometimes, in the winter off-season, Pamela accepts guests who are just looking for a place to stay and don't need any special B&B–type service. Call (910) 457–5989.

North of Southport via State Highway 133, *Brunswick Town State Historic Site* marks the first settlement in the Cape Fear area. Here you can study the remains of the colonial port town of Brunswick and the earth mounts of Fort Anderson that the Confederate Army built about 100 years later. Some of the old foundations have been excavated and are uncovered as archaeological exhibits. The mounds have survived pretty much intact since the Civil War and actually make a good spot from which to see the older ruins. A visitors center on the site has slide presentations and exhibits about the colonial town and the artifacts excavated from the ruins. This is one of those well-managed sites where you can learn about both colonial life and the Civil War, and get a sense of the continuity from the one time to the other. Brunswick Town is open April 1 through October 31, Monday through Saturday from 9:00 A.M. to 5:00 P.M., from Sunday 1:00 to 5:00 P.M. November 1 through March 31 the site is closed Monday and hours are shortened to 10:00 A.M. to 4:00 P.M. Tuesday through Saturday and from 1:00 to 4:00 P.M., Sunday. These hours may vary, so it's a good idea to call ahead (910) 371–6613. Admission is free.

About 10 miles north of Southport, still on Highway 133, you come to *Orton Plantation Gardens,* a delight for anyone who loves flowers and grand old trees. The first owners were James and Luola Sprunk, who built terraces and ornamental gardens with live oaks lining the walkways. Later, with the help of a landscape architect, additional gardens and water features were added, and the gardens were opened to the public. Blooms extend over a long season, beginning with camellias in late winter; azaleas in spring; oleander, crepe myrtle, and magnolias in summer and fall. Plantings of annuals add extra splashes of color. Orton House, a good example of Southern antebellum architecture, is an impressive feature on the property too, but it is a private residence, so you must content yourself with admiring the exterior and visiting the small family chapel that is open to the public. The gardens are open daily March through August from 8:00 A.M. to 6:00 P.M., September and November from 10:00 A.M. to 5:00 P.M. Admission is $8.00 for adults, $7.00 for seniors, and $3.00 for children. Phone (910) 371–6851.

After this, the easiest thing to do is return to Highway 17 to drive on up to *Wilmington.* People who live here call Wilmington the best-kept secret in North Carolina. They're of two minds as to whether that's

Hooray for Wilmi-Wood

*I*f you want to be in pictures, go south. Wilmington has become the hot spot for making films. More than 300 movie features, documentaries, and television miniseries have been made in the region, as well as six television series with more than 150 episodes, and many commercials.

These projects have brought such stars as Julia Roberts, Nicholas Cage, and Jamie Lee Curtis to town, along with nearly 1,000 technical crew people who live in Wilmington.

Wilmington went show-biz back in 1983, when Dino De Laurentis bought what is now Screen Gem Studios, one of the largest production studios east of Hollywood.

good or bad. The thriving, historic community has a full share of entrepreneurial types who've done much to revitalize waterfront areas and old downtown buildings. They welcome tourists and new business. Some of the old-timers would rather the community's cultural and historical attractions not become too well known, lest all the new traffic spoil the ambience.

In 1989 Wilmington, which was settled before the Revolutionary War and was the last Atlantic port open to blockade runners during the Civil War, celebrated its 250th anniversary.

Historic restoration and preservation in the official *Historic Wilmington District* have produced an appealing neighborhood that deserves more attention. One interesting approach is the *Wilmington Adventure Walking Tour,* by Bob Jenkins (910–763–1785). The tour takes about two hours. Jenkins calls it a "casual stroll on the original survey of the 1734 city." It takes in town houses, gardens, commercial buildings, churches, and fountains. The tour concludes with an 1858 theater and an 1892 courthouse and includes a twelve-minute video showing more sightseeing possibilities in the entire Cape Fear region. Tours run from April 1 through October. They leave daily at 10:00 A.M. and 2:00 P.M. from the foot of Market Street on the Cape Fear River. Look for a guide with a straw hat and a walking stick. Reservations are not necessary. Tickets are $10.00 for adults, $5.00 for children ages six to twelve.

There are two buildings in the area worth seeing inside. The beautifully restored *1770 Burgwin–Wright House* (910–762–0570) stands at the corner of Third and Market Streets. It was built in 1770 on the foundation of the abandoned Wilmington City Jail. One reason the owner chose this site and kept the foundation was because it had a tunnel running down to the water, so he could get to the boats without going outside. Open Tuesday through Saturday 10:00 A.M. to 4:00 P.M. Closed on major holidays. Admission is $3.00 for adults, $1.00 for full-time students. The *Zebulon Latimer House* (910–762–0492) at 126 South Third Street is one of the few remaining examples of a town house of the time. The same family inhabited it from its completion in 1852 until the historical society took it over in the 1960s. About 60 percent of the furnishings are the family's original belongings. Three of the four floors are open, so you can see everything from beds to china. The house also has archives and a library for those who want to study further, with a researcher available on Tuesday and Thursday. The house is open Monday through Friday from 10:00 A.M. to 3:30 P.M. Closed on major holidays. If a tour is in progress when you arrive, you may join it, be taken separately by a docent, or wait for the next group to gather. Admission is $5.00 for adults, $2.00 for full-time students.

To shift from history to contemporary attractions: If you're interested in the entertainment business, try the *Silver Screen Tours of Screen Gems Studios,* 1223 North Twenty-third Street, Wilmington 28401.

The tour takes about ninety minutes and shows a real, working movie studio that includes 115,000 square feet of stage space with nine sound stages, an urban back-street lot that has been used to depict major cities, and an orientation video.

Tours are offered only on weekends, and you must call (910) 675–8479 for reservations. The times of the tours vary, and some will be fully booked, so this requires a little planning. No cameras are allowed, and children younger than twelve are not admitted. Admission is $10. Web site: www.screengemsstudios.com/silverscreentours.html.

Another pleasant way to see the Wilmington District is to take a *Springbrook Farms* sight-seeing tour (910–251–8889) by horse-drawn carriage, with a driver who narrates as you pass the historic sites. At Christmas a nice touch is that you ride in a closed reindeer-drawn carriage, snuggled in a lap rug, for a tour narrated by Santa. Owner-operator John Pucci says this appeals especially to children and romantics. Tours leave from the corner of Water and Market Streets. Hours vary with the season, weather, and day of the week. To plan a tour, call ahead. If no one is there, you can still learn current tour hours by listening to a recording. Sometimes tours may be arranged for different times by appointment. Rates are $8.00 for adults, $4.00 for children.

One attraction that definitely deserves more attention is *St. John's Museum of Art,* at 114 Orange Street, Wilmington 28403 (910–763–0281). The museum, which is light and airy, comprises three historic buildings: a Masonic Lodge (1804), the Cowan House Studio (ca. 1830), and what was St. Nicholas Greek Orthodox Church (1943). A sculpture garden ties the complex together. The permanent collection features 200 years of North Carolinian art. The most important gift the museum has received is the original color prints of Mary Cassatt, the nineteenth-century American artist who worked with the Impressionists in France. The museum also has a dozen temporary exhibitions that change annually. Open Tuesday through Saturday from 10:00 A.M. to 5:00 P.M. and Sunday from noon to 4:00 P.M. Closed on major holidays. Admission is $2.00 for adults, $1.00 for children under age eighteen, $5.00 for families; children age five and under are free. Admission the first Sunday of every month is free.

From the inn you can walk to *Chandler's Wharf* on the Cape Fear River, a complex of restored historical warehouses and buildings with cobblestone streets, picket fences, and pretty streams. Instead of maritime businesses, the buildings now hold specialty shops and restaurants. *The Riverboat Landing Restaurant* (910–763–7227) is operated by an Italian family but offers many more seafood specialties than pasta dishes. It's a casual place where you'll feel at ease in either dressy or casual clothes, and even fussy kids do OK here because while you're enjoying fresh grouper or cioppino, they can have spaghetti or lasagna. And even though the proprietors are playing down their Italian offerings to promote their seafood (they say, "Remember, Italians are fishermen, too"), they make a wicked cannoli that no one should miss. Beer, wine, and mixed drinks are available in the lounge and dining room. In good weather some of the nicest dining areas are those on outdoor and glass-enclosed balconies overlooking the river. Prices are moderate. Open daily at 4:00 P.M. for dinner, Sunday at 11:00 A.M. for brunch. Hours vary seasonally; call for exact times.

Also in Chandler's Wharf, *Elijak's Oyster Bar,* on the waterfront, is open from 11:30 A.M. to midnight, Tuesday through Saturday. The place is known for its hot crab dip and good house wines.

Another complex of eight restored old buildings, the *Cotton Exchange* (910–343–9896), beginning on Front Street between Walnut and Grace, features almost thirty shops and restaurants, including Paddy's Hollow, a Victorian pub, and East Bank Trading Company, a shop featuring American handcrafts. Most of the shops are open from 10:00 A.M. to 5:00 P.M. Monday through Saturday and from 1:00 to 5:00 P.M. Sunday.

The restaurants are open evenings as well.

From all these points along the river, you can see the **USS North Carolina** *Battleship Memorial,* commissioned in 1941 and considered the world's greatest battleship at the time. The ship has been docked as a memorial since 1961. The self-guided tour, which takes about two hours, leads you through the crew's quarters, galley, sick bay, engine room, and pilothouse. What you see is fascinating in its technical detail. If you're the kind of person who embarrasses genteel guides in historic homes by asking what they used for toilet paper, this tour is definitely for you. A short orientation film starts you off.

A more glitzy approach to the same ship is the outdoor sound and light show, "The Immortal Showboat," offered every night at 9:00 P.M. from the first Friday in June through Labor Day. The audience sits in a 1,000-seat grandstand across from the ship's port bow, while voices, lights, music, and special-effect ordnance fire dramatize the ship's history for seventy minutes. The ship looms out of the water where Highways 17, 74, 76, and 421 intersect, 3 miles outside Wilmington. In addition to a good-sized parking lot, you'll find a center for visitors with a gift shop, snack bar, and picnic shelter. The ship (910–251–5797 or 910–350–1817) is open every day from 8:00 A.M. to 8:00 P.M., May through September. It closes at 5:00 P.M. from September 16 to May 15. Write USS *North Carolina* Battleship Memorial, P.O. Box 417, Wilmington 28402. Admission is $8.00 for adults, $4.00 for children.

The Battleship USS *North Carolina*

During the summer an alternative to parking at the battleship site is to take the **Riverboat Taxi** over from Chandler's Wharf. Originally it was a World War II U.S. Navy launch. It leaves every half hour for the battleship from 10:00 A.M. to 5:00 P.M. daily. Modest rates.

You can't get seasick on the battleship unless you have a wildly vivid imagination, and the launch ride is too short to do much damage. If you'd like to test your sea legs a bit more realistically, you could try a riverboat cruise on the **Henrietta II,** which docks at the foot of Market Street on the Cape Fear River. These cruises are party affairs, ranging from Sunday sight-seeing cruises to evening Dogwood cruises in spring, a sweetheart cruise on Valentine's Day, and weekend dinner cruises. It's all planned and public, but if you're in the mood for it, the gaiety can be a lot of fun. The original *Henrietta* was the first steam paddleboat built in North Carolina, and it ran the river between Wilmington and Fayetteville for forty years. James Seawell (no joke), the builder, named it for his daughter. The *Henrietta II* is a nearly new paddleboat and includes a dance floor and an air-conditioned dining room, in addition to the outdoor deck space you'd expect. If she can see this modern version, poor Henrietta is probably wishing herself back to the future.

Land of Ferries and Forts

*J*ust a few miles away from the historic port of Wilmington you come to a series of beaches: Wrightsville, Carolina, Wilmington, and Kure. The entire area has more historic sites and interesting spots to visit than can be included in a book covering the entire state. For folks seeking out-of-the-way places, the beaches don't offer the same secluded charm as the Brunswick Islands, but they can be fun, with enough amusement and entertainment to please the kids without doing in Mom and Dad, especially if you avoid the peak summer season. A number of historical and marine attractions are especially important and interesting.

Wrightsville Beach is 12 miles east of Wilmington. It operates as a year-round island resort and has plenty of motels and some nice, casual, moderately priced seafood restaurants.

Driving south from Wilmington on Highway 421 for a little less than 20 miles takes you to the beaches on **Pleasure Island.** This area is highly commercial and built up, but if you stick it out to Kure Beach, you'll find two attractions worth taking time to see if you're interested in the naval aspects of Civil War history and in marine life.

Three miles south of Kure Beach, on Highway 421, is *Fort Fisher National Historic Site.* The fort stood up under heavy naval attack during the Civil War, and some of the 25-foot earthwork fortifications that protected the Cape Fear River and the port of Wilmington from Union forces remain. Reading about such parapets is one thing; looking at them and musing on how they must have been built before the days of bulldozers is a more vivid experience, intensified by such touches as a reconstruction of the gun emplacement and a history trail. There's also a museum that displays Civil War artifacts and offers a slide show on the history of the fort. If you travel with a picnic cooler, you'll enjoy the picnic area on the site. Admission is free but donations are appreciated (910–458–5538). Open April through October, 9:00 A.M. to 5:00 P.M., Monday through Saturday, 1:00 to 5:00 P.M. Sunday; November through March 10, 10:00 A.M. to 4:00 P.M. Tuesday through Saturday, 1:00 to 4:00 P.M. Sunday, and closed Monday and major holidays.

Across from Fort Fisher National Historic Site, the *North Carolina Aquarium* features a 20,000-gallon shark aquarium, a whale exhibit, and a touch tank where children (and adults too, for that matter) can actually handle some kinds of marine life. There are also *koi* (carp) pools and river otters. The aquarium maintains a full schedule of special events and educational programs. It might be worth calling ahead for a schedule (910–458–8257). Admission is $3.00 for adults, $2.00 for seniors and full-time students with I.D.; free of charge for children six to seventeen. Open 9:00 A.M. to 5:00 P.M. seven days a week. Closed Thanksgiving, Christmas, and New Year's Day.

When you get this far south on the island, you will have two choices. You can take the Fort Fisher Ferry to Southport, which brings you close to the Brunswick Islands, whence you began driving, or you can backtrack up the island and take the bridge across to Wilmington, also whence you began driving. At first glance the obvious way to avoid those whences and the dilemma of decision would be to begin by taking the ferry from Southport to Fort Fisher, then drive north on the island and finally cross over to the delights of Wilmington. You may indeed decide to do it that way, especially if you're not traveling during the peak summer months. But you need to know that the ferry leaves Southport only seven times a day; crossing takes an hour; it accommodates only twenty automobiles at a time; and the time schedule may change. Trying to follow a schedule, only to end up waiting in a line that has cut off several cars ahead of you because the ferry is already full, is not the stuff relaxing vacations are made of. For more current information when you decide, phone

(919) 458–3329. Some information is also available from the **Cape Fear Coast Convention and Visitors Bureau** (800–222–4757 in the eastern United States, 800–922–7117 in North Carolina, or 910–341–4030).

Should you decide to backtrack to Wilmington, you can give the kids a pleasant break by stopping at the **Tote-em-in Zoo,** about 10 miles south of Wilmington on Highway 421. The zoo, which has been in business more than thirty-five years, features more than 100 different animals, a museum of exotic mounted specimens, and another museum of varied artifacts from around the world, including arrowheads and World War II items. Modest rates. Open from spring thaw until the first hard freeze, roughly March through November, from 9:00 A.M. to 5:00 P.M. weekdays and until 6:30 P.M. weekends. Call ahead because hours vary seasonally and according to weather (910–791–0472). Admission is $5.00 for adults, $3.00 for children two to eleven.

If you're interested in North Carolina wineries, you may want to schedule a side trip while you're in the Wilmington area to **Duplin Wine Cellars,** about an hour's drive from the coast. The winery is in Rose High, on Highway 117, about halfway between Wilmington and Goldsboro. The winery conducts tours and tastings and, of course, sells its wines. Tours are preceded by an audiovisual presentation on the history of southern wine-making. Duplin Wine Cellars (910–289–3888) is especially well known for its Magnolia, a soft dry table wine, and its scuppernong dessert wine. The word *scuppernong* is an Indian word meaning "sweet tree."

Scuppernong is the oldest grape in America, and the Duplin Cellars is the only winery in America that makes 100 percent scuppernong wine. Open Monday through Saturday, from 9:00 A.M. to 5:00 P.M. Closed New Year's Day, July 4, Labor Day, Thanksgiving Day, and Christmas Day. Write for a free newsletter: P.O. Box 756, Rose Hill 28458.

From Wilmington the best way to head north is to drive on Highway 17 for a while. Stretches of it are annoyingly full of strip-city areas where traffic is heavy and slow. Taking some of the little side roads seems like a good idea, and you can if you wish without fear of getting lost, because most of them eventually loop back to Highway 17 anyway. But the loops are disappointing. You won't find much but scrubland, little clusters of homes or mobile homes, and perhaps some tobacco fields. It's OK for a break but quickly becomes about as boring as the more direct approach on Highway 17.

One interesting stop, right on the highway shortly after you leave Wilmington, is the **Poplar Grove Plantation** (910–686–9518; Web site: www.poplargrove.com). It has an unusual history in that it not only survived the Civil War, it also became economically successful again by growing peanuts. The original plantation operated in the tradition of the times, as a self-supporting agricultural community with more than sixty slaves. The manor house burned down in 1849 and was rebuilt the following year where it now stands. When you visit the plantation, guides in period costume lead you on a tour of the manor house—a three-floor Greek Revival building—and the outbuildings, describing what daily life on the plantation was like.

Now that the plantation's restaurant, which serves lunch and dinner, has been moved from the manor house into a new building built just for the restaurant, the size and variety of exhibits in the manor house have been increased to make a complete plantation museum. The top floor displays bedrooms. On the main floor a parlor, dining room, and library are filled with appropriate period pieces. On the lower floor you'll find displays of handmade textiles, old quilts and coverlets, a floor loom, spinning wheels, and other textile-related artifacts such as an early Singer sewing machine, a clock reel, and a mother-in-law. The mother-in-law isn't going to ask to go home with you or anything; it's a device for winding yarn without an extra person to hold it.

In another room a series of displays depict agricultural activities from 1860 to 1960, especially peanut production. This was a peanut plantation, remember. The equipment includes a horse-drawn peanut planter and an assortment of hand tools, many found buried on the site. Photographs add detail to the exhibit.

When you visit you'll probably have an opportunity to watch some crafts demonstrations. The plantation has three resident craftspeople: a blacksmith, a weaver, and a basket maker. At least one of them, and often two, is always demonstrating. Some of what they make—rag rugs for instance—is for sale.

The outbuildings include a tenant house, smokehouse, herb cellar, kitchen (plantation kitchens were always in separate buildings), blacksmith shop, and turpentine and saltworks display. With or without a guide, looking at these buildings dramatically brings home some realities of history. A visitor looking at the small, roughly finished, uninsulated tenant house said, "It's hard to imagine that a whole family actually lived in here." Another visitor, seeing the mock hams, sausages, and bacons hanging in the smokehouse, wondered what the real thing would have been like in such hot weather and said, "It's a wonder everybody didn't die of food poisoning."

For children, Poplar Grove Plantation has lots of open spaces—shaded with live oaks, sycamores, and magnolias—for running; a playground; and some farm animals they can see and maybe even touch. Open Monday through Saturday 9:00 A.M. to 5:00 P.M., Sunday noon to 5:00 P.M. Admission is $6.00 for adults, $5.00 for senior citizens, $3.00 for children six to fifteen.

Continuing north on Highway 17 takes you through some very local, untouristy areas, such as Holly Ridge, where the mayor's office is also the office of Ocean Aire Realty. If you want more of a sense of the area, shortly after you pass Holly Ridge turn left on Verona Road, and following the signs, head toward Haws Run. You'll go by some pretty little houses with lovingly tended gardens, then an abandoned trailer park, and finally many occupied mobile homes on the way back out to Highway 17. This detour of only a few miles gives a view of what many small North Carolina communities near the coast are like.

Then you're into the area around Jacksonville, which is shaped and colored by ***Camp Lejeune Marine Base.*** Traffic is fairly heavy, and the area bulges with the kind of commercial development that surrounds military bases: motels, restaurants, arcades, shopping centers, and the like. But even though driving through such a section isn't as relaxing as spinning along a country road, it's tremendously instructive and sometimes funny. Most of the people you see in most of the vehicles are heartbreakingly young men with perfect posture and haircuts so short you can almost see their scalps from the next automobile. Often they're in pairs or groups, and often they're towing boats or hauling bikes. The progression of the establishments and signs they pass along the road tells a story: Foxy Lady, New Ink Tattoo Shop, Luigi's (where you can get a remarkably good Italian meal), a motel sign WELCOME MR. NUNNERY, Real Value Diamond Outlet, an assortment of churches, and The Maternity and Newborn Store.

Here's information of a more dignified nature. Camp Lejeune is one of the most complete training centers in the world and covers 110,000 acres. You may wish to stop at the Beirut Memorial, honoring those killed in Beirut and Grenada. It is outside the gate of Camp Johnson on Highway 24. You can't get onto the base without a pass, and you can't get a pass without a driver's license and registration certificate. The information center at the main gate on Highway 24 is open twenty-four hours a day (910–451–2197).

From Jacksonville you could logically continue up Highway 17 to New Bern, or you could travel east on Highway 24 toward the ocean to check out the Bogue Banks and then go on to Morehead City, Beaufort, and Atlantic, and ferry across to the Outer Banks. Better yet, if you're not hurrying, avoid this section of Highway 24, which runs along another edge of the Marine base, and continue north about 15 miles more on Highway 17, where you pick up Highway 58, which runs southeast along the side of the Croatan National Forest and is a much more pleasant drive to the coast. *Cedar Point* is a nice place to stop for a picnic or a rest and perhaps a hike along the Cedar Point Tideland Trail. You'll find camping areas and picnic tables in the shade along the water. Nearby is Cape Carteret, a little town that's probably completely solved its crime problem by locating its ABC (liquor) store right next to the police station and town hall.

Aside from learning that *Emerald Island* is a sea-turtle sanctuary, you're probably not going to find much that pleases you driving over to the Bogue Banks. The entire barrier island, which is nearly 30 miles long, has been developed commercially to the point that condos, cottages, and water slides line the beaches, and beach shops crowd one another along the highway. You may prefer to skip the Bogue Banks, stay on the mainland, and head for Beaufort.

PLACES TO STAY IN THE SOUTHERN COAST AND ISLANDS

HOLDEN BEACH
Gray Gull Motel
At the bridge
Holden Beach 28462
(910) 842–6775

OCEAN ISLE BEACH
Ocean Isle Inn
37 West First Street
Ocean Isle Beach 28469
(910) 579–0750

The Winds
301 East First Street
Ocean Isle Beach 28469
(800) 334–3581

SOUTHPORT
Riverside Motel
103 West Bay Street
Southport 28461
(910) 457–6986

Sea Captain Motor Lodge
608 West West Street
Southport 28461
(910) 457–5260

SUNSET BEACH
Sunset Vacations
401 South Sunset Boulevard
Sunset Beach 28468
(910) 579–5400

WILMINGTON
Best Western Carolinian
2916 Market Street
Wilmington 28403
(910) 763–4653
(800) 528–1238

Comfort Inn
Executive Center
151 South College Road
Wilmington 28403
(910) 791–4841

Days Inn
5040 Market Street
Wilmington 28405
(910) 799–6300
(800) 329–7466

Holiday Inn
4903 Market Street
Wilmington 28405
(910) 799–1440

Rosehill Inn
114 South Third Street
Wilmington 28401
(910) 815–0250

WRIGHTSVILLE BEACH
Harbor Inn
701 Causeway Drive
Wrightsvile Beach 28480
(910) 256–9402

PLACES TO EAT IN THE SOUTHERN COAST AND ISLANDS

CALABASH
Captain Nance's Seafood Restaurant
Riverfront
Calabash 28467
(910) 579–2574

SOUTHPORT
Sea Captain
Motor Lodge Restaurant
608 West West Street
Southport 28461
(910) 457–5263

Riverside Motel Restaurant
103 West Bay Street
Southport 28461
(910) 457–6986

SUNSET BEACH
Italian Fisherman
Causeway
Sunset Beach 28468
(910) 579–2929

WILMINGTON
Elijah's Oyster Bar
2 Ann Street
Chandler's Wharf
Wilmington 28401
(910) 343–1448

Riverboat Landing
2 Ann Street
Chandler's Wharf
Wilmington 28401
(910) 343–0200

WRIGHTSVILLE BEACH
The Bridge Tender
Arlie Road off
Inland Waterway
Wrightsville Beach 28480
(910) 256–4519

The Southern Coast and Islands Web Sites:

Cape Fear Coast
www.cape–fear.nc.us

The Crystal Coast
www.sunnync.com

The Northern Coast and Islands

Peaceful Places

our next major stop as you head north along the coast is **Morehead City,** a deep port where the Intracoastal Waterway joins the Atlantic Ocean. It is both a commercial fishing town and a summer resort area, appealing especially to sport fishers. The waterfront is more devoted to commerce than tourism, has more than 5,000 square feet of continuous wharf, and includes a lot of shipping storage space. That means the waterfront isn't really pretty; it's too commercial and busy, but the activity is authentic and interesting. As a traveler, if you aren't here to fish, you're probably here to *eat* fish. The area has plenty of moderately priced motels and more seafood restaurants than you could patronize in two weeks' hard eating. If you ask people where to go, they'll most often make the unlikely sounding recommendation of the **Sanitary Fish Market Restaurant** (252–247–3111). It's just a block from Highway 70, on Bogue Sound. This is a big, casual, family-oriented place that seats more than 600 people and serves all kinds of seafood and no alcohol. It has been owned and operated by the same family for more than fifty years. Open from 11:00 A.M. to 9:00 P.M. daily during the peak (summer) season. May close earlier at other times. Closed in December and January.

From Morehead City it's just a short drive over the Paul Graydon Bridge to **Beaufort.** The first step to having fun in Beaufort is learning to say it properly—*BOW-ford*. This separates it from that place in South Carolina spelled the same way but pronounced to rhyme with "phew." People in Beaufort, North Carolina, care and respond accordingly.

This was once a fishing village, settled by French Huguenots and English sailors more than 275 years ago. The port was active during three wars: the American Revolution, the War of 1812, and the Civil War. Today, Beaufort is a laid-back vacation area in which historic preservation and restoration have been impressive. Much of the downtown has been designated a National Historic Landmark, and the Beaufort

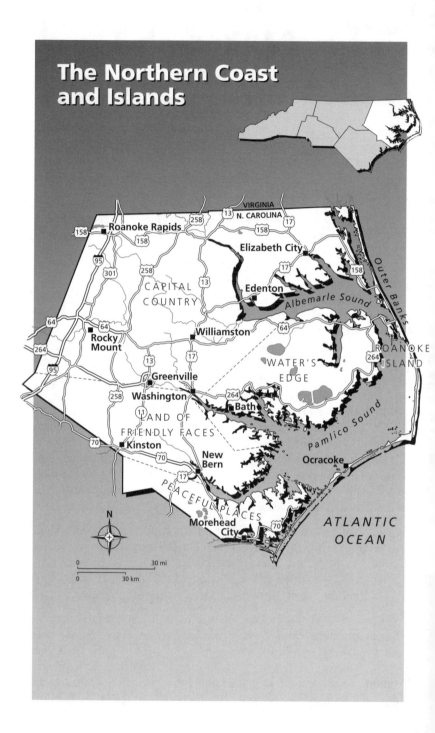

The Northern Coast and Islands

VIRGINIA
N. CAROLINA

Roanoke Rapids

Elizabeth City

Edenton

CAPITAL COUNTRY

Williamston

Albemarle Sound

Outer Banks

Rocky Mount

WATER'S EDGE

ROANOKE ISLAND

Greenville

Washington

Bath

Pamlico Sound

LAND OF FRIENDLY FACES

Kinston

New Bern

Ocracoke

PEACEFUL PLACES

Morehead City

ATLANTIC OCEAN

N

0   30 mi
0   30 km

THE NORTHERN COAST AND ISLANDS

ANNUAL EVENTS IN THE NORTHERN COAST AND ISLANDS

Emerald Isle
Annual Singing by the Sea
(mid-September)
(252) 393–8373
or 393–8956

Kill Devil Hills
National Aviation Day-
Orville Wright Birthday
August 19
(252) 441–7430

Manteo
Virginia Dare's
Birthday Celebration
August 18
(252) 473–2127

Morehead City
Annual N.C. Seafood
Festival
Waterfront
(mid-October)
(252) 726–6273

New Bern
Independence Day
Celebration
Tryon Palace Historic Sites
and Gardens
July 4
(252) 514–4900
or (800) 767–1560

Outer Banks
Annual Outer Banks Stunt
Kite Competition
Jockey's Ridge State Park
(mid-October)
(252) 441–4124
or (800) 334–4777

Historical Association has restored a number of early buildings that are open to the public.

Local art is offered in the *Mattie King Davis Art Gallery* on the grounds of the Old Town Beaufort Restoration Complex, where local artists and craftspeople display their pottery, weaving, oil painting, watercolors, and other original art. It's open April 1 through October, Monday through Saturday from 10:00 A.M. to 4:00 P.M. No admission fee.

The *North Carolina Maritime Museum,* 315 Front Street, contains artifacts ranging from fish and fossils to ships, including a model-ship collection and a collection of 5,000 seashells from all over the world. Serious boat people visit here to watch wooden boats being built and restored. Open Monday through Friday from 9:00 A.M. to 5:00 P.M., Saturday from 10:00 A.M. to 5:00 P.M., Sunday from 1:00 to 5:00 P.M. (252–728–7317). For a schedule of special events, write the museum at 315 Front Street, Beaufort 28516. Web site: www.ah.dcr.state.nc.us/maritime/default.htm. No admission fee.

One way to see the sights and learn a lot about local lore is by taking one of the *Beaufort Historic Site Tours* operated by the historical association. All tours leave from the welcome center at 130 Turner Street. Call ahead for all tour arrangements (252–728– 5225 or 800–575–7484), Monday through Saturday from 8:30 A.M. to 4:30 P.M.

The home tour includes not only old homes, but also the jail, courthouse, and apothecary shop. Tours run Monday through Saturday from 9:30 A.M. to 3:30 P.M. Admission is $6.00 for adults, $4.00 for children. A 10 percent discount for groups of thirty or more is offered.

From April 11 through October, the narrated English double-decker bus tours cover the downtown district and go out past a house that is reputed to have been a hangout for Blackbeard and his pirates in the late 1600s. The tour narrator gives a lively mix of fact and folklore. These tours run Wednesday and Saturday at 11:00 A.M. and cost $5.00

per seat. Special charters for up to fifty-six people cost $200. Charter rate for school groups is $100.

If you can get together a group of at least six people, you can book a narrated tour of the Old Burying Ground at Ann Street, where stones date back to 1709 and possibly earlier. The nar-rator tells colorful stories about unusual circumstances through which people came to be buried here. Admission is $3.00 for adults, $2.00 for children. You may walk around the grounds anytime free.

Of the several bed-and-breakfast establishments you might choose, *Langdon House,* at 123 Craven Street, Beaufort 28516 (252–728–5499), is especially congenial. This colonial home, built in 1732, is the oldest building in Beaufort operated as a bed-and-breakfast. All four rooms have private baths and queen-size beds. Two porches, one on the first and another on the second floor, invite people-watching, stargazing, and wool-gathering. Breakfast is a full show—no soggy doughnuts in a box with coffee in Styrofoam cups here. Some mornings, for instance, it's orange-pecan waffles with orange butter.

Part of the establishment's charm comes from the antiques, including paintings and musical instruments that earlier residents of the building have donated in the interests of the restoration's authenticity. A bigger attraction yet is the congeniality of the people. Jimm Prest knows the area intimately and likes to talk about it.

Langdon House is a small operation. Jimm and a little extra help usually run the show, which means personal attention that is pretty much one-on-one with guests. Want to sleep till noon and have breakfast late? Jimm's willing. He says he wishes more people understood that if you want that kind of small-town, individualized situation, you can't expect chain-motel desk service at the same time. You may call for a reservation, for instance, and get a message on the answering machine saying that Jimm's gone for groceries, a haircut, or a couple days' vacation, telling you when he'll return, and asking you to call back then—just as you'd do if you were phoning a friend.

Because he's been in the area so long, Jimm knows all the Beaufort restaurants well. For a simple meal he suggests the *Net House* (252–728–2468),

AUTHOR'S FAVORITE PLACES
NORTHERN COAST AND ISLANDS

Beaufort

North Carolina
  Maritime Museum

Langdon House

T & W Oyster Bar

Portsmouth Island

Bank of the Arts

Aurora Fossil Museum

Mattamuskeet
  National Wildlife Refuge

Weeping Radish

Wanchese

Hope Plantation

Somerset Place

a short walk away on Turner Street, where you can get broiled or lightly-battered-and-fried seafood. You'll recognize it when you get there, because of the big red crab out front.

For a more upscale menu, **Front Street Grill** (252–723–3118) has out-of-the-ordinary entrees beautifully presented with delicate sauces and garnishes. The menu changes frequently and often reflects an ethnic influence—Thai or Mexican or Greek, for instance—without actually copying any other cuisine. Reservations are strongly suggested here.

A more recently established lodging alternative in Beaufort is **The Pecan Tree** (252–728–6733), a five-room, two-suite inn on Queen Street that emphasizes the luxuries, with elaborately dressed beds, a Jacuzzi/sauna/exercise room, and a lounge. It has well-tended perennial gardens and has been popular with honeymooners.

Langdon House cooperates in handling overflow and referring extra guests with the **Captain's Quarters,** a bed-and-breakfast in a Victorian house at 315 Ann Street, Beaufort 28516 (252–728–7711 or 800–659–7111; www.beaufort–nc.com/captainsquarters). Captain Dick and Ruby Collins like to chat. Captain Dick's title comes not from the sea, as you might suppose, but from his days as an airline pilot. When you appear for your continental breakfast, he says, "Top o' the mornin' to ya!"

One could stay in Beaufort a long time just wandering around, eating seafood, and sitting on the porch reading trashy novels. But you can find more adventure if you want it, too. On the waterfront, near the North Carolina Maritime Museum on Front Street, you'll find **Captain Perry Barrow's** ferry services (252–728–4129), which will take you to **Shackleford Banks,** an island populated only with wild horses; **Carrot Island,** a good place for shelling; and on **Cape Lookout** tours to visit the lighthouse and keepers' quarters and ride a jeep to the cape point. These are great activities in good weather but miserable places on cold, stormy days—assuming you could even get a ferry to take you over then—so it's better to arrange a trip when you see how the weather is going to be. Captain Perry is a good, reliable operator who started the service because during the time he worked in real estate people kept asking him how to get to the islands. "I wanted to provide that service in

Wet Adventure

I paddled my first sea kayak in Beaufort. This is not something you start out doing gracefully. Getting into a life vest and wet suit takes some squirming. Crawling into the small open area of the kayak becomes an exercise in humility. And sitting with your legs stretched straight out in front of you seems an impossiblity.

But then somebody gives you a shove off the sloped ramp and into the water, and after a few tentative strokes, paddling this thing across the waterway to an island seems doable.

It takes a while to remember which rudder to push and even longer to get really proficient at paddling so the boat goes where you want it to. Then it all comes together and the kayak moves silently and efficiently across the water, and except for avoiding other boats and catching glimpses of the wild ponies and the birds on the islands, nothing else matters.

Be warned: Sea kayaking is addictive.

a safe, businesslike way," he says. Even if you are not particularly agile, you won't have trouble getting into the boat because he instructs you to "sit and spin": sit on the wide edge of the boat, spin around, and land your feet on the floor. He provides a sturdy ladder for easy descent onto the island beaches.

Another weather-related activity is kayaking. David and Mandy Stroud (252–728–7070) lead kayaking excursions of about four hours in calm, protected areas. You don't have to have your own kayak. The Strouds have good equipment and go through an initial shakedown routine with you to establish basic techniques and safety procedures. If you get tired and need a little help on the way back, your guide will clip a tow line from the front of your kayak to the back of his life jacket and paddle for both of you. Not only that, he'll make it sound as though you have done him a favor. "This is great, I can work off a lot of tension this way."

While you're in the area, take a half-hour drive some evening to the *T & W Oyster Bar* in Swansboro (252–393–8261). This is a local restaurant not too many tourists find. It specializes in oysters. You can get them steamed or raw. T & W serves oysters in such volume that they move them into the steamers with shovels. People who know about the place sometimes show up with their pickups to get a load of shells for their driveways. Raw oysters are served on the half shell, but you'll have more fun if you sit at the bar and order the steamed oysters, starting with maybe a half peck, although you'll probably want more. You can order them "well, medium, or rare." Rare comes to you just barely heated through. Shuckers stand behind the bar, open your oysters, and put them on your plate—dropping the shells onto a conveyor belt that moves them away somewhere. "Where are those shells going?" isn't a question that enters your mind as you're eating because, for one thing, the oysters are very good. But also, the shuckers, usually high school boys, keep up a steady stream of conversation about local goings on: who's doing what to whom, how late they stayed out last night, how long it took them to learn to shuck with any speed, how much it cost to get a tattoo. You name it, these guys have an opinion. You may get a shucker working on a case of teenage angst or a professional charmer. No matter which, it's fun.

While you're eating oysters you'll probably be invited to save one for a rooster. The shuckers make these. Each claims to have his own special version, but generally a rooster is a saltine cracker spread with horseradish; layered with Tabasco, black pepper, and an oyster; and topped with a slice of jalapeño pepper. Big men break out in a sweat eating a rooster. It's a macho thing, but any woman who wanted to try one would certainly be encouraged.

People who don't like oysters can order steamed shrimp or even burgers or fried fish, but the fun is at the bar. And don't expect any fancy booze here. The chardonnay comes in a big plastic jug labled "use this first," and the beers are your basic Bud, Bud Light choices, served in pitchers. The only proper way to end the meal is with a piece of Key lime pie, which, when it arrives, is an unlikely shade of green never intended by the Maker—but it tastes pretty good.

They'll tell you oysters are available during all the months with "R" in their names, but the more accurate description is "during the cool months." Oysters aren't good when it's hot.

T & W is open 5:00 to 10:00 P.M. daily, noon to 10:00 P.M. Sunday during daylight savings time. They close at 9:00 P.M. during eastern standard time. Closed Thanksgiving Day and December 15 through 25. Located on Highway 58 about 5 miles south of its intersection with Highway 24.

Assuming you are ready, eventually, to leave Beaufort, you should push on north almost to the end of Highway 70 East, to the little town of *Atlantic* (not to be confused with Atlantic Beach), where you can catch the ferry to the Outer Banks. Actually, you can't catch it; you're going to have to call ahead and arrange this part of your trip carefully. At *Morris Marina,* Don and Katie Morris run their private ferry business taking sightseers and fishers to various sites along the islands of Outer Banks. Don can tell stories about these places for about as long as you want to listen.

In particular, visit **Portsmouth Island.** It's uninhabited now, but 635 people once lived on the 30-mile-long island in the village of Portsmouth. Ultimately, they couldn't survive the weather, especially hurricanes. A particularly bad one in 1846 opened Hatteras and Oregon inlets and changed shipping patterns, which cut off future economic development for the village. Gradually the people left, first the young and then the old. According to Joel Arrington, writing in the magazine *Wildlife in North Carolina,* only fourteen people remained on the island in 1950; the last male resident died in 1971, after which the remaining two women gave up and moved to the mainland. The buildings of the village remain a little beat-up but intact, maintained by the U.S. Park Service.

Your difficulty in seeing the village will be that, even after you've ferried across to the island, you need a four-wheel-drive vehicle to travel the 18 miles up the beach from the ferry landing to the village, because there are no roads. But getting a ride in a four-wheel-drive vehicle in North Carolina isn't as hard as it sounds. They are ubiquitous, especially among sportsmen (and it's not sexist to leave out women here, for there are few). Enough such people like to visit the village that by planning ahead with Don Morris you should be able to arrange a ride if you don't have a 4 x 4 of your own. Indeed, the sight of half a dozen or so men in fishing clothes, sitting quietly on the benches inside the old, weathered, and abandoned Portsmouth Village Methodist Church when they're supposed to be at water's edge fishing, may be as special an experience as visiting the village. This isn't a likely place to lodge. A few cabins, locally known as "hooches," are rented, but during peak fishing seasons they're reserved as much as two years in advance. Still, if you'd like to try some truly primitive conditions on the island, it doesn't hurt to ask. For information about ferry hours and renting hooches, write Morris Marina at Star Route Box 761, Atlantic 28511; or phone (919) 225–4261.

A simpler way to visit the village, though less colorful and a bit more *on* the beaten (or should it be *rowed,* in this case?) path, is to take a skiff from Ocracoke Island that brings you directly to the spot. You need to arrange this in advance. Phone Rudi Austin (252–928–4361) or Judas Austin (252–928–4281) to charter a ferry. The more people you can round up to make the trip with you, the less it costs per person. Figure about $40 for two, round-trip, but only about $15 per person when you have three or more.

If you're not sure how to manage the trip and would like more information and advice, call the Ranger Station (252–728–2250) for enthusiastic, knowledgeable help. They have a list of all the ferrying services and can put you in touch with the one that will work best for you.

Harkers Island doesn't attract a lot of traffic. It's a people place, not yet a tourist place, where a few people still remember when hunting water-fowl for food was a natural part of daily existence, not a recreational sport. They remember carving decoys because they needed them to attract ducks, not to set up on the mantel as decorator items. The **Core Sound Waterfowl Museum** honors that Down East heritage and provides a place for carvers to practice the old art and younger people to learn it or at least see it in action.

The museum, housed in what Director Karen Amspacher calls "a little bitty house we rent for a dollar a year—a borrowed building on borrowed land," attracts visitors from all over the world.

Most days you'll find two or three local wood-carvers at work on the porch, telling stories about the days when waterfowl were so plentiful their clusters looked like islands out in the sound. When decoys got lost or drifted away, it wasn't a big deal. They just carved more as part of the daily routine. Nothing fancy about it. The early decoys didn't have to fool anybody but the flocks of birds high overhead.

A new, much larger museum is in the works—on sixteen acres at Shell Point, next to the National Park Service's Cape Lookout National Seashore headquarters near the tip of the island. It's a community effort, the money being raised by local people, with such attractions as a viewing platform on Willow Pond built by volunteers with donated materials. Whatever state the place is in when you get to Harkers, it's a heartwarming stop. The museum is open Monday through Saturday, 10 A.M. to 5:00 P.M., Sunday 2:00 to 5:00 P.M. Admission is free. For more information call (252) 728–1500.

Land of Friendly Faces

The entire area along the northern coast, the barrier islands, and the Outer Banks is a maze of toll ferries, free ferries, private ferries, and bridges. The way you organize your trips here depends on everything from the weather to how much time you want to spend driving or being ferried. Remember that a ferry is not a fast way to travel. In planning trips in this area, it sometimes works better to find a pleasant base to which you return after each foray in a new direction. Try **New Bern** as a slightly inland base from which, one way or another, you can get to a wonderful variety of places to spend a day or so. Everyone in New Bern will have ideas for you, which will certainly include *Oriental.*

Oriental is about 25 miles east of New Bern on Highway 55. It has won a reputation as the sailing capital of the East Coast and almost always has a sailing school or camp in progress. Except for a couple of antiques shops, a modest motel or two, and some simple restaurants, there's not much here except nice people. If you want to spend a night at a bed-and-breakfast here, the *Tar Heel Inn,* at 508 Church Street, Oriental 28571 (252–249–1078), has eight rooms with private baths, king- and queen-size beds, and facilities for the handicapped. The inn was built at the turn of the twentieth century and has been restored to duplicate the feel of an English country inn—with contemporary amenities. The innkeepers serve a big breakfast.

The *Cartwright House,* 301 Freemason Street, Oriental 28571 (252–249–1337), has four rooms and a suite with a fireplace, Jacuzzi, and private porch. The British innkeepers, Glyn and Tina Dykins, serve a full breakfast. Web site: www.cartwrighthouse.com.

Then again, once you're in New Bern you may not want to go anywhere else at all, not just because there's so much to see and do but also because this is one of the friendliest towns anywhere. To give you an idea, a couple staying at a bed-and-breakfast inn in the historic district was walking to a nearby restaurant where they had dinner reservations when they stopped to admire an especially nicely restored house. The owners, who happened to be on the porch, invited the couple in for a drink and showed them around. They spent so much time chatting that the couple never did make it to the restaurant.

On the outside chance that you might not be so generously befriended by strangers, stop in the tourist center at the Chamber of Commerce about 2 blocks from Highway 70, near the Trent River at the end of Middle Street, when you get to town. Signs point the way from all major entrances. Everyone here is extraordinarily friendly, too. One middle-aged travel writer who stopped in for maps and directions struck up a conversation with a teenage summer assistant. They've been corresponding ever since.

If you're an antiquer, be sure to get a copy of the brochure "Antiques Shops of New Bern," which gives particulars on more than a dozen antiques shops, complete with a map and an explanation of American furniture styles from Queen Anne (1725–50) through the arts-and-crafts and mission styles of the early 1900s.

You'll also be able to pick up full details on *Tryon Palace* Restorations and Garden Complex, where first a royal government and then an independent state government were housed. In colonial times Tryon Palace was known as the most beautiful building in America. The elaborate formal gardens as well as the elegant buildings and furnishings have been restored.

Tours conducted by guides in costume lead you through the rooms; give you a look at demonstrations of candle making, cloth making, cooking, and other period activities; and fill you in on specific facts about the buildings and their earlier, illustrious occupants. If you just want to walk around in the gardens, you can take a self-guided tour. The complex (252–514–4900 or 800–767–1560) is open year-round, Monday through Saturday from 9:00 A.M. to 4:00 P.M., and Sunday from 1:00 to 4:00 P.M. Closed Thanksgiving Day, December 24–26, and January 1. Admission is $12.00 for adults, $6.00 for students with identification. Write Tryon Palace, Box 1007, New Bern 28560.

An interesting and historical, yet cheery and comfortable place to stay in New Bern is *Harmony House Inn,* 215 Pollock Street, New Bern 28560 (252– 636–3810 or 800–636–3113). Sooki and Ed Kirkpatrick, the proprietors, bring to innkeeping the kind of personable warmth that makes business travelers who stay there regularly feel free to stop in unannounced, use the phone in the inn's office, and then hurry out to the car, saying they'll be back to spend the night on the way through tomorrow. Web site: www.harmonyhouseinn.com.

The story of the house is complex. It began as a four-room, two-story home with Greek Revival styling. As the family grew, the house was

Tryon Palace, New Bern

enlarged. Around the turn of the twentieth century, as the children grew older, two sons wanted the house, so it was sawed in half, and one side was moved 9 feet away from the other. A huge hallway and another set of stairs were put in to join the building yet divide it into two separate dwellings. Now the two hallways, front doors, and sitting areas are all part of the inn. It's furnished with antiques and reproductions created by local craftspeople, and in the parlor is an 1875 organ in perfect working order. Breakfast is always an extravaganza, including eggs, cheese, meat, cereal, and fruit. You are invited to participate in an evening social hour with white wine; sherry is put out later in case you'd like a nightcap.

Near Harmony House, *King's Arms Inn,* 212 Pollock Street, New Bern 28560 (252–638–4409 or 800–872–9306) also offers accommodations in a restored inn.

After a day of touring, you can rest awhile at one of these inns and then walk to dinner. *Henderson House,* right across the street at 216 Pollock, New Bern 28560 (252–637–4784), has been serving fine meals for nearly twenty years. The atmosphere is elegant. Dining specialties include southern peanut soup and cold apricot soup, as well as a seafood casserole, scallops, lobster, lamb, veal, and chicken entrees. All spirits are available. As you'd expect, all the desserts are homemade. Everything is delicious, the kind of dining guests at the bed-and-breakfasts talk about over breakfast the next morning. Also as you'd expect, the prices are not low. Dinner is served from 6:00 to 9:00 P.M. Tuesday through Saturday.

Much less well known than the palace are these three small museums, each within walking distance of the other.

The *Attmore–Oliver House Museum,* built in 1790, at 511 Broad Street, New Bern 28560 (parking at 510 Pollock Street), belonged at one time to Samuel Chapman, who had earlier been a first lieutenant under General George Washington. It features eighteenth- and nineteenth-century antiques, artifacts related to New Bern's history, and a Civil War museum room. There's also a collection of eighteenth-century dolls. Open Tuesday through Saturday from 1:00 to 4:30 P.M. (252–638–8558). Closed mid-December to the first weekend in April. Free.

The *Fireman's Museum,* across the corner at 411 Hancock Street, New Bern 28560, houses a collection of memorabilia of North Carolina's earliest fire company, from 1845, and of the Button Company, a rival volunteer company. The museum guide himself has been a volunteer fireman for many years. The displays include early steamers and pump wagons, large photographs, and the mounted head of an old fire horse named Fred, who, at least according to publicists, died in harness answering a false alarm in 1925. No information is offered about what happened to the rest of the horse. Open Monday through Saturday from 10:00 A.M. to 4:30 P.M.; Sunday from 1:00 to 5:00 P.M. Closed Thanksgiving, Christmas, and New Year's Day. Admission is $2.00 for adults, $1.00 for children. (252–636–4087).

At **Bank of the Arts,** 317 Middle Street (252–638–2577), about a block away, you'll find artists' exhibits in sculpture, oil, watercolor, pottery, and photography. The exhibits change every month. Originally a neo-classical bank building, it is now home to the Craven Arts Council and Gallery. The gallery has 30-foot-high ceilings with ornate colored plaster in the Beaux Arts style. Sometimes afternoon concerts, story-tellers, and folksingers are featured. Open weekdays from 10:00 A.M. to 4:00 P.M. Closed Sunday. Admission is free.

The **New Bern Trolley Cars** (252–637–7316 or 800–849–7316) combine the fun of motion with the expertise of tour guides who know the history of New Bern and tell it well. The trolley tours, which run through the historic downtown district, last ninety minutes. Tour hours vary with the seasons, so you'll do better by calling to find out what's happening during your visit to the area. Tickets are available where the trolley begins its route, next to Tryon Palace, $12.00 for adults, $6.00 for children. Tickets may be purchased on the trolley cars.

In a town as historically significant as New Bern, you could easily get overwhelmed by more historical data than you really want on a vacation, but to enjoy the area you should know at least a few basic facts. The community was first settled in 1710 by Swiss and German immigrants, who named it for Bern, Switzerland. It was capital of the colonies from 1766 to 1776 and then state capital. Economically, the area flourished mostly because of its port at the time of the Revolution, slumped during the Civil War, then recovered fairly quickly. From about the time of World War II, it has gradually restored its historical spots and become a comfortably established, low-key attraction. Irrelevant but fun to know: Pepsi-Cola was invented here, but the inventor went bankrupt during a sugar scarcity; and the official New Bern shrub is *Lagerstroemia*—crepe myrtle. The brilliant blossoms brighten most streets and home landscapes many months of the year.

Water's Edge

One interesting trip from New Bern is the drive north on Highway 17 to Washington, where you pick up Highway 264 to **Bath, Belhaven,** and **Swan Quarter.** The trip winds through mostly rural areas, although just north of New Bern on Highway 17 you'll come to a business area where you can buy supplies. Stop at the **Eagle Supermarket,** which is a lot more fun and will give you a much better sense of the local population than the little convenience stores along the way. Out front everything from bales of straw to wheelbarrows is stacked along the windows. Inside are all the standard grocery-store offerings plus some of the friendliest local employees you'll ever meet. The store is open from 7:00 A.M. to 9:00 P.M. Monday through Saturday and from 8:00 A.M. to 9:00 P.M. Sunday.

You'll find more local color just before you come to Washington, at **Chocowinity,** billed as "Home of the Indians," where the high school boasts having won a series of state and regional girls' basketball titles and cheerleading championships, beginning in 1980. It's all detailed proudly on a huge sign in front of the school. Around the corner on Highway 33 West, L Cheapos Flea Market and Scotts Collectibles and Antiques stand side by side, with old furniture, knickknacks, and odds and ends packed inside, jammed into the windows, and overflowing out onto the sidewalks. These aren't the kinds of places where you expect operating hours to remain unchanged month to month, but if you happen by when the establishments are open, you can have a lot of fun browsing, chatting, and maybe making an honest-to-goodness find. Chocowinity is a crossroads community, not set up to lure or serve tourists, so don't count on it as a place to stop, fuel up, eat, and so on. Look at it as an absolutely honest glimpse of small-town coastal North Carolina.

From here you can drive on through Washington to Bath or get to Bath by crossing the Pamlico River on the ferry, which you approach by following Highway 33 East from Chocowinity through corn and tobacco country, past a brick house with a stonework chimney that's bigger than the house, past Possum Track Road, and on to Aurora—a drive of about 33 miles. This route actually backtracks some, and you could get to Aurora faster by taking State Road 1003 from Highway 17 just outside New Bern, but then you'd miss Chocowinity. It all depends on how much exploring you want to do.

Twin Lakes Resort, 1618 Memory Lane, Chocowinity 27817 (252–946–5700; fax 252–946–1789), offers swanky camping. You have a choice

THE NORTHERN COAST AND ISLANDS

BETTER KNOWN ATTRACTIONS IN THE NORTHERN COAST AND ISLANDS

NEW BERN
Tryon Palace
(800) 767–1560

MANTEO
Lost Colony Outdoor Drama
(252) 473–3414
(800) 488–5012

ROANOKE ISLAND
North Carolina Aquarium
(252) 473–3493

NAGS HEAD
Jocky Ridge State Park
(252) 441–7132

KILL DEVIL HILLS
Wright Brothers National Memorial
(252) 441–7430

of trailer sites (some shaded), tent sites, and pull-throughs, supplying water and electricity. Also on the grounds are hot showers, campfires, laundry facilities, pay phones, ice, firewood, church services, a boat ramp, a fishing pier, water skiing, a playground, recreational facilities, a camp store, and a picnic area.

According to a chatty soul named Dianne, people sometimes bring big tents, refrigerators, and small television sets—everything they need to stay for a long time. Camping on this scale is $28 a night weekends, $23 weekdays. Primitive camping (though Linda can't imagine who'd want it) is $20 a night weekends, $18 weekdays. Ask for directions when you call.

Close to the juncture of North Carolina Highways 33 and 306, the little town of Aurora—population 700—is home to the *Aurora Fossile Museum,* on Main Street. This museum is great for kids who are turned on by hunting for artifacts and equally rewarding for anyone looking for a better understanding of the geological history of eastern North Carolina from the birth of the Atlantic Ocean to the present.

Millions of years ago this part of the state lay under the ocean. Fossils anywhere from five to twenty-two million years old are on display in the museum, along with a variety of murals and an eighteen-minute video explaining the history of the region. The fossils include giant teeth from 40-foot sharks, bones from extinct birds, and skeletons of dolphins that had necks. Some scientists speculate that the existence of the neck proves dolphins once lived on land and evolved to adapt to the sea.

The museum gets its artifacts from a large phosphate mine a few miles north of town. An exhibit in the museum shows a mock phosphate pit to illustrate how phosphate is mined and where the fossils come from. And outside the museum stands a huge pile of coarse phosphate materials through which visitors may sift for fossils. What you're most likely to find here are prehistoric shark's teeth.

The museum's director and curator, Candace Holliday, emphasizes that the museum is about more than fossils and prehistoric times. She points to a new exhibit of Indian artifacts as an example.

The museum is open 9:00 A.M. to 4:30 P.M. Monday through Friday, September through May. In June, July, and August it is open from 9:00 A.M. to 4:30 P.M. Tuesday through Friday and 9:00 A.M. to 2:00 P.M. Saturday. Closed on holidays. Phone (252) 322–4238. Web site: www.pamlico.com/aurora/fossils.

A mile or so outside Aurora, Highway 306 North turns left, bringing you to Keith Brantley's service station, the kind of place where some of the local old-timers sit around inside and talk about the weather, where whoever pumps your gas actually cleans your windshield, and where you need a key and a good kick on the door to get into the rest room. Across the road, **Brunches Restaurant** serves mostly fast food without the franchise chain atmosphere and offers excellent iced tea. The restaurant is open from 5:30 A.M. to 8:00 P.M. daily. From there Highway 306 North goes about 7 miles to the Pamlico River Ferry, which is free; the crossing takes about twenty-five minutes. From the ferry landing, go left on Highway 92 into historic **Bath,** where you come first to the visitors center.

Bath is the kind of place you fantasize about when you dream of leaving the rat race for a simpler way of life. The town, with a population not much over 200, only 3 blocks long and 2 blocks wide, is friendly and without guile; people cutting their grass or working in their gardens wave as you walk or drive by. They're proud of their history but see it with enough humor to name the state liquor store "Ye Olde ABC Package Store."

The folks in the **Historic Bath Visitors Center** at 207 Carteret Street, Bath 27889, encourage you to see the twenty-five-minute orientation film, "A Town Called Bath," before you begin a self-guided walking tour or take one of the guided tours. These begin on the hour from 9:00 A.M. to 5:00 P.M. Monday through Saturday and from 1:00 to 5:00 P.M. Sunday, from April through October 31. Winter hours are 10:00 A.M. to 4:00 P.M. Tuesday through Saturday, 1:00 to 4:00 P.M. Sunday. Tours take about an hour and a half. Modest admission charged (252–923–3971). Web site: www.pamlico.com/bath.

You can approach the history a couple of different ways. Bath was the home of Blackbeard the pirate, and some of his loot is still supposed to be buried somewhere in the area. It's also the oldest incorporated town

Whitfield's Curse

*B*ath opened the first public library in the American colonies (opened in 1700), started the first shipyard in the state in 1701, and was the state's first capital in 1744. So why did such a forward-looking town never grow the way some other seaport towns did?

Local legend has it that the townspeople rejected Methodist Evangelist George Whitfield when he came in 1774 to save their souls. They didn't want to hear his preaching, and they wouldn't give him a place to stay in town. Whitfield got back at them by placing a curse on the village: ". . . you shall remain, now and forever, forgotten by men and nations . . ."

After that the town burned three times, and even today the population stays at about 200 souls, which may or may not be saved.

in North Carolina. The Palmer–Marsh House, from the colonial period, dates back to about 1740. The St. Thomas Church, which was begun in 1734, is the oldest church in the state. It has been restored and is still used by the Episcopal Diocese as an active place of worship, although visitors are allowed to come in anytime for a self-guided tour. The St. Thomas parish had a collection in the early 1700s of more than 1,000 books and pamphlets from England, and that collection became the first public library in North Carolina.

From Bath, it's a pretty drive of 11 miles on Highway 99 to Belhaven, where you pick up Highway 264 East, crossing the Intracoastal Waterway to Swan Quarter. Most of this distance is lovely, although you'll probably see a lot of heavy equipment in some areas. In early summer hibiscus bushes bloom along the road, red and yellow cannas adorn the lawns of farmhouses and mobile homes, and apple trees bear so heavily that the fruit seems to be dripping from the laden and drooping branches.

At Swan Quarter you can either take the ferry to Ocracoke, probably the best known of the barrier islands, or you can continue driving up the coast along Highway 264 to Manns Harbor, where you cross the bridge to Roanoke Island and continue on over the Outer Banks islands. If you plan to take the ferry, a two-and-one-half-hour ride, call the Ocracoke Visitors Center (252–928–4531) ahead of time to check on current schedules and weather conditions.

Ocracoke, an old fishing village, is fun if you're willing to take a couple of days and just hang out; if all you do is drive through, you'll miss most of what it has to offer. Of course there's history. As early as 1715

Ocracoke was a port of the North Carolina colony, where Blackbeard the pirate buried his treasure and lost his head. The head got carried off to Bath; presumably the treasure's still somewhere on the island. These days, fishing, bicycling (you can rent bicycles here), and bird hunting are bigger attractions than treasure hunting. But mostly Ocracoke is a place to escape the chrome-and-plastic world of commercial tourism. You can enjoy the remnants of Old English lilting in the speech of some of the old-timers as you walk around the village, read up on local history and nature, and visit the famous pony pens where the remaining descendants of the famous Spanish mustangs are protected. For full information about the island, ferries, and the marina, contact the Ocracoke Visitors Center (252–928–4531) or the Outer Banks Chamber of Commerce, P.O. Box 1757, Kill Devil Hills 27948 (252–441– 8144). Open March through December 9:00 A.M. to 5:00 P.M. Hours may be longer during summer. ***Ocracoke Island Lighthouse*** (252– 952–5201 or 888–493–3826), on Point Road, is the oldest lighthouse still in use in North Carolina. It was built in 1823. The tower is 75 feet tall, built of brick and concrete, with 5-foot-thick base walls. The white tower serves as an entrance beacon to Ocracoke Inlet. The tower is not open to the public, but you may tour the grounds. Admission is free. Web site: www.ocracoke-nc.com/light.

The island has several motels and some bed-and-breakfast inns. One of the nicest is also one of the smallest. ***Oscar's House*** is run by Ann Ehringhaus. The name comes from Oscar, the lighthouse keeper and builder who once lived in it. The house is furnished in a style that Ann calls "comfortable and artistic." A professional photographer, she has traded some of her work with other artists, acquiring baskets, pottery, watercolors, and photographs, all of which enliven the mellow, tongue-in-groove pine walls of the house. And, as Ann says, "You can sit in the furniture. No delicate Victorian antiques."

Ann's full breakfasts feature produce from her organic garden and include everything from fresh fish to shrimp creole. It's the kind of breakfast that allows people to skip lunch. If you'd like something low-fat, vegetarian, macrobiotic, or otherwise special, Ann will accommodate you. "Cooking is my favorite part of the B&B business," she says.

A big part of the charm of staying here is getting to know Ann, who knows the island and its residents intimately. Her book, *Ocracoke Portrait,* a collection of her photographs captioned with quotations from the islanders, is an understated, elegant picture of life on the island. The inn (252–928–1311, P.O. Box 206, Ocracoke 27960) is open April through October. Special cooking workshops and photography workshops are sometimes scheduled at the beginning and end of the season. Another book to watch for is one about the complexities of innkeeping as a business and way of life. After a decade doing it, Ann is ready to write about it.

Of the several small restaurants on the island, **The Back Porch** (252–928–6401), in a shady area a half-mile north of the ferry terminal on Highway 1324, seems just right. The dining room is wood paneled, with a screened-in porch. The food is fresh, not prepared ahead, with homemade bread and desserts and subtle flavors of herb and spice that you can taste because the food isn't fried. Open daily from 5:00 to 10:00 P.M., April through November. It's good news that the restaurant now offers a cookbook of its most popular recipes.

Another popular restaurant on the island is **Captain Ben's Restaurant,** on U.S. 12, just north of the ferry terminal. The restaurant specializes in seafood; its signature dishes are shrimp scampi and Maryland crab cakes. You can enjoy wine or beer here, in a casual atmosphere. The restaurant is open April through October, from 11:30 A.M. to 9:00 P.M., serving lunch and dinner. Phone (252) 928–4741 for reservations.

No matter how much you like it, sooner or later you'll have to leave Ocracoke. A free ferry will take you from Ocracoke to Cape Hatteras and Frisco, still along the Outer Banks, where you'll find the **Native American Museum and Natural History Center** (252–995–4440) on Highway 12. The museum has a nationally recognized but too-seldom-seen collection of Native American artifacts and exhibits. In the natural history center, you'll find educational displays, special films, live exhibits, and a nature trail winding through the maritime forest. The people who work here say it's impossible to tell what the most popular exhibits are because favorites vary with each individual, but the stone artifacts attract a lot of attention, the Hopi wishing drum really does work, and people who commune with nature in the maritime forest claim some unusual experiences. The gift shop is popular, too, because it sells genuine Native American crafts. The museum is open Tuesday through Sunday, 11:00 A.M. to 5:00 P.M. To request information by mail, write the museum at Box 399, Frisco 27936. Modest admission is charged.

It's possible to drive on up the Outer Banks, but it's monotonous in some undeveloped areas, full of traffic elsewhere, and generally just not as interesting as you'd expect it to be. You might do better to ferry back across to Swan Quarter and from there drive north on Highway 264, toward Manns Harbor, where the bridge takes you across to Manteo on Roanoke Island. This trip takes you into the **Mattamuskeet National Wildlife Refuge,** a breathtaking wilderness of 50,000 acres comprising Lake Mattamuskeet, marshland, timber, and cropland. The lake is 18 miles long and about 6 miles wide, the largest natural lake in North Carolina.

In parts of the acreage, water levels are controlled mechanically to allow local farmers to plant corn and soybeans and to allow for overseeding some acres to provide food for the wildlife. The wooded areas along the boundaries of the refuge contain pine and mixed hardwoods. Some commercial logging and controlled burning are used to keep the woodlands healthy.

Headquarters for the refuge (252–926–4021) is off Highway 94, $1\frac{1}{2}$ miles north of Highway 264, between Swan Quarter and Englehard. Stopping in is a good way to learn all the possibilities of the place. At various points you can crab, fish in fresh- or saltwater, and hunt. The area begs for bird-watching, photographing, and painting. Depending on the time of year, you might spot swans, Canada geese, song- and marsh birds, and even bald eagles, as well as deer, bobcats, and river otter.

But this is a refuge administered by the U.S. Fish and Wildlife Service of the Department of the Interior and operates by its rules. You can't camp, swim, or collect exotic plants here. There are restrictions on firearms. The refuge is open from 5:00 A.M. to 9:00 P.M. daily. For full details on how to enjoy the place and lists of lodgings available nearby, write Refuge Manager, Mattamuskeet National Wildlife Refuge, Route 1, Box N-2, Swan Quarter 27885.

When you're in the area, it's fun to gas up at the **Mattamuskeet Sportsman's Center** on Highway 264, where a long-bearded proprietor and his little kids dispense information, advice, directions, and such necessities as fishing and hunting equipment, bait shrimp, worms, ice, candy, beer, and soda. Oh, yes, and food.

From Mattamuskeet Lake, Highway 264 continues through lonely marsh and woodland up to Manns Harbor and across to Roanoke Island. The main community here, Manteo, used to be a small resort area. It's growing now, not excessively, but too much to suit the longtime residents who remember when the road through town didn't turn into bumper-to-bumper ribbons of automobiles during rush hour.

Roanoke Island

ou'll remember from your grade-school history lessons that Roanoke Island is where the English first tried to establish a colony in the New World in 1585, encouraged by Queen Elizabeth I and led by Sir Walter Raleigh. They named it for Raleigh but couldn't keep it going. A year later those who had survived returned to England. In 1857 Raleigh tried again, this time including women and children in the group led by John White. Virginia Dare was born here. Then Sir Walter went sailing away for supplies. By the time he got back, three years later, the colony had vanished, leaving no signs of what might have happened to it. The **Fort Raleigh National Historic Site** memorializes the lost colony with a restoration of the old fort and a granite marker commemorating Virginia Dare's birth as the first English child born here. From June through August, the drama *The Lost Colony,* performed outdoors at the Waterford Theatre on the site, tells the story. One of Andy Griffith's acting roles in his pre-Mayberry years was as Sir Walter Raleigh in this show. Everything about this outdoor drama happens on a grand

Rain Time

he weather was cold and blustery the first time I saw a performance of The Lost Colony. *As I was getting ready to sit down, a young man's hat blew off and landed at my feet. I retrieved it and ended up sitting next to him.*

Shortly into the performance, I realized he was saying every performer's lines along with the actors—and he had it all down perfectly. He saw me notice and explained that he used to be in the show. It was common for the actors to learn each other's lines, he said, in case one of them couldn't perform and needed a stand-in.

By this time the rain was coming down pretty hard. The young man said the Indian dancers had two dance tempos—regular time and rain time. When the weather was bad, they danced faster to get the whole show finished so they wouldn't have to give back money to a rained-out audience.

This night, although the crowd sat willingly under umbrellas watching the show, the dancers just couldn't go fast enough. Pouring rain brought everything to a halt, and as we left, theater staff handed us tickets for another performance.

scale, on a stage in front of the bay so the water almost seems to be a backdrop. Many of the effects are marvels of engineering. For instance, three ships "sail" in front of the stage, moved by a combination of ropes and human energy. Moderate admission charged. Phone (252) 473–3414 or (800) 488–5012 for exact schedules. Be sure to ask what the current policy is regarding bad weather. Web site: www.thelostcolony.org.

Next to the theater, the **Elizabethan Gardens** (252–473–3234) created by the Garden Club of North Carolina as a memorial to the lost colonists, bloom from spring until fall, with roses, crepe myrtle, lilies, hydrangeas, and summer annuals. The garden features an extensive collection of old garden ornaments, some dating back to the time of the first Queen Elizabeth, as well as a sunken garden, a wildflower garden, an herb garden, and camellias and azaleas in season. Open April and May 9:00 A.M. to 6:00 P.M., June, July, and August to 7:00 P.M., September and October to 6:00 P.M., November to 5:00 P.M., December and January to 4:00 P.M., March to 5:00 P.M. Admission is $5.00 for adults, $4.50 seniors, $1.00 for children ages six to seventeen; children under six are admitted free.

Complete your history lesson by visiting the **Elizabeth II State Historic Site,** across the bridge and opposite the Manteo waterfront. The museum (252–473–1144) contains exhibits depicting life in the sixteenth century, including a reproduction of a sailing vessel similar to what would have been used to bring the first colonists to Roanoke in 1585. A twenty-minute multimedia program gives you the feel of those early voyages and

All the Town's a Stage

*I*f you strike up a conversation about The Lost Colony *with some of the local people in Manteo, you'll quickly discover that the show is a town industry. It has its share of famous people, like Andy Griffith, on the stage, but at one time or another, many of the townspeople also appeared in the show, treating it as their summer job. Others have worked as crew and stagehands, helped maintain the costumes, answered telephones, made reservations in the office, and taken tickets at the gates.*

I stood with three women ranging in age from about thirty to early sixties as they compared notes. They'd all played one of the same female parts at different times. They mentioned the character's name, but I didn't recognize it from having seen the show, so you probably have to know the script to remember it. I could tell that being in the show had been a magical experience, if a strenuous one, for each of them, and while they didn't really want to work that hard again, they still missed it.

Elizabeth II

what it would have been like to live on the ship. In the summer costumed actors portray early marines and colonists. After seeing the film, you may tour the ship. Operating hours vary seasonally. Moderate admission is charged. Write to *Elizabeth II* State Historic Site, Manteo 27954.

In downtown Manteo (named for an Indian of Roanoke who went back to England with the early sailors) on Highway 64/264, you can pick up a bit of local family history by staying at ***Scarborough Inn*** (252–473–3979), run by longtime residents of the island. Six rooms in the inn and four in the annex are furnished with comfortable old furniture that has been in the family, or at least in the community, for generations. It's not fancy stuff but the kind of things you remember from visiting old Aunt Lizzie or Great-grandma. Nearly every piece has a story that Rebecca and Fields Scarborough, who love to talk, will tell you gladly. The rooms are simple but comfortable. Two units over the barn are outfitted with king-size beds. Each room has a private bath, a small refrigerator, and a coffeemaker with coffee provided. No breakfast is served, but Rebecca leaves a couple of packs of doughnuts by the coffeemaker. Rates include the use of bicycles for exploring the island.

Across the road from Scarborough Inn, the ***Weeping Radish*** specializes in authentic German food served by waitresses in Bavarian costume and accompanied by a variety of dark and light beers from the Weeping Radish microbrewery, all to the tune of Bavarian folk music. The pub and restaurant operate on varying schedules depending on the season. Tours of the brewery are available on a varying schedule. Phone (252–473–1157) for details.

For more elegant accommodations and dining, try **Clara's Seafood Grill** on the waterfront. According to the Scarboroughs, Clara's, in the waterfront condos overlooking rows of sailboats and yachts, makes the best crab cakes in town. Advertised on the menu as "more crab than cake," these hefty crab cakes are coated with a tempuralike batter that barely contains the large lumps of crab bursting from the cake. Homemade whole-wheat rolls, an imported beer or some wine, a house salad with strawberry vinaigrette, and a rich Kentucky Derby fudge pie complete a sumptuous meal, all for a little more than $20. The atmosphere is upscale, but casual dress is appropriate. Clara's (252–473–1727) is in the condo division at the corner of Sir Walter Raleigh and Queen Elizabeth Avenues. Open daily from 11:30 A.M. to 9:30 P.M. in summer and noon to 8:30 P.M. the rest of the year. Sometimes closed for a few weeks in winter.

You might put what you don't spend at Clara's toward a special night at the **Tranquil House Inn.** The inn, on the Shallowbag Bay waterfront in downtown Manteo, whispers *luxury* when you enter—clearly a fine-wine-and-cheese kind of place. The building is a reproduction of a typical nineteenth-century Outer Banks inn, with added contemporary conveniences a nineteenth-century traveler wouldn't even have dreamed about. Because of the pale cypress woodwork, glass, and stained glass throughout, the inn's interior seems almost as bright and sunny as the docks outside. The inn has an upscale gourmet restaurant with a fine wine list. In the guest rooms you'll find not only the expected amenities such as television and telephone but also Oriental carpets, fine furnishings, and hand-tiled bathrooms. Rates, commensurate with the luxurious atmosphere, vary seasonally and include a buffet breakfast (252–473–1404 or 800–458–7069). Web site: www.tranquilinn.com.

The other community on Roanoke Island, **Wanchese** (named for another Indian who took off for England), doesn't seem to know it is surrounded by tourists. Most of the people of Wanchese fish for a living. Driving on Highway 345 South to the village, you pass modest homes—many with a boat in the yard—battered vans, worn pickups, and lots of churches, flowers, and pets. Signs in some of the yards invite you to buy hand-carved duck decoys, driftwood, wood crafts, and nursery plants. All the people you see in the community will talk to you pleasantly and seem to enjoy your watching them work on the docks.

Fisherman's Wharf Restaurant (252–473–5205), a large, unpretentious restaurant on the wharf, surrounded by pilings, wild stands of Queen Anne's lace, and rolls of chicken wire, specializes in broiled and fried seafood and Wanchese crab cakes at modest prices. From your table you can watch the same fishing fleets that probably caught what you're eating. Sometimes broadcasts from a religious radio station drift through a speaker at the door. Open from noon to 9:00 P.M. Monday through Saturday, from mid-April through October or later, depending on the weather.

Before you leave Roanoke Island, take time to visit this branch of the *North Carolina Aquarium,* about a mile north of Manteo, off Highway 64. Here you get a close-up view of live marine life, including sharks, eels, and sea turtles. A touch tank, as the name implies, lets you feel live crabs and starfish. The aquarium maintains a full calendar of special events, from seafood-cooking workshops to field trips and cruises. The aquarium has been closed for renovation but is expected to reopen by press time. For a current schedule, write the aquarium, Roanoke Island, Manteo 27954, or call (252) 473–3493.

From Manteo, a short drive across the bridge on Highway 64/264 takes you to Bodie Island (which isn't really an island anymore but a location along the northern section of the Outer Banks), where it's worth stopping to see the Bodie Island Lighthouse, operating since 1872. Aside from Coquina Beach, a good beach for swimming and fishing, you won't find many attractions here. A turn to the south, however, takes you to Hatteras Island, home of the tallest lighthouse in America, the *Cape Hatteras Lighthouse.* When the Cape Hatteras Lighthouse was built in 1870, it stood thousands of feet from the Atlantic Ocean. But erosion gradually brought the sea closer and closer. In the last decade, experts said the lighthouse would soon fall into the ocean if it were not somehow protected. After lengthy controversy about what to do and how to do it, Congress authorized nearly $12 million to move the lighthouse away from the shore line, preserving it as a historic structure.

In June 1999 the old lighthouse was moved 1,300 feet inland, barely an inch at a time, while North Carolinians watched reports of the progress on the Internet and on nightly television news.

Now the lighthouse stands 3,000 feet from the ocean at high tide, about the same distance as when it was first built, and is open for visitors. If you're up for climbing more than 260 steps, you can stand on a balcony at the top to survey the area.

Cape Hatteras Lighthouse

What used to be the lighthouse keeper's home is now a visitors center where you can check out exhibits about local history and pick up a map for a self-guiding nature trail that begins nearby.

In the summer season the lighthouse is open every day from 10:00 A.M. to 4:00 P.M. In the off-season it closes earlier. The visitors center is open from 9:00 A.M. to 5:00 P.M. daily. Admission is free. Call (252) 995–4474 for details. This area is undeveloped because the protected Cape Hatteras National Seashore comprises Hatteras, some of the southern end of Bodie, and Ocracoke. Here you can see natural beaches and their attendant wildlife, seashells as they wash ashore and accumulate, and vegetation dwarfed and gnarled by salt and wind but not threatened by macadam, all without water slides. For more information on the area, write the Superintendent, Cape Hatteras National Seashore, Route 1, Box 675, Manteo 27954, or call (252) 473–2111. At the north end of Hatteras Island, ***Pea Island National Wildlife Refuge,*** an area of nearly 6,000 acres, is a place to see more than 250 different species of birds, watch the ocean, and view old shipwrecks near shore. The refuge has observation decks about 5 miles south of the Oregon Inlet Bridge. For details phone the information office (252–473–1131).

It's a different story turning north from Bodie Island. You drive through the kind of beach-strip conglomeration of motels, restaurants, gas stations, fast-food chains, and beach shops that typifies most popular beach areas. As a follower of unbeaten paths, you might choose to skip it, unless you're interested in seeing the ***Wright Brothers National Memorial*** at Kill Devil Hills, which marks the spot where Wilbur and Orville Wright first got off the ground in powered flight on December 7, 1903. The visitors center here has full-sized copies of the brothers' glider and their first plane. The brothers' workshop and living quarters have been re-created too. Open daily from 9:00 A.M. to 6:00 P.M. Winter hours may be shorter. Admission is $2.00 per person or $4.00 per car (252–441–7430).

Just south of Kill Devil Hills, on the U.S. 158 Bypass in Nag's Head, *Jockey's Ridge State Park* (252–441–7132) makes a good place to stop, play in the sand, and get some exercise. This is the highest sand dune on the East Coast, where prevailing winds generally range from 10 to 15 miles an hour. Kite flying here is just about perfect. Hang gliding is popular, too. The park has a picnic area and a shelter, as well as swimming and fishing on the sound.

Enjoy a more rural setting at *Nags Head Woods Preserve* (252–441–2525), 701 West Ocean Acres Drive, Kill Devil Hills 27948. This is a 1,400-acre maritime forest with more than 5 miles of hiking trails. It also has a visitors center and a gift shop, and you can arrange kayak field trips in the summer. The preserve is open from 10:00 A.M. to 3:00 P.M. Monday through Friday. Closed on major holidays.

Kill Devil Hills is a destination resort area, probably the kind of thing you're trying to avoid. But if it seems appropriate to spend the night, try *Cypress House,* a big, square, blue-green beach house run by Karen Roos and Leon Faso. It was originally a sea captain's hunting and fishing lodge. The six guest rooms are done in cypress, with white ruffled curtains and ceiling fans. It might surprise the sea captain that the rooms have private baths and color television. The inn is open year-round. Rates include a full breakfast (252–441–6127).

Once you get this far north on the Outer Banks, it makes more sense to keep driving north on Highway 158 across the bridge onto the mainland than it does to backtrack. Following Highway 158, you can pick up Highway 17 South at *Elizabeth City.* Elizabeth City merits at least a brief stop, if only because it is at the site of a canal dug in 1790 with the unlikely name of Dismal Swamp Canal. A Coast Guard installation nearby and the local shipyard make this clearly a working, rather than a vacationing, area. The town, however, has a number of interesting historical buildings that are easy to check by taking a walking tour. For a map write the Chamber of Commerce, 502 East Ehringhaus Street, P.O. Box 426, Elizabeth City 27907, or call (252) 335–4365. Web site: ecacc@interpath.com.

The *Museum of the Albemarle* (252–335–1453), about 3 miles south of town on Highway 17, provides information on the area, known as the Historic Albemarle Area, along with displays of artifacts and exhibits related to local history. (Colonists first revolted openly against the English monarchy here.) Open Tuesday through Saturday from 9:00 A.M. to 5:00 P.M. and Sunday from 2:00 to 5:00 P.M. Closed Monday and major holidays. Admission is free.

Returning Home

Another interesting spot in Elizabeth City is the *Historic Main Street District,* one of four National Register Historic Districts in Elizabeth City. It has the largest number of brick antebel-lum commercial buildings in the state. The early nineteenth- and twentieth-century storefronts are now home to specialty shops, restaurants, art galleries, and antiques shops. Free brochures for a self-guided tour of the district are available at the Museum of the Albemarle.

And you don't have to have a boat to enjoy the *Mariner's Wharf* (252–335–4365) on the Intra-coastal Waterway waterfront where boats are offered free dockage for forty-eight hours. The "Rose Buddies" greet each boat with a rose and a welcome to Elizabeth City.

The next community along Highway 17, Hertford, the Perquimans County seat (population only about 2,000) is on the Perquimans River, which feeds into Albemarle Sound. It's worth a stop to visit the *Newbold-White House,* believed to be the oldest house in North Carolina, probably built sometime between the early 1660s and 1685. The house has been restored, preserving much of the original hand-work of the brick chimneys and walls and some of the woodwork. Though not the original, the furnishings are authentic pieces dating from the seventeenth century. Open from March to the week before Christmas, Tuesday through Saturday, 10:00 A.M. to 4:30 P.M. Sunday 2:00 to 5:00 P.M. Other times by appointment (252–426–7567). Modest admission charged.

You can learn a lot about the character of the area by taking two tours here, the *Historic Hertford Walking Tour* (252–426–5657), Hall of Fame Square, Church Street, Hertford 27944, and a self-guided driving tour of the *Old Neck Rural Historic District* (252–426–7567). Web site: www. perquimans.com.

The walking tour takes you by old waterfront homes and the 1828 Perquimans County Courthouse and into a district of antiques stores and cafes. The Historic Hertford District is listed on the National Regis-ter of Historic Places. A free tour booklet is available from the Perquimans County Chamber of Commerce, P.O. Box 27, Hertford 27944, where you can also get a free map for the driving tour of Old Neck Rural Historic District, New Hope Road, and Old Neck Road. The driving tour runs through a National Register Historic District and into the countryside, past old plantation homes.

As an alternative plan if you are pressed for time, you may decide to skip the northern Outer Banks and go back from Roanoke Island on Highway 64, which takes you across the Alligator River and through the *Alligator River Refuge* (it's not clear whether the refuge protects people from alligators or the other way around) where you'll find lots of wildlife, picnic areas, and boating access. Either way, make your next stop Edenton, the first capital of colonial North Carolina. From Highway 64, take Highway 32 North. On Highway 17, keep going about 15 miles west from Hertford.

Capital Country

Although *Edenton* is in no way backward, it has managed to retain the calm and slower pace that we associate with earlier times and has done an outstanding job of preserving its historical sites and promulgating the facts.

Blackbeard lived here, even though he hung out in Bath and maybe left his treasure there. This would have been good pirate country. It was a busy port town in the eighteenth and early nineteenth centuries. During the Revolutionary War supplies were shipped from here to Washington's army farther north.

Edenton had some of the earliest female political activists, too. In 1774 fifty-one women gathered in the courthouse square to sign a declaration vowing not to drink English tea or wear English clothing.

To steep yourself in colonial and Revolutionary War history, you have a choice of a guided or self-guided walking tour or a trolley tour. Pick up a walking-tour map for a quarter, or join a guided tour for a modest fee at the *Historic Edenton Visitors Center,* 108 North Broad Street, Edenton 27932 (252– 482–2637; www.edenton.com). A free audiovisual presentation gives you some orientation in the area's history. The Barker House (ca. 1782) was the home of Thomas Barker, a colonial agent in England, and his wife, Penelope, one of those ladies who boycotted English tea and clothing.

Call the visitors center also to arrange a guided walking tour of Historic Edenton. It takes a couple of hours. The tour includes four interesting buildings: Chowan County Courthouse, one of the oldest in the country, built in 1767; the Cupola House, noted for its elaborate Georgian woodwork inside; the James Iredell House State Historic Site, built in 1773, home of the first attorney general of North Carolina; and St. Paul's Episcopal Church, built in 1736. You may also purchase tickets to go into individual buildings apart from the tours.

In addition to the walking tours, you can take a guided trolley tour, which goes into the outskirts of town as well as through the downtown. Walking tours leave several times a day. They include time inside some of the homes. The cost of tours is moderate and varies according to their length and the number of homes visited. The visitors center is open from 9:00 A.M. to 5:00 P.M. Monday through Saturday, 1:00 to 5:00 P.M. Sunday. Shorter hours in winter. You'll know you're at the visitors center when you see the flag with a teapot flying in the doorway.

Because it's so pleasant, full of flowers, friendly people, and lovely waterfront vistas, spending the night in Edenton rests and relaxes you.

The Lords Proprietors' Inn (252–482–3641), at 300 North Broad Street, Edenton 27932, has earned a reputation as one of the most elegant and gracious inns in the state. The inn comprises three separate restored homes in the historic district, grouped around a lawn and gardens and the Whedbee House, on a brick patio, where continental breakfast is served. Each of the twenty rooms has private bath, cable television, videocassette player, and telephone.

All the guest rooms are light and airy. The common rooms have lots of open space, beautifully refinished old floors, and many whimsical decorating touches.

A few steps away, at 304 North Broad Street, Edenton 27932, you'll find you have an entirely different lodging alternative. The *Governor Eden Inn* (252–482–2072), four rooms with private bath and television in an old neoclassical family home, gives you the feeling of stopping in to spend the night with a friendly relative. Joy and Barry Caron, proprietors, offer complimentary afternoon refreshments and serve a full breakfast.

As for places to eat when you're in town, you're in for a true off-the-beaten-path experience at *Lane's Bar-B-Que* on Highway 32 on the south side of town. For the most fun, sit at one of the five tables in the front rather than in the larger dining room in back. Up front you can enjoy the company and comments of the local workers, such as the men from nearby Edenton Utilities, as they have lunch and swap wisecracks.

"Boy, did it rain or did it rain?"

"It was so bad I had to get up in the trees and swing to the truck."

The restaurant serves burgers and a variety of home-cooked platters, but the barbecue deserves first place on your list of choices. Open from 11:00 A.M. to 8:30 P.M. every day.

A popular restaurant in Edenton is *Broad Street Restaurant & Pub,* 705 North Broad Street, Edenton 27932. This is a rustic place with knotty pine walls, serving good Italian food. Everything, from the soup and entrees to the desserts, is freshly prepared on the premises. Adult portions are generous; there's also a children's menu. This is a nice place to enjoy a glass of wine or a cocktail before your meal, too. The restaurant is open Monday through Friday from 11:30 A.M. to 10:00 P.M., Saturday from 5:00 to 10:00 P.M. Closed Sundays and holidays. Phone (252) 482–8173.

When you study North Carolina history, much of it seems to be about war campaigns, documents, and declarations. Two plantation tours in the area give you a more personal look at history on the day-to-day level.

Hope Plantation, about 20 miles west, in Windsor on State Highway 308, 4 miles west of the highway bypass, re-creates rural domestic life in northeastern North Carolina during the colonial and Federal periods. The plantation belonged to Governor David Stone, who also served in the state House of Commons and later as a U. S. senator. Stone owned more than 5,000 acres, planted mostly in wheat and corn. The plantation had all the mills, shops, and work areas necessary to be self-sufficient.

The two homes on the plantation, one dating from 1763, the other from about 1803, are examples of architecture that combines medieval English, Georgian, and neoclassical traits, reflecting the changing needs and knowledge of North Carolina colonists. Touring them, you see examples of how they might have been furnished, based on research about the plantation. The project continues to develop, so that eventually you'll be able to study a reconstruction of the kitchen on its original foundation, inspect relocated and restored outbuildings, and examine historically authentic vegetable and flower gardens. Moderate admission charged. Open Monday through Saturday from 10:00 A.M. to 5:00 P.M. and Sunday from 2:00 to 5:00 P.M. Closed Thanksgiving Day. For full information write to the plantation at 32 Hope House Road, Windsor 27983, or call (252) 794–3140.

The second plantation also deserves much wider attention. *Somerset Place,* a nineteenth-century coastal plantation near Creswell, belonged to Josiah Collins, a successful merchant who came to Edenton from England in 1774. He and other investors formed the Lake Company, which acquired more than 100,000 acres of land next to Lake Phelps. They dug (or, more accurately, had slaves dig) a 6-mile-long canal through an area known as the Great Alligator Dismal, to join the lake to the Scuppernong River and drain the swamps. When things were going well, gristmills and sawmills produced rice and lumber to ship down the canal in flatboats. But the flooding it takes to grow rice bred mosquitoes that made the slaves sick, so eventually the plantation grew corn and wheat instead.

Collins bought out his partners in 1816 and at his death passed the property on to his son. Later, Josiah Collins III took over. It seems Josiah Three, who went to Yale and graduated from law school in Connecticut, had a head for business. He turned Somerset Place into one of the state's largest plantations, working more than 300 slaves by 1860. Most North Carolinians didn't own slaves; Collins was one of only four planters in the state with more than 300.

The great fascination in visiting Somerset Place lies in the uncommonly detailed records the Collins family kept, especially about the black people on the plantation. The records detailed not only births, deaths, and marriages, but also jobs and skills. Thus today we know that the cook was Grace and that one slave, Luke Davis, had only one job, cleaning carpets. We know that two sons of Collins III were playing with two slave boys one winter when all four boys drowned in the canal.

Additional information comes from the accounts of Dr. John Kooner, a physician who used to stay at the plantation for several weeks at a time, treating the slaves and the Collins family. He described an elaborate African dance that slaves Collins had imported directly from Africa apparently taught to the rest of the slave community. They performed it every year at Christmas, beginning at the great house, snaking to the overseer's house, and ending up at the slave quarters. Everyone on the plantation participated, either as a slave dancer or a spectator.

Archaeological exploration has turned up the remains of slave houses, a hospital and chapel, and the plantation's formal garden, as well as the original brick boundary walls.

This kind of priceless information continues to come to light at Somerset Place, where personable and knowledgeable guides work hard to pass it on. You won't experience a routinized, canned tour here.

Ultimately, the Civil War did in the plantation. The Collins family died elsewhere, and today the site is run by the state.

Somerset (252–797–4560) is open April 1 through October 31, Monday through Saturday from 9:00 A.M. to 5:00 P.M., Sunday from 1:00 to 5:00 P.M.; November 1 through March 31, Tuesday through Saturday from 10:00 A.M. to 4:00 P.M., Sunday from 1:00 to 4:00 P.M. Closed Monday during winter when hours are shorter. All hours may vary; for details contact the site manager (P.O. Box 215, Creswell 27928). Admission is free. At Creswell, the turn for the plantation is marked with a sign. The address is 2572 Lake Shore Road, Creswell 27928.

It's a quick drive from here to the office and main parking lot of **Petti-grew State Park** (252–797–4475), 2252 Lake Shore Drive, Creswell 27928, bordering on Lake Phelps. Actually, Somerset Place State Historic Site lies within the park, too. And a hiking trail from the parking lot takes you to the Somerset Place buildings in about five minutes. The trail continues to the Pettigrew cemetery. Another part of the trail, known as "Carriage Trail" because the Collins family used to like taking carriage roads along the route, leads to an overlook from which you can tread a boardwalk through the cypress woods. Some families like to settle in a picnic area in the park, then walk over to the historic site, rather than starting out at Somerset Place.

A park entrance and parking lot are 9 miles south of Creswell, off U.S. 64 on State Route 1166. One of the park's main draws is fishing—largemouth bass, yellow perch, and pan fish are plentiful. The lake is also good for shallow-draft sailboats, canoeing, and windsurfing. The park forest has a variety of deciduous trees, along with wildflowers and lower shrubs, all in enough variety to keep nature travelers with botanical interests happy. As for wildlife, a variety of waterfowl, owls, and other birds of prey, and lots of small woodland animals, including deer, frequent the area. Pettigrew has a few campsites but no hookups.

Finally, you can inspect some displays of prehistoric Indian culture, including dugout canoes, that will help give you a sense of the area's history over a long period of time. The park is open from about dawn to nightfall, varying with the season. Call ahead to check hours for your visit. Admission is free.

PLACES TO STAY IN THE NORTHERN COAST AND ISLANDS

BEAUFORT
Beaufort Inn
101 Ann Street
Beaufort 28516
(252) 728–2600

Inlet Inn
Corner Queen
and Front Streets
Beaufort 28516
(252) 728–3600

Elizabeth Inn
307 Front Street
Beaufort 28516
(252) 728–3861

KILL DEVIL HILLS
Best Western
Mile Marker 8.5,
State Road 12
Kill Devil Hills 27948
(252) 441–1611

Holiday Inn
1601 Virginia Dare Trail
Kill Devil Hills 27948
(252) 441–6333

KITTY HAWK
Beach Haven
4104 Virginia Dare Trail
Kitty Hawk 27949
(252) 261–4785

MANTEO
Duke of Dare Motor Lodge
100 South Virginia
Dare Road
Manteo 27954
(252) 473–2175

Tranquil House Inn
405 Queen Elizabeth Street
Manteo 27954
(252) 473–1404

MOREHEAD CITY
Best Western
Buccaneer Inn
2806 Arendell Street
Morehead City 28557
(252) 726–3115

Comfort Inn
3100 Arendell Street
Morehead City 28557
(252) 247–3434

Hampton Inn
4035 Arendell Street
Morehead City 28557
(252) 240–2300
(800) 467–9375

NEW BERN
Comfort Inn
218 East Front Street
New Bern 28560
(252) 636–0022

Days Inn
925 Broad Street
New Bern 28560
(252) 636–0150

Holiday Inn Express
3455 Clarendon Boulevard
New Bern 28562
(252) 638–8266

OUTER BANKS
Hatteras
Holiday Inn Express
58822 Highway 12
Hatteras 27943
(252) 986–1110

PLACES TO EAT IN THE NORTHERN COAST AND ISLANDS

BEAUFORT
Net House
Turner Street
Beaufort 28516
(252) 728–2002

The Spouter
218 Front Street
Beaufort 28516
(252) 728–5190

The Northern Coast and Islands Web Sites:

New Bern
www.newbern.com

Outer Banks
www.outer–banks.com/visitor–info

Oregon Inlet Fishing Center
www.oregon–inlet.com

Kitty Hawk Kites, hang gliding
www.kittyhawk.com

KILL DEVIL HILLS
Flying Fish Cafe
2003 Croatan Highway
Kill Devil Hills 27948
(252) 441–6894

Port-O-Call Restaurant
504 South Virginia
Dare Trail
Kill Devil Hills 27948
(252) 441–7484

MANTEO
Clara's Seafood Grill
400 Queen
Elizabeth Street
Manteo 27954
(252) 473–1727

1587 Restaurant
405 Queen Elizabeth Street
Manteo 27954
(252) 473–1587

MOREHEAD CITY
Mrs. Willis' Restaurant
3002 Bridges Street
Morehead City 28557
(252) 726–3741

Sanitary Fish Market
and Restaurant
501 Evans Street
Morehead City 28557
(252) 247–3111

NEW BERN
Henderson House
221 Tryon Palace Drive
New Bern 28560
(252) 638–3205

Pollock Street Delicatessen
208 Pollock Street
New Bern 28560
(252) 637–2480

OUTER BANKS
Hatteras
The Great Salt Marsh
Restaurant
Ocracoke Ferry at Hatteras
Landing, Highway 12
Hatteras 27943
(252) 995–6200

The Upper Piedmont

Sir Walter's Country

You should probably get here soon if you want to enjoy the Raleigh area. Although the population hovers around several thousand more or less than 200,000, depending on your source, the entire area is developing or at least spreading out rapidly, especially in the direction of Durham. Driving along rural roads, you often come upon heavy equipment and newly cleared land. Tomorrow that land will be home to a new development. But the area is so rich in history, culture, and amenities that it would be a shame to skip it.

Raleigh, the state capital, named for Sir Walter Raleigh, offers a variety of historical sites, museums, and fine old architecture in addition to the government buildings downtown.

Plan on stopping at *Historic Oakwood,* at North Person Street between Jones and Boundary, if you're interested in Victorian homes. This historic district of more than 400 homes, many restored, is considered one of the best examples of an unspoiled Victorian neighborhood in the country. Pick up a free walking-tour map that includes some history and descriptions of some of the buildings at the Capital Area Visitors Center, 301 North Blount Street. The center (919–733–3456) is open Monday through Friday from 8:00 A.M. to 5:00 P.M., Saturday from 9:00 A.M. to 5:00 P.M., and Sunday from 1:00 to 5:00 P.M. Closed Thanksgiving, December 24 and 25, and New Year's Day.

The Oakwood Inn, 411 North Bloodworth Street, Raleigh 27604, offers you an opportunity to spend the night in an 1871 Victorian home in the heart of the historic district. The proprietors, Bill and Darlene Smith, know a lot about the area and keep maps with lots of information about the old houses on hand to guide you through the historic neighborhood. The inn, which has six guest rooms, is attracting increasing numbers of business travelers during the week and because of that has put telephones in every room and makes cable television available in your room.

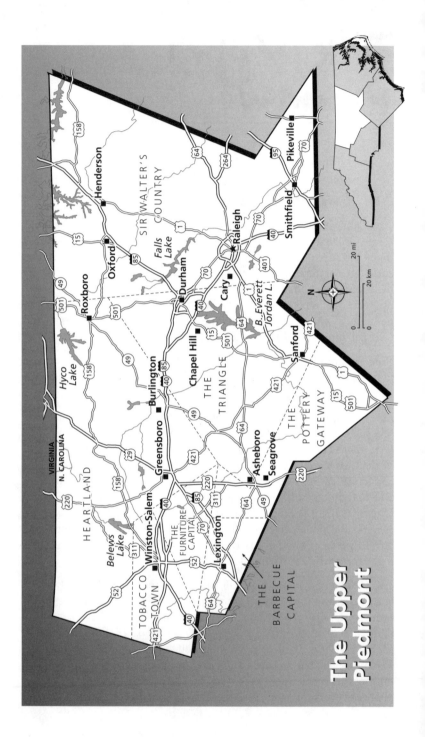

The Upper Piedmont

THE UPPER PIEDMONT

ANNUAL EVENTS IN THE UPPER PIEDMONT

Old Salem
Reenactment of original
Fourth of July held in 1783
July 4
(336) 721-7300
Winston-Salem
Annual Piedmont
Crafts Fair
(mid-November)

The most recent additions are gas-log fireplaces in every room. Oakwood breakfasts fall in the gourmet category: croissant French toast, pumpkin pancakes, orange waffles, and so on. Breakfast is included in the rates. Phone (919) 836–9263 or (800) 267–9712; Web site: www. members.aol. com/oakwoodbb/.

As for the museums, several deserve your attention. The *North Carolina Museum of History,* 5 East Edenton Street, 4650 Mail Service Center, Raleigh 27699–4650, concentrates on exhibits, artifacts, and dioramas related to state history, transportation, and, of course, the Revolutionary and Civil Wars. It also has good exhibits about women in North Carolina. A recent addition is a huge exhibit about health and healing as it has been practiced in different cultures and times in the state. It covers everything from polio hospitals to herbal medicine. Guided tours are available Monday through Friday, but you need a reservation. Located at 109 East Jones Street, the museum (919–715–0200) is open Tuesday through Saturday from 9:00 A.M. to 5:00 P.M. and Sunday from noon to 5:00 P.M. Closed major holidays. Admission is free.

The *North Carolina Museum of Natural Sciences* is between Jones Street and Edenton on North Salisbury Street (919–733–7450). Here you divide your attention between stuffed and skeletal remains of what once was and living specimens of what still is from across the state. In the whale hall a 50-foot whale skeleton hung from the ceiling dominates the exhibits. The prize for live interest probably goes to a python. For twenty-five years the python of note was 17-foot-long George, but he died of cancer when he was twenty-eight years old. Hapi, a mere baby at about ten years and 15 feet, succeeds George. Hapi's acquisition interested North Carolinians enough to be written up in *Carolina Country* magazine. The living conservatory here is filled with live monarch butterflies and ruby-throated hummingbirds, in a re-creation of a dry tropical forest that also has cacti, heliconias, and orchids. Web site: www.naturalsciences.org. Museum hours are the same as those at the museum of history. Admission is free.

Black history is beginning to receive organized, formal recognition in this area. The *African-American Cultural Complex,* 119 Sunnybrook Road, Raleigh 27602, displays a large collection of items created by African-Americans in three houses along a nature trail. They include innovations in science, art, business, medicine, politics, and sports. Web site: www.aaccmuseum.org. Call (919) 212–3598 for details.

The ***Martin Luther King Memorial Gardens*** (919–834–6264), 1500 Martin Luther King Jr. Boulevard, Raleigh 27602, features a life-size statue of Dr. King and a two-tone granite water monument honoring twenty-five pioneers in civil rights and education in a setting of more than 8,000 flowers. The King Memorial Wall surrounds the statue and includes 2,400 bricks inscribed with the names of people who have helped support the facility. The park is open twenty-four hours a day. Admission is free. Web site: www.king-raleigh.org.

Also allow time for the ***North Carolina Museum of Art*** at 2110 Blue Ridge Avenue (take the Wade Avenue exit off Interstate 40), 4630 Mail Service Center, Raleigh 27699-4630. The building, designed by the architect Edward Durrell Stone, who designed the John F. Kennedy Center in Washington, D.C., and the original Museum of Modern Art in New York, is important; so are the eight major collections. Arranged in chronological order, they cover 5,000 years of art, displaying work by artists from Botticelli to Monet to Andrew Wyeth. You'll also find exhibits of Jewish ceremonial art along with Greek and Roman sculpture. Tours are available at 1:30 P.M. A cafe and gift shop operate during museum hours. The museum also offers varied, changing programs of festivals, films, and performing arts events for the family. The museum (919–839–6262, extension 2154) is open Tuesday through Saturday from 9:00 A.M. to 5:00 P.M. (until 9:00 P.M. Friday) and Sunday from 11:00 A.M. to 6:00 P.M. Closed Monday. Admission is free. Web site: www2.ncsu.edu/ncma.

Another approach to art is ***Artspace,*** 201 East Davie Street, Raleigh 27601 (919–821–2787), a nonprofit visual arts center in downtown Raleigh with more than twenty-five working studios where you can watch artists at work and also visit shows in two galleries. Artists sell work out of their studios as well as from the galleries and in the gift shop. Artspace is open from 10:00 A.M. to 6:00 P.M. Tuesday through Saturday. The first Friday of every month, Artspace is open until 10:00 P.M. Web site: www.artspace.citysearch.com. Admission is free.

Attending to your dinner, a restaurant in the area really appeals to the kinds of people who read a book like this. ***Jean-Claude's Cafe*** serves French country food in a small, unassuming dining room, mostly to local folks who believe they're keeping the place a secret. The restaurant is in North Ridge Shopping Center, unlikely as that sounds for such a find. (Take the Old Wake Forest Road exit from the beltline and go north 3 miles on what becomes Falls of Neuse Avenue.) The menu includes a country pâté that could be a meal in itself; soup du jour specialties,

THE UPPER PIEDMONT

AUTHOR'S FAVORITE PLACES IN THE UPPER PIEDMONT

North Carolina State University Arboretum

Cedar Creek Gallery

Hillsborough

Mt. Airy

Harley Museum

Seagrove

Old Salem

Selma

Museum of Early Southern Decorative Arts

Furniture Discovery Center

Nahunta Pork Center

Ava Gardner Museum

such as cream of pumpkin; and entrees such as French sauerkraut with pork and mixed sausages to make your mouth water and bust your belt, at surprisingly moderate prices. You can order nice wines and imported beers here, too. Open Tuesday through Saturday from 11:00 A.M. to 2:00 P.M. and 5:30 to 9:00 P.M. Closed Sunday and holidays (919–872–6224).

People who enjoy Jean-Claude's also like the ***Irregardless Cafe,*** at 901 West Morgan Street, Raleigh 27603. When they describe it, people tend to call it the "vegetarian restaurant," but it does serve chicken and fish as well as the vegetarian entrees. Don't be fooled by the sprouts in the salads. These aren't old hippies or young health-food nuts; they're folks who've figured out how to get the best flavor out of fresh ingredients with the least amount of doctoring. To dispel the notion that you're doing something that's good for you, you can order anything you like from the full bar. The homemade desserts will keep you on the sinful side, too. Open for lunch Monday through Friday from 11:30 A.M. to 2:30 P.M.; dinner Monday through Thursday from 5:30 to 9:30 P.M., Friday and Saturday to 10:00 P.M. Sunday brunch 10:00 A.M. to 2:30 P.M. Call (919) 833–9920 for a mouthwatering description of the day's dinner menu. Call (919) 833–8898 to make reservations.

If you like gardens and plants and farmers, you'll want to add several more stops to your itinerary—the ***Raleigh Farmers Market*** and the ***North Carolina State University Arboretum.*** The Farmers Market, 1301 Hodges Street in the warehouse section of town, draws crowds of locals with fresh produce sold by local truck farmers. Even if you're traveling and don't want to haul a lot of carrots across the state, it's fun to wander around watching the people and sampling the wares. Depending on your taste in fresh fruits and vegetables, it might be a little more fun to visit here during spring strawberry season or summer peach time than, say, for fall turnips or winter squash, but the market is open year-round from 5:00 A.M. to 6:00 P.M., every day but Sunday. The arboretum at North Carolina State University, 4301 Beryl Road, Raleigh 27605 (919–515–3132, take the Hillsborough Street exit off the beltline), grows thousands of plants from around the world. In addition to special interest areas, such as the silver and white garden and a Japanese garden, a long perennial garden shows what it's possible

Courtesy in the Capital

*A*s a newspaper reporter, I sometimes have to spend time in the courthouses in Raleigh. Full of lawyers, clerks, defendants, and mounds of paperwork, this is nobody's favorite place. And I've been around a lot of overworked, unpleasant people in a lot of courthouses, so I went into the state and county courthouses here with a chip on my shoulder.

I got lost. I got into the buildings but couldn't figure out what exit to use to find my car. Here are the people who helped me and smiled while they were doing it: two clerks, three guards, and a lawyer. The lawyer went with me on the elevator and through some back halls to a shortcut that got me out to the parking lot where I'd left my car. As the door was closing on the building, he actually waved bye.

to grow outside in North Carolina every month. Open daily from 8:00 A.M. to dusk. Admission is free.

For a nice break from the city, head north, either on Highway 1 or on Highway 401 and Highway 39, to Henderson, not far from the Virginia border. The *Kerr Lake State Recreational Area,* 269 Glasshouse Road, Henderson 27536 (252–438–7791), is a 50,000-acre lake that stretches from North Carolina into Virginia, with 800 miles of shoreline. You'll find everything from picnic areas to camping facilities and hiking trails. Admission to the park is free, but there is a fee for camping: $17 for electrical and water or $12 for nonelectrical, just water, for both tents and recreational vehicles. The Vance County Tourism organization sponsors July 4 fireworks and a Labor Day Parade of Lights flotilla.

While you're in the area, treat yourself to the *Cedar Creek Gallery,* 1150 Fleming Road, a workplace and sales outlet for top-quality craftspeople. Their brochure says, "Expect to be overwhelmed," and that's not hype. The gallery displays are spread through many rooms. Much of the work is pottery, but you'll also find fine glass, handmade stereopticons, stringed instruments, jewelry, and toys that are too splendid to put into the hands of kids. The quality is so outstanding that people tend to walk along talking in hushed tones, though that's not at all the demeanor of the artisans themselves. In the rear of the gallery, the *Museum of American Pottery* displays the entire range of local pottery, from the old folk pottery of places such as Cole and Jugtown to the works of contemporary studio potters. The exhibits include information about basic potting procedures and such things as salt glazes, too. From Henderson go south on Interstate 85, take the second Butner exit (186), turn left on Highway 15

North, turn right at the first crossroads, and left on Fleming Road to the gallery. Open daily from 10:00 A.M. to 6:00 P.M. (919–528–1041). Web site: www.cedarcreekgallery.com.

As a final indulgence in this area, stop at **Bob's Bar-B-Que,** on Highway 56 between Creedmore and Interstate 85. Not only can you get good North Carolina barbecue here, but you can also dig into a serving of bunter stew, made with beef, pork, limas, and potatoes. The traditional beverage is iced tea, sweet or unsweetened, served in plastic cups with the name of the restaurant on the side. Open Monday through Saturday from 10:00 A.M. to 8:00 P.M. (919–528–2081).

From Raleigh you can go off in a number of directions, all with their own peculiarities and pleasures. U.S. Highway 70, toward Goldsboro, takes you to **Selma, Pikeville,** and **Smithfield.** You can easily stop in all three places on the same day, though if you are an antiques lover, you may decide to devote a day to the town of Selma.

Signs from Highway 70 (as well as from I–95 and I–40) will direct you to Selma, a small town that has pulled itself from the doldrums of empty old buildings to become an antiques mecca. The story begins in 1997, when Bruce Radford, town manager, was trying to figure out a way to restore the town to its earlier vibrancy. The town needed a theme, he thought. And it came to him during a golf game. He swung at the ball and got an inspiration, more or less at the same time. The golf ball went into the woods, but his idea flourishes.

Who Cares about Royalties Anyway?

I was sitting in Bob's Bar-B-Que enjoying a barbecue sandwich and fried onion rings, my usual treat here, when I noticed an unusual amount of activity going on as some customers paid their bill at the cash register. The woman went out to the car and came in carrying a book I recognized right away as North Carolina: Off the Beaten Path. She showed it to the proprietors, who were surprised.

They didn't know they were in the book.

I walked over to the counter and asked, "Do you like that book?"

Fortunately they said they did, so I told them, "I wrote it."

They acted suitably impressed, then the woman said to me, "I'd ask you to autograph it, but I didn't buy it. I checked it out of the library."

A Mellow Fellow

*W*hen I talked to Bruce Radford the other day about how things continue to prosper in Selma, the mellowness of his voice reminded me of the first time I talked to him on the telephone, before I'd been to Selma to meet him. I said that he had "a radio voice."

"Actually," he said, "I have a radio face."

He doesn't. He's a nice-looking man, but what a great line!

Using some financial incentives, promise of advertising support, and a lot of local enthusiasm, the town of Selma has seen its downtown buildings restored as antiques malls and shops, many with living quarters upstairs, artisans' studios, and shops for such antiques-related activities as upholstering.

The town is already into the swing of it and will probably grow fast enough to cease being off the beaten path before long. While you are searching for antiques, take the time to stop in *Short's Grill,* a lunch place in the center of town where you can get a burger all-the-way made of fresh ground beef, served with a fountain Coke that tastes like Coke tasted in the old days. For further information about Selma, call the town hall (919) 965–9841.

In this same area, *The Nahunta Pork Center,* 200 Bertie Pierce Road, Pikeville 27863, is a family operation that has grown from early slaughterhouse days, when they supplied hogs to barbecue houses, into a plant that includes a retail store where you can buy pork products so fresh that you can almost still hear the squeal. The difference in flavor between this and grocery store meat that has spent several days in storage, transit, and case-life is obvious after a single bite. The sausage is made from an old family recipe, as is the barbecue coating sauce the store sells.

When Nahunta Pork Center went retail, a lot of people predicted the Center wouldn't make it because there weren't enough customers in the area. They were wrong. In 1984 it claimed to be America's largest retail pork store. It had 40 employees and processed about 100 hogs a day.

Today the Center claims to be the largest all-pork retail displayer in the eastern United States.

The same old family home, with the same carpet and a bit of the furniture still there, now serves as offices. The center employs about 80 people and processes up to 150 hogs a day. Part of the beauty of the place is that it's oriented to small farmers, not agri-industry producers. The Nahunta Pork Center is especially known for its hand-rubbed country hams. The center is open from 8:00 A.M. to 5:30 P.M. Monday through Friday, 8:00 A.M. to 3:00 P.M. Saturday. Phone (919) 242–4735.

When you're through here, hop back on Highway 70 and follow the signs a few miles to Smithfield and the **Ava Gardner Museum.** Ava Gardner was born in this area, lived here when she was young, and is buried here. The museum was started by Tom Banks, who met Ava while she waited for rides near the campus of Atlantic Christian College, which he was attending, in the little town of Wilson.

Later he became a publicist on one of her movies, *My Forbidden Past.* No matter what else he did in a career that took him from New York to Florida, he kept up with what was happening to Ava, making scrapbooks of newpaper clippings about her. He also collected photographs, posters, audio and video cassettes from her movies, and anything else he could find. In the 1970s he visited her in London and told her he was going to donate everything to start a museum in her honor.

In 1981 he bought the teacherage in Smithfield where she had lived when her mother taught school. He moved his collection there and opened the museum in 1982.

Since then the museum's had a few different locations, and the collection has continued to grow with donations of costumes, Ava's good china from her years in London, even her collection of Frank Sinatra records, until there are now more than 100,000 items. Everything is well

---

Oink

*L*arry Pierce, manager of Nahunta Pork Center, wearing the white smock and hat that is standard dress for anyone going into any of the buildings where pork is handled, is headed into the ham house. As he opens the door he turns slightly and says, "You know about the chicken and the pig planning what each will contribute to an important breakfast?

"The pig says, 'I'm contributing bacon.'

"The chicken says, 'I'm contributing eggs.'

"The pig says, 'You're making a commitment. I'm making a sacrifice.'"

And grinning at his own pork humor enough to wiggle his thick brown mustache, Pierce goes on into the chilly building.

Tar Heel Movies

*N*orth Carolina makes more movies, TV shows, and TV series than any other states except California and New York. Among the movies that have been filmed at the coast in North Carolina are Forrest Gump, The Fugitive, Days of Thunder, *and* The Color Purple.

Scenes from Nell, The Last of the Mohicans, *and* Patch Adams, *were filmed in the Blue Ridge Mountains.*

displayed and fun to see; even people who don't ordinarily like museums have a good time here. Admission is $2.00. Phone (919) 934–5830. The museum has moved from its location on South Third Street to a larger building next to the old Belk department store, downtown on Market Street. Call for details.

The Triangle

In a sense, **Durham** is closer to Raleigh than it used to be. With both communities expanding laterally, it's not hard as you drive between the two places to imagine that they'll soon run together. Durham is a tobacco town; Duke University was endowed by and named for the Duke family, which made Durham a tobacco center.

Although tobacco is not as important in the area as it once was, criticizing smokers is not a good way to make friends here. The Duke family pioneered in marketing cigarettes in America. You can understand something of the mystique and importance of tobacco by visiting the **Duke Homestead State Historic Site and Tobacco Museum,** established on the Duke family farm. Take the Guess Road exit off Interstate 85 to 2828 Duke Homestead Road. Depending on when you're here, you'll see tobacco being planted, cultivated, harvested, or prepared for market and have the opportunity to participate in part of the processing.

On the property, the old family house, two tobacco factories, a curing barn, and a packhouse show you how it used to be. In the visitors center, tobacco-related exhibits include advertising, signs, machinery, and an old cigar store Indian. A twenty-minute film, *Carolina Bright* (the local name for brightleaf tobacco), describes the history and importance of tobacco in the state in a more positive light than most of what you see and hear today. Admission is free. Open April through October,

Monday through Saturday from 9:00 A.M. to 5:00 P.M., Sunday from 1:00 to 5:00 P.M.; November through March, Tuesday through Saturday from 9:00 A.M. to 5:00 P.M. and Sunday from 1:00 to 5:00 P.M. Closed Monday, Christmas Day, and Thanksgiving. Hours change, so it's a good idea to call ahead (919–477–5498).

Duke money also made possible a dominant institution in this area, *Duke University.* In 1924 a six million dollar gift from the family made it possible to expand what was then Trinity College. A large endowment and subsequent grants followed. The result is Duke University's two large campuses spread west and east of Durham, with great stone buildings and acres of grass and woods seeming to be enough for a huge student population. In fact, everything is large except the student body. Enrollment is in the neighborhood of 10,000 students, most of whom have to walk a lot to cover the large distances. The campuses are called, appropriately enough, East Campus and West Campus. You get to East Campus by following the signs from U.S. 15/501 bypass to State Road 751 onto Duke University Road. The Georgian buildings of the original college are here.

To get to West Campus take the Hillsborough Road exit from Interstate 85 and go east on Main Street. On the West Campus the massive Gothic *Duke University Chapel* dominates (919–684–2572). James Duke, founder of the university, planned it that way. In March 1925, when he was walking the woods that have become West Campus, he designated the highest ground as the chapel site, saying that he wanted the central building of the campus to be "a great towering church" so dominating it would have a spiritual influence on the young students who studied there. This edifice is worth a visit.

Horace Trumbauer of Philadelphia, who designed Duke's mansion on Fifth Avenue in New York, was the architect. The chief designer was Julian Able, the first black architect graduated from the department of architecture at the University of Pennsylvania.

Duke chose to have the church built of gray stone from a quarry in nearby Hillsborough. The result is a Gothic church patterned after the original Canterbury Cathedral. A 210-foot tower soars skyward, housing a fifty-bell carillon. A 5,000-pipe organ was built into the rear of the nave several decades after the chapel's construction.

The organ, designed by Dirk Andries Flentrop of Holland, is an eighteenth-century organ of classical design, constructed of solid wood and using no electricity except to power the blower. It was built in Holland, where it was played to assure its quality. It was then totally dismantled,

Duke University Chapel

with each pipe wrapped separately, and shipped to Duke University. After the organ's first official use at Christmas 1976, one critic wrote that the organ "breathes music." In daylight the red, green, and gold trim on its mahogany seem to combine with the glow of its 5,000 long slender pipes.

Sunlight streams through seventy-seven stained-glass windows. These and the ornamental lead and gold symbols in the doors of the building were designed and created by G. Owen and Bonawit, Inc., of New York.

Instead of kings and saints at the portals, the chapel memorializes Protestant heroes such as Luther, John Wesley, Thomas Jefferson, and Robert E. Lee.

James Duke, his brother Benjamin, and their father Washington are entombed in a small memorial chapel. Statues, showing all three men lying comfortably pillowed and gracefully draped, are carved in marble atop their tombs beneath the windows. Charles Keck of New York was the sculptor.

The elaborate ironwork of the gates to the memorial chapel was done by William H. Hackson Company of New York.

THE UPPER PIEDMONT

BETTER KNOWN ATTRACTIONS IN
THE UPPER PIEDMONT

RALEIGH
North Carolina State Capitol
(919) 733-4994 or 733-3456

WINSTON-SALEM
Old Salem
(336) 721-7300
(336) 725-1516

Fine woodwork throughout the building was done by Irving and Casson, A. H. Davenport Inc., Boston; the stone carving was by John Donnelly, Inc., of New York.

It may seem strange that so much work in this southern chapel was done by New York and Boston craftsmen until you realize that James Duke was living in New York when the project was in process.

The chapel is open daily from 8:00 A.M. to 5:00 P.M. during the school year. Hours are shorter in summer. Interdenominational worship services are at 11:00 A.M. on Sunday.

The **Sarah Duke Memorial Gardens** (919-684-3698) have lots of open grass for kids to romp on and paths through wooded areas, as well as all kinds of seasonal flowers, a gazebo, and a lily pond. The gardens are open every day from 8:00 A.M. to sundown. Admission is free. Web site: wwwhr.duke.edu/dukegardens.

Another stop to feed your fascination with natural science is the **Museum of Life and Science & Magic Wings Butterfly House,** 433 Murray Avenue, Raleigh 27602. Spread over seventy-eight acres, the museum has a variety of science and nature displays, including a mock-up of the Apollo 15 and a nature center with native animals. A train ride through the outdoor park gives you a chance to see everything from bears and wolves to farm animals. And the tropical butterfly house, the largest museum butterfly house east of the Mississippi, features species from Asia, Africa, and Central and South America. Open from 10:00 A.M. to 6:00 P.M. Monday through Saturday, noon to 6:00 P.M. Sunday from Memorial Day to Labor Day. Closes an hour earlier in the off-season. Closed New Year's Day, Thanksiving, and Christmas. Admission is $8.00 for adults, $7.00 seniors, and $5.50 for children. Miniature train ride is $1.00 extra. Phone (919) 220-5429. Web site: www.ncmls.citysearch.com.

Two attractions in Durham pay homage to the role of African-Americans in the region. **Hayti Heritage Center,** 804 Old Fayetteville Street, Durham 27536, features works and artifacts of African-Americans, visual arts galleries, and dance and community meeting spaces. Both contemporary and traditional art, by local, regional, and national African-American artists, is on display. Hayti was once a focal African-American marketplace with thriving neighborhoods. The center is downtown, easy to find by taking Expressway 147 to exit 12. It is open from 9:00 A.M. to 5:00 P.M. Monday through Friday, 9:00 A.M. to 3:00 P.M. Saturday. Weekend hours may vary depending on special events and activities. For details call (919) 683-1709. Web site: www.hayti.org.

Historic Stagville, 5825 Old Oxford Highway, P.O. Box 71217, Durham 27722, is a center for African-American studies and a place to learn about African-American plantation life, culture, and society before the Civil War. Historic Stagville has an eighteenth-century plantation house, part of which contains offices, with the rest open to the public. Four slave houses and an 1860 barn are on the property as well. Displays and research here emphasize the various cultures from which the slaves came, forming a new African-American culture in which self-reliance flourished. The barn, for instance, was built by master-craftsmen carpenters: slaves. Research here also demonstrates that there was more to the lives of the slaves than working all day for the master, although they certainly did that. But in their own community and homes, they also cultivated vegetable gardens, participated in athletic events, and took part in community affairs. Artifacts found on the property suggest that slaves brought from various parts of Africa kept some of their traditions and secret religious practices, which they used to create a new African-American culture. Historic Stagville is open from 9:00 A.M. to 4:00 P.M., Monday through Friday. Admission is free. Phone (919) 620–0120.

While you're in the Triangle, take a picnic to the *B. Everett Jordan Lake,* a 47,000-acre lake created by the United States Army Corps of Engineers for flood control. All water recreation is available at some part of the lake—boating, swimming, and fishing, as well as hiking and camping. As you drive around in the area, you'll probably notice several different roads, all marked with signs, leading into access areas. One is Highway 64 at Highway 51, which leads to several recreation areas. Another is off Highway 64 going north on Highway 15/501, a point southwest of Durham, which takes you from Pittsboro, through Bynum and into Chapel Hill, home of the *University of North Carolina at Chapel Hill.* Chapel Hill and Durham are so close together that residents frequently live in one community and work in the other. The area south of Chapel Hill is still fairly rural and is a popular living area for university people with an itch to rusticate.

About 8 miles south of Chapel Hill, on U.S. 15/501, just outside the community of *Pittsboro,* you'll find one of the most unusual examples of gentrified rural living imaginable. *Fearrington Village,* Pittsboro 27312, built around what used to be a barn, silo, farmhouse, and a few outbuildings, now comprises an inn with thirty-one rooms, a restaurant, a market and cafe, a series of shops, a residential area with town houses and freestanding homes, and such services as a pharmacy, bank, and beauty shop. It really is a village—an upscale one—in the middle of perennial gardens and fields dotted with cows. Not just any cows, of course: Scottish Belted Galloway cows, black at both ends and white in the middle, like walking Oreo cookies. Nobody milks these cows or eats them. They're pets. Or stage setting.

More than twenty-two years ago, R. B. and Jenny Fitch bought the Fearrington family dairy farm and started work on a planned community here. They didn't tear down existing buildings, and they built new ones to fit in unobtrusively. For instance, the granary became the market, deli, and cafe. The old milking barn houses a home-and-garden shop. The Potting Shed, in the old corncrib, sells plants propagated from the Fearrington gardens.

Living here isn't for anybody with shaky finances, and neither is staying at *Fearrington House Inn,* with rates starting at about $165 and running to more than $325 a night. The prices at the *Fearrington House Restaurant* or the *Fearrington Market Cafe,* however, are comparable to those in restaurants anywhere, and the inn offers every creature comfort you can think of, in rooms decorated in English style.

Activities such as touring the gardens, which are wonderful, are free. And you can browse in McIntire's, a good independent bookstore, shop for wine and gourmet treats, pick up handmade pottery and jewelry, and perhaps attend a reading by a well-known author in the renovated barn.

The Fearrington House Restaurant is open Tuesday through Saturday from 6:00 P.M. to 8:00 P.M. The Fearrington Market Cafe is open Monday through Friday for lunch and dinner, Saturday and Sunday for brunch. For more information call (800) 733–2785. Web site: www.fearrington.com.

The town of Pittsboro is worth wandering through, too. It has lots of antiques shops and the kinds of stores that cater to people fixing up old houses, as well as a natural foods store and a small restaurant. This is the kind of place where "real" farmers still mix on the sidewalks with men in Bermuda shorts and Birkenstocks.

Chapel Hill, almost the geographical center of North Carolina, is recognizably a college town, the kind in which the campus and the town meet at a wall running along the campus green, where students sit on the wall to see and be seen, and where the businesses across the street are mostly campus oriented. Visitors actually tour the campus, less because of its history than because it is so Norman Rockwellish, sort of an artist's conceptualization of a campus, with trees and grass and historic buildings—even some ivy here and there.

In the college atmosphere, **Womancraft,** a retail gallery of area artisans, seems to be just what you'd expect. Forty or so craftswomen sell their work in the cooperative. The offerings range from Appalachian mountain crafts such as basketry to sophisticated stained glass and stitchery. You'll find handmade quilts, weavings, jewelry, pottery, artwork, and sculpture. The children's toys and clothes are especially popular with shoppers. The shop doesn't have the hit-or-miss feeling that tends to pervade some cooperatives, probably because it is so well established. Womancraft is in its third decade in business.

The crafters take turns working in the shop; they hire no outside help.

Carrot Stuff

*W*ell over a decade ago, my husband and I ate at the Fearrington Market Cafe for the first time. We both took a fancy to the cold carrot concoction served with our sandwiches. When I asked about the recipe, the waitress said the carrots were so popular they sold them in the deli. She also told me the recipe was in Jenny Fitch's cookbook, The Fearrington House Cookbook, which had been published not long before and was for sale in the market. She suggested I go take a look at the recipe, but I decided the only decent thing to do was buy the book.

The recipe is titled "Carrots in Smooth Tomato Sauce," and the main ingredient in the sauce is canned tomato soup. My crest was fallen. This was during one of my "purist" food periods, and I tried everything to make the recipe with something other than canned soup, but nothing else worked.

Ultimately, I capitulated and made very good carrots in smooth tomato sauce. I

took the dish as my contribution to a communication studies department party at UNC/Charlotte while I was teaching there.

The head of the department was ecstatic. It was his favorite, he said. His roommate used to make it all the time. Did he know what the recipe was called? I asked.

"No," he said. "We just called it 'carrot stuff.'"

To make "carrot stuff," steam sliced carrots until just crispy-tender. Mix them with chopped onion and green pepper and pour over them a sauce made by combining a can of tomato soup with $^1/_2$ cup salad oil, $^3/_4$ cup vinegar, 1 cup (or less) sugar, and a dash each of Worcestershire sauce and prepared mustard. The carrots taste better if you refrigerate them overnight before serving. (Note: Use as much carrots, onion, and green pepper as you'd like.)

This means that whenever you shop, you have the opportunity to talk with some of the people who have made the things you're inspecting. Items are arranged in appealing displays throughout the space rather than each member's work being confined to a particular booth. The shop is a pleasure to visit anytime, but it is especially rewarding around holidays. They take pains to offer seasonally appropriate items for Christmas and other special times. The shop (919–929– 8362) is at 1800 East Franklin Street in the East Gate Shopping Center. That's on Highway 15/501 South, east of Highway 86 heading toward Carrboro. Open Monday through Friday from 10:00 A.M. to 8:00 P.M., Saturday from 10:00 A.M. to 6:00 P.M., Sunday from 1:00 to 6:00 P.M.

Make a quick 12-mile side trip north on Highway 86 to **Hillsborough,** where a lot of history is condensed in a small area. Hillsborough was a capital of colonial and revolutionary North Carolina and a center of politics. During the Revolution troops of Cornwallis grouped for deployment here. The state convention to ratify the federal Constitution met here in 1788; in 1865 the Confederate general who signed the surrender of the Civil War headquartered here. Colonial, antebellum, and Victorian architecture mingle comfortably along the streets. The Hillsborough Historical Society likes to say that the town is a living, not a reconstructed, community.

The town has become more aggressive about advertising to attract tourists in the past few years. One of the town's ads says it is "an easy day trip from just about anywhere." This is true, but Hillsborough is also rather removed from other attractions in the area, sitting, as it does, almost at the Virginia border. But there's enough to do here to make a side trip worthwhile.

To pick up a map for a walking tour, stop at the **Orange County Visitor Center,** 150 East King Street, Hillsborough 27278. You can also get information about shops, museums, and restaurants in the area. Call (919) 732–7741 for details.

One interesting site in Hillsborough is the **Burwell School Historic Site,** 319 North Churton Street, Hillsborough 27278. The house and outbuildings were built about 1821 and served as a school for women— they called it a "female school" back then. The house includes furnishings from the days when the Reverend and Mrs. Burwell lived in and ran the school there. The property has a nice formal garden as well. Call (919) 732–7741 for details. Admission is free.

The **Montrose Gardens,** at 320 St. Mary's Road, Hillsborough 27278, were begun in the 1800s by Governor William Alexander Graham and his wife, Susan Washington Graham. The complex now includes rock gardens, sunny and shady gardens, and woodland. Call (919) 732–7787.

At the opposite extreme, **Occaneechi Indian Village,** downtown on South Cameron Avenue by the Eno River, is a reconstructed village with huts, a cooking area, and a sweat lodge that appear as they would have from the late 1600s and up to about 1710.

If you decide to spend the night in Hillsborough, you have your choice of several standard motels and an old inn that has been operating continuously as an inn for 240 years. **The Colonial Inn,** 153 West King Street, Hillsborough 27278, built in 1759, has eight rooms and serves lunch and dinner. The food is family-style southern cooking, served by a staff dressed in colonial costumes. Call (919) 732–2461 for details.

Hillsborough House Inn, 209 East Tryon Street, Hillsborough 27278, is an upscale bed-and-breakfast in a restored Italianate mansion on seven acres in an historic district. It has five rooms and a suite. The creature comforts include a fireplace, whirlpool, swimming pool, and nature trail. Call (919) 644–1600 or (800) 616–1660. Web site: www. hillsboroughinn.citysearch.com.

South of Chapel Hill on Highway 15/501, shortly after you pass the access roads to the lake between Bynum and Pittsboro, two more women practice their craft in a ramshackle building beside the road. Neolia and Celia Cole make pottery in the North Carolina production tradition, specializing in spongeware, a soft brownish glaze called "butterware," and a shocking red glaze. The pots at **Cole's Pottery,** 3410 Hawkins Avenue, Sanford 27330, are not the sleek stylish pieces of studio potters but the made-for-use mugs, bowls, pitchers, and teapots of the kind that served local people for daily use in earlier days. The sisters also make a variety of miniature tea sets and vases. They sign each piece with a comment like, "Love, Neolia Cole," and "Let me go home with you." Their stock, like that of most North Carolina potters, fluctuates with demand. Sometimes they can hardly keep up, and the shelves will be sparsely filled; other times pots crowd every available inch. Nobody gets upset if you stop in, look around, and leave without having bought anything. Open Monday through Friday from 8:00 A.M. to 5:30 P.M. and Saturday from 8:00 A.M. to 3:30 P.M. (919–776–9558). New potteries spring up regularly in this area and their numbers grow steadily, so when you drive through, you will certainly see signs for some items not mentioned here that will be worth a look. Generally, the newer places produce studio-art pottery rather than traditional folk pottery.

From Pittsboro it's an easy drive of no more than 40 miles west on Highway 64, mostly through rural countryside, to *Asheboro.*

Asheboro, a little community of something more than 16,000, is home to the *American Classic Motorcycle Company and Museum* (336–629–9564), a meeting spot for Harley-Davidson enthusiasts at 1170 U.S. Highway 64. Ed Rich, proprietor, distinguishes between enthusiasts and bikers. "The bikers, they're more the party types. The enthusiasts are into history and restoration."

Rich started collecting old Harley-Davidsons in 1971 and has been building the collection ever since. He bought most of the bikes in the 1980s, then cut down on the number of purchases when their cost went up in 1988.

He opened the museum in 1980. The collection of thirty-one bikes fills the second floor of his store. A long row of old bikes gleams behind a glass-enclosed display area. One of his treasures is a red 1936 model El61 knucklehead, only one of two known to exist in original condition. It has the original paint and 17,000 miles on the odometer.

Knuckleheads, shovelheads, blockheads, and flatheads have engines fitting those descriptions. If you get confused you can buy a magnet replicating each kind of engine head in miniature.

The museum also has a collection of toys, old advertisements, and other memorabilia, including a picture of a smiling young Elvis on *his* Harley.

You don't have to know anything about Harleys to enjoy this place. It's enough to enjoy the enthusiasm of others. Rich and his mechanic, Larry Kessler, are almost missionaries when it comes to teaching people about the world of Harleys. "A lot of heritage and history go with it," Rich says.

Going in every direction from Asheboro, you have wonderful possibilities.

The Pottery Gateway

Although the area bustles with activity, don't look for anything special in the way of food or lodging. Steakhouses and a few motels are about all you'll find, but these are pleasant and entirely acceptable when you just need a meal and a night's sleep, not an experience.

For an *experience,* go to the south side of Asheboro on Highway 220, where signs and arrows direct you to the *North Carolina Zoological Park.* The zoo (336–879–7000 or 800–488–0444) is big, on more than 1,000 acres, though not all are being used yet. It's famous, and it's

What We Do for Love

Larry Kessler is proof that a good mechanic is made, not born. For eleven years he drove a truck coast-to-coast, averaging 4,500 miles a week. He lived in Columbus, Ohio. One Friday night when he and a friend were having a cold beer in the garage, they hatched a plan to go to the Harley-Davidson school in Orlando, Florida. They agreed that first one, then the other, would do it.

Kessler went first. He, his wife, and child moved to Orlando, struggling to earn enough money for Orlando's high rents and food. Kessler's wife worked, and he worked too—whenever he wasn't in class. "I didn't sleep much," he says.

They bought their food a day at a time, sometimes not sure they'd be able to eat the next day. At one point Kessler was ready to give up and go back to Columbus, but his friend insisted on helping him financially.

"The thing is, I'm here and he's still in Ohio, so only half the plan worked out," Kessler says. Was it worth it? Kessler looks up from the shiny machine he's working on and grins, "When I'm done with this, I gotta go ride it."

certainly not far off the beaten path. Go anyway. It got to be big and famous because they're doing such a good job with the concept of keeping the animals in natural environments without bars. Sometimes a natural gulf separates the people from the animals, sometimes a clear barrier. For instance, the aviary, under a glass dome, houses hundreds of exotic birds along with thousands of tropical plants. In other sections you can watch elephants, herds of antelope, and even crocodiles, all apparently blissfully unaware of an audience or confinement.

If you are traveling with an eye to understanding the state of North Carolina, the North Carolina Streamside exhibit is special. It depicts the wildlife and habitat from the mountains to the coast in a series of displays with everything from fish and snakes to otters splashing in a pool. The impression you get in many of these displays is that someone has simply glassed in a slice of nature and set it there, but in fact you're looking at artfully created ponds, streams, and woodlands, all suited to creatures displayed there. It isn't really natural. For instance, the "rocks" in the habitats of some indigenous snakes are really made of lightweight molded composition with heaters inside that keep the temperature exactly right for the snakes. A few live plants grow, but many of the "trees" and "bushes" have been fabricated with stunning accuracy. And on the back side, doors open to allow attendants access to the habitats for feeding and caring for the animals.

Seeing everything involves walking a couple of miles or more, but for a modest fee you can ride in a tram that follows the same route as the footpaths. There is also a modest admission fee to the park itself. Open Monday through Friday from 9:00 A.M. to 5:00 P.M., and Saturday and Sunday from 10:00 A.M. to 6:00 P.M.

From the natural to something near the ultimate in machinery, the **Richard Petty Museum** displays race cars, trophies, and films of famous races on the grounds of Petty's garages. Most of the awards belong to Richard, but some belong to Lee Petty, his father. Sometimes the garages are open for tours. Showcases commemorate Petty's 200th win and his 1,000th start. If you know about NASCAR racing fans, are aware of the intense partying that goes along with any race day for some of them, and have seen the huge banners advertising Goody's Headache Powders that go up at convenience stores on big race weekends, you may find humor in the Goody's Mini-Theater and Photos. Among the displays are a Chrysler Hemi engine and several race cars, all number 43. (Every car Richard Petty drives is number 43.)

Racing is so important in North Carolina that the results of all races in which local drivers participate are broadcast on local television sports news. Petty is a much-loved North Carolina hero. He has received honorary degrees from North Carolina colleges. It would be a mistake, however, to suppose this is a uniquely North Carolina phenomenon. Among Petty's artifacts are letters of congratulations from Presidents Ford, Reagan, and Bush.

Petty's racing days have ended, but his reputation as the king of racing remains intact. Even if you neither know that Petty is the king of racing nor care a fig for the sport, you might find spending some time among people who do a fascinating cultural experience. Signs off Highway 220 near the zoo signs south of Asheboro at the Level Cross exit direct you to the museum. Modest admission fee; children under twelve free. Open Monday through Saturday from 9:00 A.M. to 5:00 P.M. (336–495–1143).

You could spend all day at the zoo; the Richard Petty Museum needs only an hour or so; the next attraction, **Seagrove,** and the potteries could take a week.

The Seagrove area is rural. You need to plan ahead for food and lodging. The nearest motels are in Asheboro, a little less than 30 miles north of Seagrove. Comfort Inn (336–626–4414) and Days Inn (336–629–2101) are at the juncture of U.S. 64 and U.S. 220 bypass. **Hampton Inn Hotel** (336–625–9000 or 800–426–7866) is at 1137 East Dixie Drive, Asheboro 27203.

Restaurants are in such short supply in pottery country that several potteries have picnic tables for shoppers who bring lunch. A good restaurant in Seagrove, on U.S. 220, is the *Jugtown Cafe* (336–873–8292). The food ranges from subs, croissant sandwiches, and burgers to country-cooking plate specials with several vegetables. The food is good and prices are moderate. The cafe is open Monday through Thursday from 5:00 A.M. to 2:00 P.M., Friday and Saturday from 5:00 A.M. to 8:00 P.M., and Sunday from 7:00 A.M. to 2:00 P.M. These hours may vary seasonally.

Before you start, accept the fact that it's physically impossible to stop at every pottery in one day. It was impossible a few years ago when they numbered in the thirties; now that there are more than one hundred, your only alternatives are to choose your stops selectively or to plan several trips. New places open regularly, so don't limit your stops to those mentioned here.

The people whose job is to promote tourism in the area have all but thrown up their hands in despair over keeping up with the growing number of potteries or with trying to tell you when they are open. As Susan Smith of Randolph County Tourism puts it, "If somebody decides to go to the beach for a week, they just close down and go."

This is not true of all the potteries; many run thoroughly professional businesses with enough staff to keep things going even during vacations. But as Dan Triece of Dirt Works Pottery explains, potters in the area these days fall into roughly three groups: those open seven days a week, those open five days a week (usually Tuesday through Saturday), and those that operate on weekends. The weekend potters generally have other jobs and throw pots as a hobby.

Another recent development is the opening of consignment shops in Seagrove, where work by various potters is for sale. This is a good way to see the work of several potters at one stop, but you'll miss the action of the actual potting.

An efficient way of deciding which potteries to visit is to stop at the North Carolina Pottery Center, at the junction of U.S. 220 and S.R. 705. The center displays the work of potters from all over the state, and you can discover whose work you like without stopping at every single pottery. A free map of area potteries is available in the lobby. Admission is $3.00 to see the entire display. The center is open Tuesday through Saturday, from 10:00 A.M. to 4:00 P.M.

Originally this part of the country attracted production potters who

Potting in North Carolina

made the storage jugs, pitchers, crocks, and bean pots farmers used every day because both the heavy red clay for potting and the timber stands for fueling the kilns were right here. No doubt local moonshine was one of the products that got stored in the jugs. A rich culture developed around potting, complete with family traditions in design and glazing. Some potters, such as Ben Owens, earned reputations for being excellent turners.

As other materials came along for making utensils to cook and store food, the potters turned more to producing items for tourists. But the actual potting stayed basically the same. Over three and four generations, feuds and disagreements came up, and sometimes a member of a famous potting family, such as the Owens, would splinter off to start an independent pottery.

The old families continue making the same kinds of pottery today. Tourists and gift shop owners buy it up faster than the wheels at Cole and Jugtown and Owens can turn.

Newcomers fill out the scene with more artistic studio pottery, which is usually more elaborately shaped, decorated, and glazed. These pieces take longer to make.

Some of the new potters are local young people who have studied in the well-respected program at Troy Technical College nearby. Others, transplants from elsewhere, have been attracted by the concentration of potters that draws customers and ensures support. It would be wrong to say that all new potters make studio pottery and all old-timers practice production pottery, however. You'll find a good bit of crossover. The best thing to do is simply look at the work, talk to the potters, and make your choices.

Many of the materials these days are shipped in from elsewhere rather than dug from local ground, and some kilns are fired by oil, gas, or electricity rather than wood. But the atmosphere is still that of a unique culture engrossed in a hands-on kind of work.

Some people say the old-timers don't think much of the new crowd because they're too fancy. Some people say the newcomers look down on the "production mentality" of the old families. Those attitudes may exist, but what you'll usually hear is encouragement from the long-established potters for the new ones, and deep respect and admiration from the newer people for the speed and accuracy with which a good production potter can turn. As one young man said, "I've been futzing with this lid for two hours now. Those guys would've finished a dozen pots in that time."

Wherever you stop, talk to the people. They're used to it, they like it, and it's an integral part of the experience. As you do, you can't help noticing the arthritic hands of some of the old potters. As a younger artisan explained it, "My pots will never be quite as good as theirs, because you need to keep wetting the clay with *cold* water for the very best results, and I use warm water. I've seen what twenty and thirty years of cold water and clay does to your hands. I'm afraid I'm not quite that dedicated."

The largest concentration of potteries begins on Highway 705, off Highway 220. The state road numbers are clearly marked, so it is easy to follow the map through the countryside, traveling from one pottery to another. No two are alike, nor are their wares. Part of the fun is in the discovery and surprise; you don't need full information ahead of time about each place, but the following are a few guaranteed to be special. They are all marked on the free maps available at every pottery.

Phil Morgan Pottery (336–873–7304) features Phil's elegant crystalline glazes on porcelain and his wife's more traditional earthenware, much of it in pleasing muted rose and blue tones and decorated with flowers. These people love to talk and can give you what seems like a complete course in the intricacies of crystalline glazing. Although more people are producing crystalline these days, Morgan is still considered a master.

Potts Town Pottery (336–879–4295) is a new endeavor by Jeff and Linda Potts. Linda's grandmother was a Cole—the Potts say they represent the ninth generation of Coles, famous traditional folk potters. They use local clay and produce traditional earthenware tableware and serving pieces. Some of the glazes, especially the blue, resemble those of the old Cole pottery, but you will see differences in sheen.

Ben Owens Pottery (336–464–2261) displays the work of Ben Owens III, who was recognized as a boy for having superior talent, on a par with that of his grandfather. Young Ben works as an artist, producing shapes and designs inspired by Egyptian and Japanese work. His pots are on display in museums around the country. The display rooms usually aren't heavily stocked, but you do find an interesting variety, presided over by a proud papa who can explain Ben's work in detail.

At *Westmoore Pottery* (336–464–3700), open only since 1977, Mary and David Farrell make reproductions of the earthenware and salt-glazed stoneware typical of the eighteenth and early nineteenth centuries. They also make stunning reproductions of Moravian pottery as well as create new designs in the old traditions.

Mary can throw a pot or apply a Moravian-design slip trail without a flaw and chat with customers at the same time. The couple and the pottery have received national attention in more than one country-oriented magazine for their work and the unique new home they built behind their new pottery. Their work is especially popular with people involved in authentic historic restoration and representation.

The people at *Cady Clay Works* (336–464–5661), John Mellage and his wife, Beth Gore, produce pieces with vibrant colors and contemporary designs. They usually have some spectacular, extra-large bowls that are surprisingly lightweight for their size.

At *Walton's Pottery* (336–879–3270), Don and Susan Walton make lead-free stoneware pottery that you can safely subject to the oven, microwave, and dishwasher. The Waltons have some gorgeous glazes and unique contemporary designs. They make some small, oval dishes with straight sides that are just right for individual servings of gratinéed casserole-type foods. Also, you can buy some unusual jewelry, such as earrings—hand cut, glazed, and fired—here.

DirtWorks Pottery (336–873–8979, closed Monday in January and February) is the permanent showroom of Dan Triece. Triece has won awards in the Southeast, especially for his copper luster raku. He also works in stoneware, ranging from pastels to midnight blue. The shop also carries woodcrafts, basketry, jewelry, and other North Carolina crafts as well as work by other regional potters.

Turn and Burn (336–873–7381) produces unusual handcarved face jugs and snake jugs inspired by jugs made locally in the 1600s satirizing political problems. David Garner, who says he grew up so surrounded by the craft he can't remember the first time he saw a pot made, has been potting for twenty years, the past eight in his current location. His current favorite jug shows Ross Perot's face upside down.

Milly McCanless of **Dover Pottery** (336–464–3586) is one of the newer potters, too. Initially, she got into it because she had a dollhouse and wanted to learn to throw miniature pots for her miniature dining table. In the process she discovered that she was also good with big pots. She saw that while there wasn't much market for miniatures, she could sell as much full-sized pottery as she could produce. She's especially known for pieces beautifully decorated in painted floral and bird designs. "It's functional art. I love the idea," she says. Millie's husband, Allen, has been working with crystalline and raku glazes and has some handsome pieces for sale. He's known for his intricate designs. Sharon Williams is also a working potter at Dover. Often when you stop, you are helped by one of the McCanless children, who are becoming potters in their own rights. The business has grown so much, Milly says, that she does much less potting herself these days.

Jugtown (336–464–3266) operates somewhat more commercially than the other potteries, including handwoven rugs and placemats, hand-made toys, and other North Carolina folk crafts in its retail stock. The Jugtown stoneware is uniform enough in appearance to look nice beside the more regular, mass-produced commercial dinnerware and seems practically indestructible. Most of the pieces reflect traditional local styles and glazes. There is a bathroom here, too. That may seem like a small thing, in the abstract, but after you've spent some time driving these country roads where you don't find pit stops every few miles, it's something to appreciate. You may also enjoy eating your picnic lunch at the tables under the trees provided for visitors.

The hours of the various potters may vary by a half-hour or so in opening and closing, but most are open from 8:30 A.M. to 4:30 P.M. Tuesday through Saturday. Nearly all are closed Sunday. The best time to go is Friday afternoon, when most of the kilns are opened to bring out the new pots. Saturday morning is a good time, too, but by afternoon the wares will already be thinning out. It's almost a waste of time to go around Christmas or in late summer. The shoppers then simply buy faster than the potters can pot.

Although some early glazes contained lead, today's are lead-free and safe for table use. If you have any concerns about lead, ask in the pottery.

Heartland

*A*nother possible trip from Asheboro is the short hop up High-way 220 to *Greensboro,* a pleasant city with a historic down-town and lots of surprises. There's some Revolutionary War history here, in a strange sort of way. Cornwallis won a battle against General Nathanael Greene's American troops, but in the process he lost so many men that he ultimately had to surrender at Yorktown. The Guilford Courthouse National Military Park, 6 miles north of Greensboro on Highway 220, commemorates the loss and the win with exhibits on the battlefield and displays and films in the visitors center (336–288–1776). The center is open daily from 8:30 A.M. to 5:00 P.M. The gate to the tour road closes at 4:30 P.M. Admission is free.

Drawing on more recent events, Greensboro holds special significance for blacks. In 1960 black students from *North Carolina A & T State University* (originally the Agricultural and Mechanical College for the Colored Race) began the first sit-ins at Woolworth's segregated lunch counter. A & T is Jesse Jackson's alma mater, and he still comes to town from time to time.

On the campus of North Carolina A & T State University, the *Mattye Reed African Heritage Center* displays African masks, paintings, black history books, and art objects. Open Monday through Friday. Call for current hours (336–334–3209; www.nps.gov/guco). Admission is free.

Less than 10 miles east of Greensboro, the *Charlotte Hawkins Brown Memorial* (336–449–4846), a still-developing state historic site, hon-ors Dr. Brown's fifty years as head of another school for blacks, Palmer Memorial Institute. The buildings are gradually being restored, and plans are to make the memorial a center for contributions of North Car-olina blacks, including a research center with collection and computer facilities devoted to North Carolina black history. Dr. Brown's house has been restored, and some of her original furniture is being reuphol-stered. Open Monday through Saturday from 9:00 A.M. to 5:00 P.M., Sunday from 1:00 to 5:00 P.M. April through October. Winter hours are Tuesday through Saturday from 10:00 A.M. to 4:00 P.M. and Sunday from 1:00 to 4:00 P.M. Admission is free. For further information on develop-ment of the site, write P.O. Box B, Sedalia 27342.

Local history from the time of the early Indians to date shapes the dis-plays at the *Greensboro Historical Museum,* 130 Summit Avenue, Greensboro 27401, in what used to be the First Presbyterian Church. In a re-creation of nineteenth-century Greensboro, the museum displays a general store, the drugstore where William Sydney Porter (O. Henry) once worked, a post office, a law office, a firehouse, a cobbler's, and a blacksmith's.

Other exhibits include room settings from historical homes, an exhibit of household items and clothing of Dolley Madison (a Greensboro native before she became First Lady), and a collection of antique automobiles. Open Tuesday through Saturday, 10:00 A.M. to 5:00 P.M., and Sunday from 2:00 to 5:00 P.M. Closed holidays. (336–373–2043). Admission is free. Web site: www.greensboro.lib.nc.us/museum.

If you're traveling with kids (or even if you're not, come to think of it), don't miss the *Natural Science Center,* 4301 Lawndale Drive, Greensboro 27401 (336–288–3769), where you can easily spend a day immersing yourself in the sights and sounds of everything from dinosaurs to star systems. This is a "participation museum," where you don't have to tell the kids to look, not touch. For instance, you can put your hand into a real dinosaur footprint, pet and feed animals in the zoo, observe sunspots in the live solar observatory, and turn your imagination loose in the planetarium. The transparent anatomical mannequin, which you might want to save until after lunch, lets you study what goes on inside the skin of the human body. The museum is open Monday through Saturday from 9:00 A.M. to 5:00 P.M. and Sunday from 1:00 to 5:00 P.M. The zoo is open Monday through Saturday from 10:00 A.M. to 4:30 P.M. and Sunday from 12:30 to 4:00 P.M. A moderate admission fee covers the museum and zoo. Planetarium shows daily at 3:00 P.M. are $1.00 extra.

When you've had enough of indoor attractions, Greensboro has three gardens worth some attention, collectively known as the *Greensboro Gardens.* The Greensboro Arboretum, Bog Garden, and Bicentennial Garden feature most of the plants native to the Piedmont region. The arboretum is on West Market Street at Lindley Park. It has nine labeled collections of indigenous species. The bog garden is at the corner of Hobbs Road and Starmount Farms Drive and features a variety of plants that thrive in wet areas. The Bicentennial Garden is at the corner of Cornwallis Drive and Hobbs Road. It emphasizes mass plantings of bulbs, annuals, and perennials, along with flowering trees and shrubs. Admission to the gardens is free. Call (336) 373–2199 or (800) 344–2282 for more information.

If you are interested in regional folk art and pottery, you should know about two Greensboro collectors with galleries in their homes. Mike Smith and his family run the *At Home Gallery,* and Mike's cousin,

THE UPPER PIEDMONT

Lynn Melton, has a gallery to display and sell the pottery she has been collecting for thirty years. Smith's emphasis is on the type of art that has come to be called "self-taught" and sometimes "visionary" and "outsider." The artists he represents include Sarah Rakes, G. C. DuPree, M. C. Jones, Mose and Annie Tolliver, Mary T. Smith, and Jimmy Lee Sudduth. To the beginning collector, some of this art looks like something your kids could do, but on closer inspection, there's a lot more to it. Lynn Melton specializes in regional pottery dating back to the earliest days of potters here. She has everything from swirl pottery (striped with mixed clays in colored swirls around the pot, in the throwing process) to face jugs of every description. You have to make an appointment to visit Lynn and Mike because the galleries are in their private homes. To see a sample of At Home Gallery's art, check the Web site: www.athomegallery.com. To make an appointment, e-mail him at athome98@aol.com or call (336) 664–0022. To contact Lynn, e-mail her at LMELTON222@aol.com.

Drop your weary head on a pillow at the Greenwich—a small, older, European-style hotel downtown—or at the Greenwood Bed and Breakfast, in one of Greensboro's first suburban areas, about 10 blocks from the business district. *The Biltmore-Greensboro Hotel,* 111 West Washington Street, Greensboro 27401 (336–272–3474), has had what the cliché makers would call "a checkered past." It was built to be corporate headquarters for a textile company in the 1800s, then was used as a post office, and later was turned into a hospital during World War II. In the twenty years before it was rescued and renovated, it had been either a house of ill repute or a flophouse, depending on whose story you believe. A little of both may have been true. Now the lobby is a pretty little area of brass and crystal chandeliers and eighteenth-century reproductions and art. The rooms are tasteful and comfortable, with small refrigerators to cool your traveling comestibles.

The *Greenwood Bed and Breakfast,* 205 North Park Drive, Greensboro 27401 (336–274–6350 or 800–535–9363), a stick-style home built in the early 1900s, has also been renovated. Old oaks and the neighborhood park surround the home with greenery and shield the backyard swimming pool from the curious. Inside, wood carvings and art collections from around the world attract your attention. The proprietors, Bob and Dolly Gerton, serve a continental breakfast with fruit and homemade breads, which is included in the rates. The inn has three guest rooms and a two-room suite, all with private baths.

From here you can easily make a side trip up U.S. Highway 29 to Reidsville for a tour of the **Chinqua-Penn Plantation** museum. The home of Thomas Jefferson and Beatrice Schoelkopf Penn, it was three years in planning and construction. The couple moved into the main house in December 1925, where they lived until "Jeff" died in 1946. Beatrice stayed on until 1965.

The Penns were wealthy and built their home, a 27-room house designed in a Y shape, as a place to live and do things, a place to keep their ever-growing collections of art and antiques. But they built it for themselves, not as a place to impress other people. All the Penns' furnishings and personal items are still in the house, and all the structures on the property, including a greenhouse and a pagoda, are pretty much the way the Penns kept them.

This makes a unique museum. While only a few years old, it has caught the imagination of local people, staff, and volunteers. Part of the fun of touring Chinqua-Penn is interacting with the enthusiastic guides who obviously love the place.

The Chinqua-Penn Plantation is open 9:00 A.M. to 5:00 P.M. Tuesday through Saturday, noon to 5:00 P.M. Sunday. Tickets are $13.00 for adults, $12.00 for seniors sixty-two and older, and $6.00 for children six to eighteen. Children under five admitted free. Tickets for the landscape and gardens only are $6.00. Chinqua-Penn is west of Reidsville near U.S. Highway 29 and 158, halfway between Greensboro and Danville. From U.S. Highway 29 by-pass, exit at Highway 14. Travel north on Highway 14 for 3½ miles to Salem Church Road. Turn left. At the stop sign, turn right onto Wentworth Street. Chinqua-Penn is immediately on your right. Phone (336) 349–4576 for more information; or visit their Web site: www.chinquapenn.com.

From here you may want to go back to Greensboro to pick up I–40.

Tobacco Town

From Greensboro you're looking at a drive of only about 20 miles west on Interstate 40 to Winston-Salem, the tobacco town. It would be hard to overstate the influence of the R. J. Reynolds Tobacco Company. While Richard Joshua Reynolds was directing a rapidly growing business and hiring increasing thousands of people in the tobacco factories, his wife, Katharine, set about a long series of community improvement activities for the benefit of those same families. With Reynolds money and Moravian artistic influence, the area developed into a cultural center that still ranks high in the country today.

Perhaps the most audacious Reynolds act in later years was the lock-stock-and-barrel move of Wake Forest University from Wake County to Winston-Salem in 1950. President Truman came to wield the shovel in the groundbreaking ceremony. The **Museum of Anthropology,** on the campus, is billed as the only museum devoted to the study of world cultures, covering Africa, Asia, Oceania, and the Americas. Call (336) 758–5282 for details.

To learn more about the tobacco industry and the Reynolds influence in it, stop at the **R. J. Reynolds Tobacco U.S.A.** plant 3 miles north of Greensboro on Highway 52 for a guided tour of the plant that produces 450 *million* cigarettes a day, and a stop in the museum that depicts the development of the industry. Notice the heavy sweet smell of tobacco that permeates the air. Line workers who are close to the actual tobacco products will tell you that the smell gets into their clothes and remains so strong that when they get home after work, they may shuck their work clothes at the doorway to keep the smell out of the house.

As background on the R. J. R. dynasty, you should read the book by Patrick Reynolds (who has come out strongly against using tobacco) and Tom Shachtman, *The Gilded Leaf: Triumph, Tragedy, and Tobacco—Three Generations of the R. J. Reynolds Family and Fortune.* Larry Hagman (who played ruthless J. R. Ewing in the *Dallas* television series) wrote of the book that it made *Dallas* look "like a bowl of warm milk toast." Be careful about trying to discuss the book while you're here, though. Criticizing tobacco in a community built upon it rouses the ire of some residents. So does speaking ill of the First Tobacco Family.

About half a century ago, the town was shocked when Zachary Smith Reynolds, usually called Smith, son of R. J. and Katharine, was shot through the head during a boozy party at the family home, less than a year after his marriage to the torch singer Libby Holman. Apparently Smith Reynolds caught Libby flirting (or more) with a friend, fighting erupted, and Smith either shot himself or was killed by Libby. Newspapers suppressed much of the story at the time, and even today, polite society doesn't talk about it, though that hasn't stopped brazen authors from writing about it. An interesting source, should you decide to pursue the subject further, is the biography, *Libby Holman: Body and Soul,* by H. D. Perry.

After studying the impact of Reynolds and tobacco, turn your attention to the Moravians. Moravians came from Pennsylvania to settle the area in 1753. They built Salem as a totally planned, church-governed community in 1766. Winston wasn't founded until 1849. In Salem, arts and crafts flourished; in Winston, it was tobacco and textiles. By the early 1900s the two towns had grown together and consolidated. It would be hard to say whether tobacco or the Moravians left the greater mark on the area, nor is it really pertinent; in the early days tobacco wasn't a dirty word, and nobody saw anything wrong with a strong relationship between church and chew.

If you see only one attraction here, it certainly should be **Old Salem,** a Moravian town restored so carefully that when you walk the streets and go into the buildings, you feel as though you've entered a time warp. To give you an idea of the pains staff people take with getting it right, people responsible for demonstrations of cooking and household activities take turns preparing research papers and consulting old diaries, journals, and letters to discover exactly how the households might have run. Unlike traditional historians who mainly study battles, politics, and industrial development, these re-creators also try, as well, to piece together the elements of day-to-day life. This isn't the only historic site where such activities are going on, but it's hard to imagine one where they're being treated any more earnestly or where the subject matter is any more fascinating. This attention to detail extends even to the food cooked from old Moravian recipes. The original recipe used fresh ginger root, but gingerbread recipes in later years have shifted to powdered ginger because it's easier to find and keep. The Old Salem recipe still specifies fresh, grated ginger. At the **Winkler Bakery,** costumed bakers make cookies and bread in a wood-fired brick oven. The baked goods are for sale.

Costumed guides in the old kitchen cook in the huge fireplace and iron with flatirons heated there, all the while sweating genuine sweat—a fascinating reminder in this age of air-conditioning that just getting from one day to the next once took a lot of energy. Among the demonstrations offered in Old Salem are music from an organ built in 1797, potting, baking, and spinning.

Not all the buildings in the historic district are restored as tour buildings. Some are private homes. The presence of automobiles and real people living real lives doesn't seem to detract from the atmosphere; indeed it simply makes it feel more alive. Whatever tours you take, start at the visitors center (336–721–7300 or 888–348–5420). Moderate to high admission fees, depending on how many features you wish to tour. Get tickets for all Old Salem tour attractions at the visitors center, open

Old Salem

from 9:00 A.M. to 5:00 P.M. Monday through Saturday and from 12:30 to 5:00 P.M. on Sunday.

The gardens at Old Salem are reputed to be the best-documented, restored community gardens in America. Their authenticity is possible because the Moravians kept meticulous records. Many of the gardens have been re-created on their original sites and produce the same varieties of vegetables, flowers, and herbs described in old records. The attention to horticultural detail goes beyond the garden squares to include old cultivars of fruit trees in orchards, flowering vines on fences, and native trees in the landscape.

Having toured Old Salem, you'll need to eat at the **Old Salem Tavern Dining Rooms** at 736 South Main Street in the district (336–748–8585). Continuing the sense of reenactment, costumed staff serve Moravian-style cooking by candlelight. Specialties include game and gingerbread from the old recipes. For the faint of palate, standard beef and chops entrees are also available. All spirits served. The restaurant is open for lunch from 11:30 A.M. to 2:00 P.M. Sunday through Friday and from 11:30 A.M. to 2:30 P.M. Saturday; for dinner from 5:30 to 9:00 P.M. Monday through Thursday and from 5:30 to 9:30 P.M. Friday and Saturday.

Also in Old Salem, the **Museum of Early Southern Decorative Arts** (336–721–7300 or 888–348–5420; Web site: visit@oldsalem.org) gives you a close look at the results of extensive research into the regional decorative arts of the early South. The exhibits include furniture, paintings, textiles, ceramics, silver, and other metalware. You can't just wander in here. Guides take you through the building in small groups. You may buy tickets at the Old Salem Visitors Center. Museum hours are Monday through Saturday from 10:30 A.M. to 5:00 P.M. and Sunday from 1:30 to 5:00 P.M. You can spend the night in Old Salem at the 1840 *Augustus T. Zevely Inn,* a privately owned bed-and-breakfast at 803 South Main Street, Old Salem 27101. This fine old brick building is furnished with pieces of the Old Salem Collection so that it feels much as it would have in the 1840s. Some of the twelve guest rooms have fireplaces. Some also have microwaves, refrigerators, and whirlpools, which, of course, feel nothing at all like the 1840s but are kind of nice after a day of walking. Rates begin at about $80 per double room. Phone (336) 748–9299 or (800) 928–9299.

An alternative end to a day in this historic manufacturing and artistic town is a night's lodging at *Brookstown Inn,* a restored 1837 textile mill (336–725–1120 or 800–845–4262). The history of the inn matches that of the city for interest. Moravians opened the Salem Cotton Manu-facturing Company and later sold it, and the buildings were subse-quently used as a flour mill and then as a moving-company storage house. The conversion to an inn created large guest rooms with odd nooks and crannies and high ceilings. An upstairs wall is covered with the graffiti (protected by an acrylic plastic sheet) of the young factory girls who boarded there. A boiler room with catwalk now serves as a restaurant in which one of the old boiler faces is a focal point. The decor is early American, with many handmade quilts and country accents. Rates include wine and cheese in the parlor, homemade cookies and milk, and continental breakfast in the dining room.

While you are in the Winston-Salem area, take a few minutes to drive to the old *Shell gas station* at the corner of Sprague and Peachtree Streets. You'll know you're there when you come to a huge orange and red structure shaped like a seashell, with two old gas pumps standing in front. This old gas station sold Quality Oil products in the 1930s and then fell into disuse and disrepair. It had a big crack sealed with a

Sweet Stuff

Southerners have a notorious sweet tooth. The tea-drinking habits of North Carolinians are a good example. We drink tea iced—year-round, not just in summer. We put sugar in it and call it "sweet tea"; if you want it any other way, you have to say so by ordering "unsweet tea." Even then, if you don't want a mouth-ful of sugar, taste just a little sip when the tea comes, because the request for unsweet tea is so rare servers may well bring you the sweet kind out of habit.

strip of black tar, and vandals had broken windows and fixtures and littered the ground.

Sarah Woodard, who wasn't even born when the station was in its glory days, oversaw the renovation, which was completed in 1997. Almost any time you stop in, some old-timers who remember when the station was operating are apt to be standing around reminiscing about earlier times. One of them, Sidney Teague, says he always thought the Shell was the prettiest thing in town—and he still does.

As you leave the area, to move swiftly back into the twenty-first century you might stop at the *Sciworks,* 400 West Hanes Mill Road, 7¹/₂ miles north of the intersection of Interstate 40 on Highway 52 on Museum Drive off the Hanes Mill Road exit. The participatory exhibits cover natural science and physical science and technology. A three-dimensional solar system display puts you in the middle of the planets, and a model of the moon shows the landing sites of Apollo. Children especially enjoy the saltwater touch tank and the petting zoo. Admission is $8.00 for adults, $6.00 for children ages six to nineteen, $6.00 for senior citizens fifty-five and older, $4.00 for children ages three to five; children younger than three are free. The museum (336–767–6730) is open Monday through Saturday from 10:00 A.M. to 5:00 P.M. and Sunday from 1:00 to 5:00 P.M. Admission is free the second Friday of every month from 4:00 to 8:00 P.M.

The Barbecue Capital

Also on Highway 52, about 20 miles south, the town of *Lexington* is a must-stop for barbecue freaks. More than a dozen restaurants in this little town serve pork barbecue (if it's made with anything else it isn't really barbecue!) "Lexington style," which means with a pepper-vinegar sauce. The sauce, which is always added later rather than simmered with the pork, contains only hot pepper and vinegar. And it never, never contains mustard. That's South Carolina barbecue. In the eastern part of the state, barbecue restaurants sell something made with pork and a sweet tomato sauce. *They* call it barbecue, but of course it isn't really. Sometimes you'll see signs in other parts of North Carolina advertising Lexington barbecue, but as anyone in town will tell you, to be authentic, it's got to be made by roasting pork shoulder over a wood fire in Lexington. Also, it has to be served with red slaw, not the white or yellow stuff. And that's just the way it is.

Lexington's most popular celebrity is Bob Timberlake, the painter and designer, whose ideas have mushroomed into a multi-million-dollar

How the Experts Rate North Carolina Barbecue Blind Taste Judging				Judge No. _____ Code No. _____
	Poor	Fair	Good	Very Good	Excellent
Appearance	2 4 6 8	10 12 14 16	18 20 22 24	26 28 30 32	34 36 38 40
Tenderness	2 4 6 8	10 12 14 16	18 20 22 24	26 28 30 32	34 36 38 40
Taste	4 8 12 16	20 24 28 32	36 40 44 48	52 56 60 64	68 72 76 80

Total Score: _____

Key:
Appearance: Texture, color, fat to lean ratio, burnt meat.
Tenderness: Moist and tender vs. dry and tough.
Taste: Sauce too hot, too mild, or excessive vs. a pleasing blend of sauce and meat.

business. Timberlake grew up in the area, made contact when he was young with Andrew Wyeth and, with Wyeth's encouragement, decided to try to paint for a living. His style is something of a cross between Norman Rockwell's nostalgia and Wyeth's detailed realism. Mostly Timberlake paints scenes from the farm and lake where he lives. His prints sell these days for more than he once got for his originals. The early prints bring as much as $3,500. And an original Timberlake painting may bring up to $50,000.

Timberlake has thrown his energy into designing everything from upholstery fabric and men's shirts to log cabins. His furniture company provides employment for thousands of people in the area as do his other ever-growing enterprises. He has created a series of dolls made to look like his grandchildren. "It just keeps pouring out," he says. The best way to get a glimpse of the scope of Timberlake's activities is at the *Bob Timberlake Gallery* (800–244–0095), which opened in 1997. It is a combination gallery, museum, and salesroom. You can see everything from his new furniture to his earliest paintings. The gallery is at 1714 East Center Street. From I–85 take exit 94, then drive west on Highway 64. Signs direct you. The gallery is open Monday through Friday 10:00 A.M. to 6:00 P.M., Saturday 9:00 A.M. to 5:00 P.M., closed Sunday. Admission is free. Web site: www.bobtim berlake.com.

The Furniture Capital

igh Point is mostly about manufacturing and selling furniture. The town, already active in the lumber business, first got into furniture building in the early 1880s, when a local lumber salesman noticed the big difference between the price of wood as it left the sawmill and the price it brought once it had been shipped away and turned into furniture. Sensibly, he and two local merchants risked all they had to start a furniture company close to the source of the wood. It was the right idea in the right place at the right time. Sales took off and the future was set. Today High Point has 125 furniture manufacturing companies.

Unless you are professionally involved in the furniture business, avoid High Point in April and October, when for the better part of two weeks in both months the town hosts the Southern Furniture Market, usually referred to simply as "market." Said to be the largest furniture show in the world (it fills 150 buildings and between five and six million square feet), this trade show attracts interior decorators and furniture retailers—in other words *buyers*—from all over the world. More than 1,500 furniture company exhibitors show up for each market show. Multiply that by the staff each company brings to work the booths and add all the buyers who come looking for the latest goodies, and you get an image of a town, normal population on the shy side of 70,000, so overloaded that if it were a ship it would sink. Finding a place to stay or to eat is a challenge.

A valuable museum in the area is the **Springfield Museum of Old Domestic Art,** established in 1935 in the third meetinghouse of the Springfield Meeting, 555 East Springfield Road (336–889–4911). Museums, like history books, tend to focus on extraordinary events, wars, and politics and not on the commonplaces of day-to-day life. This museum is an exception. Here you can inspect the artifacts of daily life that have been used in the neighborhood for 200 years or more—spinning equipment, utensils, farm items, clothing, pictures from homes, toys, and a slew of fascinating odds and ends. The curator says, "Most of what we have has been donated by local Quakers."

She likes to emphasize most of the items that were so commonplace in their day, objects crudely made to fill an immediate need. If you didn't know the way in which many of them had been used, you probably could never figure out what they were for. Such artifacts simply cannot be replaced.

One example is the log lifter. It looks like a crutch for a giant. Log lifters were devices created to get logs from the ground to high points in the walls when building log cabins. One man stood at each end of the log with a lifter and heaved.

Another example is a homemade Noah's Ark, with all the animals two-by-two. This was a Sunday toy, made during the time when children in the community weren't allowed to play on Sundays with their regular toys or do much else. It was carved about one hundred years ago by Yardley Warner for his twins, probably because he sympathized with the children's restlessness and wanted to make them a religious toy to keep them occupied on Sundays.

Another uncommon exhibit is the 4-foot-long tin horn the coachman blew at each stop of the stagecoach along the Old Plank Road. The number of blasts blown told people at upcoming stops, such as Nathan Hunt Tavern, what passengers would be wanting when they got there. Old Plank Road was built between Fayetteville and Winston-Salem by laying down boards next to one another to form a firm-surfaced highway. Part of the old road is now Main Street. A plank from the road and a notched mile marker are also in the display. A traveler in the dark could stop at the marker and feel the number of notches on it to know how far it was to Nathan Hunt Tavern. A model shows a stagecoach on a plank road with markers to give you an idea how it all worked.

Visiting here is more like going into an attic than a museum. "There's so much stuff, and you can handle it. You don't get the feeling of things resting on velvet that you can't touch," the curator says. The museum is open by appointment. Admission is free.

The *High Point Historical Museum,* 1805 East Lexington Avenue (336–885–6859), exhibits more traditional kinds of material related to the town's history, including military displays. There is also a display of old telephones that takes you back to before Ma Bell, a collection of furniture made in High Point, and, appropriately, woodworking tools that take you back to the first manufacturing in town. Also on the property are the restored 1786 John Haley House, a weaving house, and a blacksmith shop. Demonstrations are offered in these buildings on weekends. The museum is open Tuesday through Saturday from 10:00 A.M. to 4:30 P.M. and Sunday from 1:00 to 4:30 P.M. Other buildings are open only on weekends. Admission is free.

The next two attractions are in the same building at 101 West Green Drive, but they really don't have much to do with each other. *The Angela Peterson Doll and Miniature Museum* (336–885–3655) contains more than 1,700 dolls collected by Angela Peterson from around the world. She picked up everything—crèche dolls, a Shirley Temple collection of 120 dolls, and Bob Timberlake dolls, as well as enough dollhouses and furnishings to create a miniature village. Before the collection was housed here, it was in several rooms of the retirement home where Peterson lived. In fact, she said she chose that particular place to live after "auditioning" a number of possibilities because this place expressed an active interest in her doll collection. The home may have ended up being more interested than she was. Somewhere along the way, when she was in her late eighties or early nineties, she began referring to the collection as "the damned dolls," because it took so much work to keep their costumes clean and properly pressed. The dolls were moved into the building on West Green Drive after her death. The museum is open 10:00 A.M. to 4:30 P.M., Monday through Friday and 1:00 to 4:30 P.M. Sunday. Admission is $3.50 for adults, $3.50 for people age sixty-five and over, $2.00 for children six to fifteen. Combination ticket with the Furniture Discovery Center is $8.00.

At the *Furniture Discovery Center* (336–887–3876), in the same building as the doll museum, you can learn more than you realized there was to know about how furniture is designed and made. The center, which has been around less than a decade, is a place for entertainment and education. It was started partly as a substitute for tours of specific furniture manufacturing plants, a practice that has been abandoned because of safety hazards and liability problems.

Actually, you can learn more about how furniture is made and about its history in the center than you could touring a factory, because the displays are set up to explain industry issues concerned with everything from eight-way-hand-tied cone coils to ergonomics.

Here are some of the topics the exhibits cover: furniture market history, miniature bedroom displays, Drexel salesmen's miniatures, wood and trees, furniture designed to fit people rather than spaces, upholstery fabric, and furniture reproductions.

The exhibits are numbered to guide you through the offerings in a logical manner, giving you a sense of the flow of production. Signs explaining the exhibits are conspicuously posted.

The museum offers a variety of hands-on experiences. You can try the air-powered tools, sit in the chairs of the ergonomics exhibit, study a half-built love seat, and play with the computer design program to see what various fabric colors and patterns look like on different-shaped furniture pieces.

For kids one of the most popular exhibits is Harvy Hardwood, the talking tree, who gives recorded lessons about hardwoods and their uses.

Another popular exhibit is the wood exhibit, a series of eleven different wood panels with appropriate leaves etched on the outside. You guess the kind of tree, lift the panel, and read the description to see if you are right. The center is open Monday through Friday, 10:00 A.M. to 5:00 P.M., Saturday from 9:00 A.M. to 5:00 P.M., Sunday from 1:00 to 5:00 P.M. Closed Monday October through April. Admission is $5.00 for adults, $4.00 for senior citizens and students over fifteen years, $2.00 for children six to fifteen; children under six are free with accompanying adult. Web site: www2.hpe.com/discovery.

A pleasant place to stay while you're in High Point is *The Premier,* a six-room bed-and-breakfast inn at 1001 Johnson Street, High Point 27260 (336–889–8349). It's a completely renovated 1907 neo-Colonial home in the center of High Point's historic district. The house used to be known as Mrs. Jones's house and accommodated female schoolteachers in what were considered modest quarters then. The ladies would scarcely recognize the place today.

The decor is luxurious and eclectic, reflecting the taste of a good designer with a flash of humor. Old botanical prints and Dali prints hang side by side in rooms with classic quilts, Oriental rugs, antique wicker, and comfortable contemporary chairs. The colors lean toward pastels, grays, and white, with surprising splashes of turquoise. In one downstairs bedroom, four huge white posts that were originally part of the side porch mark the four corners of a luxuriously festooned bed. The posts are painted so that blooming vines seem to grow toward the ceiling.

Breakfast is lavish, with lots of fresh fruit, the inn's now-famous French toast (one version of which has Bailey's Irish Cream in the batter), and other out-of-the-ordinary entrees.

Partly because of the efforts of a previous innkeeper, the house is surrounded with good perennial borders, so that you enjoy peonies, foxgloves, daisies, and the like, brightening the area along the privet hedge. The back doorstep of the house looks toward the historic district, which features in its old buildings a growing number of specialty shops, including a children's shop, a nature shop, a bookstore, and a gourmet shop. Whatever stores are in business when you visit here, the "boutique row" is always fun to browse through.

The inn has attracted celebrities but has done it so quietly that folks didn't know they were in town. Cher is reported to have stayed here. While it's easy to see that she would enjoy the inn, one wonders what in the world she was doing in High Point in the first place.

Within walking distance of the inn, you can dine at **Noble's,** at 114 South Main Street, High Point 27260 (336–889–3354), a restaurant described by one local resident as "nouvelle American but kind of French and almost four-star." You'll find such offerings as grilled salmon with lobster sauce, veal with chef's sauce, and game such as quail or pheasant, always interestingly prepared. The restaurant has a full liquor license and an excellent wine list. Open Monday through Thursday, from 6:00 to 10:00 P.M. and Friday and Saturday from 6:00 to 11:00 P.M.

A five-minute drive takes you to another popular restaurant, the **Atrium Cafe** (336–889–9934), in the furniture mall at 430 South Main Street, High Point 27260. The prices are reasonable. The restaurant serves the specialties you'd expect—chicken, seafood, and so on—but it is famous for its duck. All spirits are available if you're thinking of making it the kind of special meal that demands a certain drink or a glass of wine. Open from 11:00 A.M. to 4:00 P.M. for lunch and 5:30 to 9:30 P.M. for dinner. Hours may change, so call ahead.

**PLACES TO STAY IN
THE UPPER PIEDMONT**

ASHEBORO
Comfort Inn
825 West Dixie Drive
Asheboro 27203
(336) 626–4414

Hampton Inn
1137 East Dixie Drive
Asheboro 27203
(336) 625–9000

DURHAM
Comfort Inn University
3508 Mt. Moriah Road
Durham 27707
(919) 490–4949

Courtyard by Marriott
1815 Front Street
Durham 27705
(919) 309–1500

Hampton Inn
1816 Hillandale Road
Durham 27705
(919) 471–6100

Red Roof Inn
5623 Chapel Hill Boulevard
Durham 27707
(919) 489–9421

GREENSBORO
Battleground Inn Motel
1517 Westover Terrace
Greensboro 27408
(336) 272–4737

Comfort Inn
2001 Veasley Street
Greensboro 27407
(336) 294–6220

Courtyard by Marriott
4400 West Wendover
Greensboro 27407
(336) 294–3800

Days Inn
120 Seneca Road
Greensboro 27407
(336) 275–9571

Holiday Inn Express
3114 Cedar Park Road
Greensboro 27405
(336) 697–4000

HIGH POINT
Biltmore Suites Hotel
4400 Regency
High Point 27265
(336) 812–8188

Super 8 Motel
400 South Main Street
High Point 27260
(336) 882–4103

RALEIGH
Best Western
Hospitality Inn
2800 Brentwood Road
Raleigh 27604
(919) 872–8600

Brownstone Hotel
1707 Hillsborough Street
Raleigh 27605
(919) 828-0811

Courtyard by Marriott-
Raleigh Wake Forest
1041 Wake Towne Drive
(Near I-40 beltline)
Raleigh 27609
(919) 821-3400
(800) 321-2211

Holiday Inn State Capital
320 Hillsborough Street
(Downtown)
Raleigh 27603
(919) 832-0501

Red Roof Inn Raleigh
3520 Maitland Drive
Raleigh 27603
(919) 231-0200

Sleep Inn
2617 Appliance Court (near
I-440 and
Capital Boulevard)
Raleigh 27604
(919) 755-6005
(800) 753-3746

WINSTON-SALEM
Courtyard by Marriott
3111 University Parkway
Winston-Salem 27105
(336) 727-1277

Hampton Inn
1990 Hampton Inn Court
Winston-Salem 27103
(336) 760-1660
(800) 426-7866

Innkeeper
2115 Peters Creek Parkway
Winston-Salem 27103
(336) 721-0062
(800) 466-5337

Salem Inn
127 South Cherry Street
Winston-Salem 27101
(336) 725-8561
(800) 533-8760

**PLACES TO EAT IN
THE UPPER PIEDMONT**

ASHEBORO
Bamboo Garden
Oriental Restaurant
405 East Dixie
Asheboro 27203
(336) 629-0203

CARY
Horowitz' Delicatessen
107 Edinburgh South
Macgregor Village,
Cary 27511
(919) 467-2007

DURHAM
Pappa's Grill
1821 Hillandale Road
Durham 27705
(919) 286-1910

GREENSBORO
Gate City Chop House
106 South Holden Road
Greensboro 27407
(336) 294-9977

Lucky 32
1421 Westover Terrace
Greensboro 27408
(336) 370-0707

HIGH POINT
Act I Restaurant
130 East Paris Avenue
High Point 27262
(336) 869-5614

The Upper Piedmont Web Sites:

Durham
www.dcub.durham.nc.us

Greensboro
www.greensboronc.org

Lexington
www.web.infoave.net/lexington

Raleigh Visitors Bureau
www.johnstonco-cub.org/smithfield.nc/

Thomasville Tourism Commission
www.ucoml.com/thomasville

Village Cafe
1141 East
Lexington Avenue
High Point 27265
(336) 886–2233

RALEIGH
42nd Street Oyster Bar
508 West Jones Street
Raleigh 27603
(919) 831–2811

Glenwood Grill
2929 Essex Circle
Raleigh 27608
(919) 782–3102

Simpson's Beef
and Seafood
5625 Creedmoor Road
Raleigh 27612
(919) 783–8818

WINSTON-SALEM
Lucky 32
109 South Stratford
Winston-Salem 27103
(336) 777–0032

Nobel's Grille
308 Knollwood Street
(Nation's Bank building)
Winston-Salem 27103
(336) 777–8477

Paul's Fine Italian Dining
3443-B Robbinwood Road
Winston-Salem 27106
(336) 768–2645

The Lower Piedmont

Statesville

n less than an hour, you can drive west on Interstate 40 from
Winston-Salem to *Statesville,* where you'll find several delight-
ful stops known mostly to local folks. *Farm House Gardens* is on the
east side of town on Highway 70 (704–873–2057). If you like garden-
ing and houseplants, you'll find that you simply must buy some plants
here, even if it means driving 500 miles home with them in the back
seat. Kay Kincaid, the main Farm House gardener, started the business about ten years ago with the encouragement of her husband,
Randy, as the obvious expression of her lifelong passion for plants. "I
always loved plants. So did my mother and before her, my grandmother. When I was little, I spent all my time around the farm at my
grandmother's knees in the garden," she says. The force of that passion produced a nursery-greenhouse-gift shop combination that
stuns you with the variety and quality of the offerings. This isn't the
kind of place where anybody counts the number of plants for sale or
measures in terms of how many greenhouses are open (that number
changes with the seasons anyway).

Farm House Gardens surely isn't the largest retail plant operation in
North Carolina, but it is the place you go for the special plants you
haven't been able to find anywhere else. In spring you can buy tomato
plants and pepper plants, but that's rather like choosing peanut butter in
a gourmet shop. The perennials fill benches and the spaces under them
and are lined up along the paths of the back gardens. In the greenhouses
houseplants, including little myrtle topiaries and several different maid-
enhair ferns, tempt you to exceed your budget with every step you take.
All the common herbs and many more that are hard to find are here, too,
along with Japanese maples in great variety, enough different hostas to
fill a small catalog, and rare dwarf shrubs. One gardener, nursing sore
feet the day after a visit to Farm House Gardens, complained that she'd
been there for four hours and hadn't seen everything.

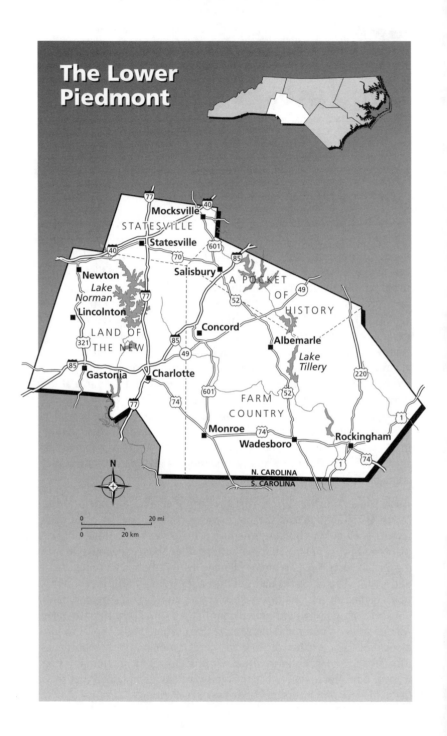

The Lower Piedmont

STATESVILLE

A POCKET OF HISTORY

LAND OF THE NEW

FARM COUNTRY

Mocksville
Statesville
Salisbury
Newton
Lake Norman
Lincolnton
Concord
Albemarle
Lake Tillery
Gastonia
Charlotte
Monroe
Wadesboro
Rockingham

N. CAROLINA
S. CAROLINA

N

0   20 mi
0   20 km

THE LOWER PIEDMONT

ANNUAL EVENTS IN THE LOWER PIEDMONT

Charlotte
Southern Ideal Home Show
(mid-October)
(800) 849–0248

Gold Hill
Gold Hill Founder's Day
(late September)
(704) 279–5674

Salisbury
Uniquely Rowan Mayfest
(early May)
(704) 638–9887

Autumn Jubilee
(early October)
(704) 636–2089

Statesville
National Balloon Rally
(mid-September)
(704) 873–2892

As if the variety weren't enough, you deal with people who so obviously love and know the plants that it's more like swapping cuttings with Aunt Elizabeth than a commercial transaction. If you mistakenly zero in on a not-for-sale stock plant and are crushed that you can't have it, Kay or one of her helpers will cut off a little start for you and tuck it into the soil of another plant you've purchased, along with instructions, if you need them, on how to root the slip. If you're one who boasts that you have a black thumb and can kill anything, don't go here. They mean for your plants to thrive, and any other attitude would be an insult. At the outdoor sales station they keep a hand-lettered sign listing the people who are mad at them. The way to get on the list is to sign it. A *great* joke. Open from 9:00 A.M. to 5:00 P.M. Monday through Saturday. Closed Sunday. Write Route 7, Box 27, Statesville 28677.

Don't leave Statesville without seeing the *Arts and Science Center,* 1335 Museum Road, Statesville 28625 (704–873–4734). This is a truly local museum, and the story of its beginning and growth makes you feel good. The center is housed in a turn-of-the-century building that was the Statesville waterworks until 1940. In 1956 a group of local citizens decided that the area needed a museum and put their energy and money into making it happen. Today it operates with a $100,000-a-year budget that allows for three full-time professionals on the staff. Enthusiasm for it practically shoots out the ears of people working there. The museum features ten temporary exhibits a year, runs thirty-five educational programs in association with the local school system each year, and displays 3,000 objects in the permanent collection. The glassware pieces number more than 1,000. The staff say the quality of the items varies, but it's important to have it all. "Somebody has to save all those Avon pieces." Plans for the future include identifying all the glassware. A geologist has already put in a marathon rock-identification day to tag and group the 500 rocks in the collection.

In the small toy-and-doll collection, you'll see a Victorian doll with brown eyes—a rarity, because Queen Victoria had blue eyes, and most dolls were modeled on her.

One of the museum's founders insisted that it deal with science as well as art to attract people not interested in the arts. To help fill that need, two partly restored pioneer cabin sites have been included. Nature trails have been developed outside for short walks.

But what captures the imagination of the public here is the homeless mummy. Well, it has a home now, but nobody has been able to say for sure how it got there. They know she died when she was thirty-five years old, that her remains are 2,000 years old, and that she was mummified at a time when practitioners were getting a little sloppy about the process, but all people know about her recent history is that the museum and the mummy have both been there since 1956. Nobody knows where the mummy came from before that. One staff member said, "A lot of the people involved are still alive, but not all of them remember where the trucking company went to get things. One woman who might know has long since moved, and we can't find her."

The best rumor about the mummy is that another museum rejected it because it was cursed. Maybe it was a good curse. Good things certainly have been happening while Ms. Mummy has lived at the Arts and Science Center. Open Tuesday through Friday, 10:00 AM. to 5:00 P.M. and Sunday from 2:00 to 5:00 P.M. Closed Monday. Call to check on Saturday hours. Admission is $1.00.

Take time to wander around Statesville's historic downtown. Many of the commercial buildings and homes are on the National Register of Historic Places, including the 1892 City Hall, considered by preservationists to be a fine example of the Richardsonian Romanesque style. Stop next at the **Fort Dobbs State Historic Site** (704–873–5866), 438 Fort Dobbs Road, Statesville 28625, the site of a French and Indian War fort with archaeological sites, artifacts, nature trails, and recreational facilities. Open April through October, Monday through Saturday, 9:00 A.M. to 5:00 P.M., Sunday 1:00 to 5:00 P.M., November through March, 10:00 A.M. to 4:00 P.M. Tuesday through Saturday, Sunday 1:00 to 4:00 P.M.

This next stop isn't near anything else. Although it is located a ways north in the High Country (almost at the Virginia border), the most direct way to get to **Mt. Airy** is to drive a couple of hours from Statesville straight up I–77. Mt. Airy is **Andy Griffith's home town.** As a visitor you can approach it in one of two ways—visiting a shrine to Andy Griffith in his incarnation as Sheriff Andy Taylor, the Hero of Mayberry, or experiencing the spirit behind the Mayberry Fiction.

How long Mt. Airy will remain off the beaten path is anybody's guess. The thing is, local people are starting to live the fiction. Griffith has always insisted that Mayberry was not really based on Mt. Airy, and while he did

THE LOWER PIEDMONT

go back there from time to time when his parents were alive, he doesn't any more. He retired to Manteo. But ever since Tanya Rees, of the Surry County Arts Council, got together with Jim Clark, publisher of *The Bullet: Official Newsletter of the Andy Griffith Show Rerun Watchers Club,* to create Mayberry Days with tours and contests and parades, Mt. Airy keeps moving toward becoming Mayberry.

There is an old jail. It really is the old Mt. Airy jail. You can tour it. It bears no resemblance to the Mayberry jail, but the old squad car outside looks an awful lot like Sheriff Taylor's.

The most authentic place in Mt. Airy is probably *Snappy Lunch,* 125 North Main Street, Mt. Airy 27030, which, according to its menu, is "Mt. Airy's Oldest Continuous Eating Establishment at the Same Location Since 1923!! Home of the Famous Pork Chop Sandwich." Mentioned by Andy on the show, they tell you. Snappy Lunch seems to have translated straight from fact to fiction. It looks the same as it did at the time of the show: wooden booths, grill in the window, pictures on the wall. The famous pork chop sandwich still sells for $2.40, even though the tourist trade would pay more, because as Mary and Charles Dowell, who own the restaurant and work here see it, they are "making it OK." Call (336) 786–4931.

CHARLOTTE
Charlotte Hornets Basketball
(704) 522–6500

Charlotte Knights
Baseball Stadium
(704) 357–8071

Discovery Place
(704) 372–6261

NORTH CAROLINA/SOUTH CAROLINA BORDER
Paramount's Carowinds
Theme Park
(704) 588–2600
(803) 548–5300
(800) 888–4386

Right next door is *Floyd's Barber Shop.* It used to be called City Barber Shop, but the proprietor, Russell Hiatt, got on the bandwagon. Lots of people come in not just to get a haircut but also to take Hiatt's picture. He doesn't mind at all. But in turn, he whips out his Polaroid and takes two pictures of the customers, one for them to take home as a souvenir and one to add to the collection on the wall.

The *Andy Griffith Museum* in the visitors center, 615 North Main Street Mt. Airy 27030, (800–576–0231 or 336–789–4636), contains several rooms of memorabilia, including the white suit Griffith wore as Matlock. Both a walking tour of some of the town's older neighborhoods and a guided step-on tour are available.

As for *Mayberry Days,* it's hard to give exact dates because the thing keeps growing, but they're always in late September. For specifics, call the Surry County Arts Council (800–286–6193). Mt. Airy Web site: www.visitmayberry.com.

Braggin' Rights

A clerk in the Rockford General Store is trading one-liners with a customer about how small the town of Old Rockford Village is. The customer wins with, "This town is so small that the person who left the porch light on last December won a prize for best Christmas decorations."

Now, to get a taste of a more authentic version of rural North Carolina, get out your N.C. Transportation map and look at the blue highways just off U.S. 601, south of Mt. Airy. Go south on the blue highway that crosses N.C. 268 at Level Cross. This takes you into rural Surry County. Comparatively speaking, you might consider Mt. Airy the "urban" part. Head for the little town of Rockford and *Old Rockford Village.* This is what country folk used to call a "poke and plum" spot: Poke your head out the window as you drive, and you're plum out of town.

The focal point here is Annie Barnett's *Rockford General Store.* It's a hard place to define—partly touristy, partly a local source for everything from lye soap to pickled eggs and homemade fried apple pies, as well as more than one hundred kinds of old-fashioned candy. The store meanders in several directions, with wooden-floored rooms filled with reminders of earlier times. Outside the store on the porch, a red wooden bench invites you to sit, and a checkerboard is set up with rocks as playing pieces, ready for anybody who wants a game. Annie Barnett is something of an entrepreneur and arranges special events from time to time. You just never know what might be going on. The best way to find out, and to make sure the store will be open if you want to stop in, is to call ahead (336) 374–5317.

Whether you actually go into the store or not, driving these back roads gives you a glimpse of rural North Carolina as it really is, not as parts of it have been gussied up for tourists. Driving along these two-lane macadam roads with the car windows down, you can hear a "bobwhite, bobwhite, bobwhite" bird call. The warm air in summer smells of recently cut hay, although the fields are planted mostly in corn and tobacco. New orange Allis Chalmers tractors, sometimes standing right beside old ones, dot the landscape.

This stretch has as many trailers as conventionally built homes, and cable TV probably doesn't come out this far, because TV satellite dishes stand in many yards. Here and there an old log building has been restored. Others are crumbling to the ground. Driving these miles slows you down and reminds you that not everyone lives strapped with cell phones and pagers. From these roads you can drive easily over to U.S. 601 South and head down to Salisbury.

A Pocket of History

From Statesville, head east on Highway 70 for twenty or thirty minutes to *Historic Salisbury.* Two kinds of people live here—those whose families have been in place for generations and those who have moved in recently, mostly from up north. Both share an almost smug conviction that theirs is one of the most congenial, historically interesting communities in North Carolina. I say *almost* smug because they're right. Although this is one of the oldest towns in the area, and the entire 23-block downtown community of commercial and residential buildings dating from 1820 to 1920 is on the National Register of Historic Places, it receives relatively little attention from outside. The Historic Salisbury Foundation and an active group of supporters are trying to change that.

They point to the 1898 Grimes Mill, a roller mill with all its original machinery in five floors; the Civil War Salisbury Confederate Prison Site and National Cemetery, where the largest number of unknown Civil War soldiers are buried; and the restored Railroad Depot. All of them are open to the public.

Then there's the Historic Salisbury walking tour, which includes the homes in the National Register Historic District. Some of these homes are open to the public. The *Dr. Josephus Hall House,* 226 South Jackson Street, Salisbury 28144, for instance, is a large, 1820 antebellum house that sits among old oaks and boxwoods that have been in place nearly as long as the house. Dr. Hall was chief surgeon at the Salisbury Confederate Prison during the Civil War. After the war the Union commander used the house as headquarters. Somehow the grounds and the interior escaped the destruction typically associated with Yankee occupation in the South, and the Hall House contains nearly all its original furnishings. Open Saturday and Sunday from 2:00 to 5:00 P.M. Modest admission fee (704–636–0103).

Just about a block away, the *Utzman-Chambers House* museum, 116 South Jackson Street, Salisbury 28144, is a notable example of architecture from the Federal period. It shows the life of a prominent local family during the early 1800s. An early nineteenth-century garden features four formal beds of flowers and herbs native to the Piedmont in 1815. Open Thursday through Sunday from 1:00 to 4:00 P.M. Admission is $3.00 for adults, $1.50 for children. Call (704) 633–5946 to arrange a tour.

The **Rowan Museum,** which used to be part of the Utzman-Chambers House, is moving its exhibits related to Rowan County history to the old courthouse, 202 North Main Street, Salisbury 28144. The old courthouse building was built in 1857, for the princely sum of $15,000, and was used as a court building until 1914, when it became the community building. Since then, at one time or another, it has served as almost everything for which the town needed a building: public library, American Red Cross headquarters, chamber of commerce, and adult night school. When the flu epidemic hit the town in 1918, the community building became an emergency hospital and kitchen. Until the move is complete, the museum's exhibits are still in the Utzman-Chambers House. To check on the status of things, call (704) 633–5946 or check the Web site: www.vnet.net/rowanmuseum.

The Rowan Museum includes another house a few miles outside of town that gives you a glimpse of early country life in the county. **The Old Stone House,** built by Michael Braun between 1758 and 1766, reflects the traditions of the German Rhinelanders who settled in the county in the early 1700s. Braun came to the area from Philadelphia, Pennsylvania, and the stone house will look familiar to anyone who has traveled the county roads in Pennsylvania and seen houses built on the Quaker plan. The house has been beautifully restored, and the museum is working to continue developing the property. The house is furnished with a collection of North Carolina and Pennsylvania pieces and looks much as it probably would have when Braun lived in it. One piece, a weaving loom in an upstairs room, has been in the house as long as anyone can remember.

To get to The Old Stone House from Rowan Museum, turn right on Innes Street, and go $4^1/_5$ miles (Innes Street becomes Highway 52 South) into Granite Quarry, and turn left on East Lyerly Street, which is also called Old Stone House Road. The house sits on the right, beside the road, about $^3/_5$ of a mile farther on. Admission is $3.00 for adults, $1.50 for children. The house is open from 1:00 to 4:00 P.M. Saturday and Sunday, April through November. The hours may change and sometimes you can arrange to see the house at another time. Call the museum at (704) 633–5946 for more information.

Moving from the historic to the contemporary, the **Waterworks Visual Arts Center,** at the corner of West Kerr and Water Streets, features changing exhibits of contemporary art. The outdoor sculpture garden is especially pleasant on clear, sunny days. The gallery is in a building that was first used as the Salisbury Waterworks and then as the city police station. Its large open spaces are especially suited to displaying art. Open Tuesday through Friday from 10:00 A.M. to 5:00 P.M., Saturday from 9:00 A.M. to 4:00 P.M., and Sunday from 1:00 to 4:00 P.M. Closed Monday. Nominal donations are suggested.

In downtown Salisbury, which you really must see for its remarkable old factory, old train station (where Amtrak now stops), and business buildings, you can break the fast-food habit by having a bite of lunch at *Spanky's,* an old-fashioned ice-cream parlor that serves not only homemade ice-cream concoctions, but also good soups, salads, deli sandwiches, and cheesecake (704–638–0780). Spanky's actually makes seventy-five different flavors of ice cream, but the owner explained, almost apologetically, that they keep only twenty-five flavors on hand at a time! The restaurant is in an old building that in 1859 was the tallest in North Carolina. Open Monday through Saturday from 9:00 A.M. to 8:00 P.M., and Sunday from noon to 8:00 P.M.

One heartwarming attraction is *O. O. Rufty's General Store* (800–611–6055), 126 East Innes Street, Salisbury 28144. Web site: www.oorufty.com. The store has its original wood floor. The place is a little dusty and dimly lit. Although it's become something of an attraction, people still learn about the store mostly by word of mouth and, colorful and old-timey as it

Humiliation

I had just begun exploring the area around Salisbury and Spencer. People kept asking me if I'd been to the **Spencer Shops** yet. I wasn't in a big hurry to find them, because shopping isn't my idea of a good time, but eventually I figured that anything so many people mentioned would be worth a visit. The idea of gift shops in an old transportation museum seemed OK.

I went into the museum office and after checking all the signs, asked the receptionist where the gift shops were. Was it like a row of specialty shops in converted train buildings or what? I asked.

Her face changed from polite-receptionist to local-citizen-horrified-at-such-ignorance. The Shops at Spencer, she said, are machine shops where mechanics once repaired Southern Railway's steam locomotives. Those trains hauled passengers and such freight as furniture, textiles, and tobacco, and the shops at one time employed nearly 3,000 people.

Gift shops, indeed! Sniff.

Confederate Monument

may be, it's still a place where local folks actually shop. You can buy everything from kindling to marbles here. Hard candies it would be hard to find anywhere else are sold by weight. You scoop them from big jars into small brown paper bags. The store has all kinds of cooking utensils, glassware, knickknacks, hoop cheese, country ham, shoes, pocket knives, Christmas decorations, candles—in short, if you want something strange, you have a good chance of finding it at Rufty's. If you want something as practical as a pressure cooker, you can find that, too. Oliver Oscho Rufty, who started the store in 1905, taught his sons, "If you don't have it, you can't sell it." The store has an annual attic and basement tour Saturday and Monday of Labor Day weekend. Rufty's is open 7:30 A.M. to 6:00 P.M., Monday through Saturday. Rufty's has recently added a grocery store and restaurant serving old-fashioned southern cooking buffet-style.

While you are on Innes Street, orient yourself so the winged *Confederate statue* in the center of town is to your back, turn left on Main Street (or turn right if you are facing the statue), and drive a few minutes into the neighboring town of Spencer to visit the **North Carolina Transportation Museum** (704–636–2889) on 411 South Salisbury Avenue, Spencer 28159. This is the site of what was once the largest service facility or shops for Southern Railway Company. The museum's collection includes all kinds of transportation-related artifacts—antique automobiles, railroad cars, and an airplane. The roundhouse, with thirty-seven bays, is an inevitable hit with train enthusiasts. You can watch a video about the railroad in the visitors center. Train rides in restored cars are available when there are enough people. Admission to the museum is free. Train rides are $5.00 for adults, $4.00 for children and senior citizens. Train rides and museum hours vary seasonally. It is a good idea to call ahead.

Right across the street *The Little Choo Choo Shop* (704–637–8717), 500 South Salisbury Avenue, Spencer 28159, is a serious, well-stocked model-railroad shop handling supplies for scales from "G" to the tiny "Z." They buy, sell, trade, and repair. One room is devoted to books and videos about model railroading, and you can get top-notch advice from the people who work here, too. One small room is filled with wooden toy trains to occupy kids while you browse among the grown-up toys. The store is open Tuesday through Saturday, 10:00 A.M. to 5:30 P.M.

In the same block, *La Dolce Vita* (704–636–8891), at 518 South Salisbury Avenue, Spencer 28159, does a better-than-average job with Italian food. They offer a variety of fish and chicken dishes, lots of pastas, and an eggpglant parmigiana that is splendid. The red sauces are light and fresh tasting, and you can order a variety of wines and beers. The service is pleasant, and many local businesspeople eat lunch here during the week. Open for lunch and dinner every day but Sunday.

Or for an absolutely authentic local dining experience, go on out to *Martin's Barbeque,* 615 Salisbury Avenue, Spencer 28159. It's actually more accurate to speak of "chowing down" than of "dining." This is a place where waitresses may call you "honey" and somehow manage to carry everything you ordered to the table, apparently in one hand. The restaurant serves three meals. Breakfast includes grits or rice and gravy or homestyle potatoes or apples. A traditional order would be eggs with country ham, grits, and biscuits. If you're not quite up to it, lighter choices are available. Lunch and dinner continue in a similar vein, with hickory-smoked barbeque or a foot-long hot dog being the traditional choices and some version of "meat and three" coming in a close second. That means something like fried fish or country-fried steak and gravy with three vegetables. Pinto beans, fried okra, and slaw would definitely be local choices. The restaurant is open Monday through Saturday, 5:30 A.M. to 9:00 P.M. Phone (704) 636–1773.

One interesting side trip from Salisbury is a quick jog south on I–85 to *Cannon Village at Kannapolis.* Cannon Village is a shopping outlet now, but it and the town are a fascinating, almost unspoiled glimpse of a once-prosperous mill town.

Another interesting dimension is that Fieldcrest-Cannon has been taken over by Pillowtex. The community is once again full of talk about strikes and unions and finally, after numerous union attempts to get in, the employees have voted yes. Many Southerners don't like or trust unions and rarely vote them in.

Early Kannapolis

*T*hey say George Washington never slept here—but he could have. The area attracted many important travelers, and Washington passed through at least once. Francis Asbury, the English preacher who brought the Methodist faith to the United States, also stopped here several times. The "Great Road" between Charlotte and Salisbury in Colonial days ran through the center of Kannapolis, just about where Cannon

Village is now. One favorite stopping place was Murph's Inn, which stood near what is York Avenue today.

Earlier, Catawba and Waxhaw Indians traveled about the same route as they made trading trips between South Carolina and Virginia. They probably stopped at springs near what are now the South Main underpass, the east side of the North underpass, and the west side of Woodrow Wilson School.

The first thing you notice about Cannon Village and its outskirts is that everything matches—not sheets and towels or skirts and blouses, but the white-trimmed brick shops and brick sidewalks, bounded by the great brick walls of the Fieldcrest-Cannon mill buildings; the brick schoolhouse, the church, and even the supermarket that are part of the larger community. About the only things that aren't brick are the mill houses—tidy, modest, mostly white homes that reflect pride of ownership in their neatly clipped hedges and mowed lawns. You pass these homes that run along the railroad tracks and the streets of Kannapolis on your way into Cannon Village.

Cannon Village is at the center of the town of Kannapolis. The village is a center for off-price, outlet, and specialty shopping, especially home furnishings, with nearly fifty shops where you can buy everything from lamps to leggings. Back in 1887 this was a mill town founded by Charles Cannon as a community for the employees of Cannon Mills.

In the early 1980s Fieldcrest Corporation and Cannon Mills combined, and Fieldcrest's founder, Benjamin Franklin Mebane, restored the buildings along Oak Avenue, West Avenue, and Main Street to create a shopping complex that is a mix of colonial and early twentieth-century structures trimmed by full-grown trees and green strips of lawn. Cannon Village has everything you'd expect in an outlet center, but it's more pleasant than most because you walk outside to get from shop to shop in a place that still has the feel of a town. There's plenty of parking, conveniently arranged throughout the village rather than in one huge lot. The shopping area itself is pedestrian oriented, with tree-shaded sidewalks, appealing shop windows, and several places to eat. One of the most popular is **Baker's Dozen,** a bakery where the shelves are full of baked goods in the morning and everything is gone by dinner. With such rapid turnover everything has to be fresh.

For shopping, as you might expect, one of the most popular stores is the **Fieldcrest-Cannon Store,** an outlet where you can find a good selection and good bargains in their own brand of bath towels and bedding, the main products of Fieldcrest-Cannon mills. The store is arranged so that the first-quality merchandise is in front, with irregulars and seconds in the rear of the store. In both areas they carry many groupings, all clearly marked. You can go into this shop and buy draperies, a bedspread, a dust ruffle, and sheets—all matched—and get them at a nice discount. You can also find matching pillows and shams as well as loose fabric from which you can sew whatever else you need. If you need help getting it all together, you'll find the staff are all friendly and helpful. In addition to textiles, Cannon Village has more than 250,000 square feet of furniture arranged in showcase settings where you can buy furniture at significant discounts. For instance, **Baker Furniture Factory Clearance Store** carries an assortment of pieces in styles ranging from traditional to contemporary, as well as appropriate accessories such as lamps and decorative items. The first floor is given over to Baker's own brand. On the second floor you'll find other brands, too. In the rear of the Baker store, you'll find loose fabrics that have been used for their own upholstery at good prices.

Another popular furniture store, **Carolina Interiors,** displays ready-to-go rooms. The showroom takes up an entire city block. If you wanted to, you could buy everything a room needs, from the rugs to the rocker, in this one store. The bargain basement has odds and ends—one chair, or an end table or coffee table with an imperfection—heavily discounted.

Waccamaw, one of the best-known discount stores in the Carolinas, has a store in Cannon Village with an especially good selection of dried and silk flowers and seasonal decorating items as well as kitchenware, dishes, and home-decorating accessories. The antiques mall is another good place to find items for decorating. Although you can't predict exactly what will be in stock at any time, collectibles and small antiques usually make up a big part of the inventory.

The whole family will enjoy the multi-image show in the one-hundred-seat auditorium of the **Cannon Village Visitor Center and Museum,** 200 West Avenue, Kannapolis 28081. The show, which runs about twenty minutes, begins and ends with frankly commercial promotions of Fieldcrest-Cannon Mills, but the information about the early development and eventual union of Cannon and Fieldcrest Mills is fascinating, as is the explanation about modernization in the textile industry. In the same building a museum display traces the development of textiles from some early Inca cotton to present day fabric woven on high-speed, air-jet looms.

Two special events scheduled during the year are also geared to the whole family—the **Christmas celebration** and the **Scarecrow Festival.** The Scarecrow Festival is held the last Saturday in October. Some of the streets are blocked off to form an area for vendors—as many as 100 to 150—who display and sell their handcrafts. The Christmas celebration runs from Thanksgiving to Christmas and features costumed carolers, rides in old-fashioned horse-drawn carriages, and visits from Santa Claus. The village is decorated with seasonal greenery and red ribbons that call to mind the gentle activities of earlier times. But, at the same time, the offerings of the stores are up-to-date and priced to give shoppers savings of 30 to 70 percent at a time when a chance to save is most welcome. In a sense that's what Cannon Village is all about—a marriage of the old and the new, a union of commerce and aesthetics in a town that feels like old times even as it keeps up with changing times.

Cannon Village is open seven days a week year-round except for Thanksgiving, Christmas, and Easter. Furniture stores are closed Sunday. For more information call (704) 938–3200. The Fieldcrest-Cannon exhibition and theater show are free. The theater show is presented every hour, on the hour, from 10:00 A.M. to 3:00 P.M. The Cannon Village Visitors Center is open Monday through Saturday 9:00 A.M. to 5:00 P.M. and Sunday 1:00 to 6:00 P.M. How to get there: From I-85 take exit 63 or 58, and follow the signs to Cannon Village.

When you are through here, you can get back on I-85 and head back to Salisbury. You might spend the night, at **Rowan Oak House,** 208 Fulton Street, which offers Victorian elegance in a 1902 Queen Anne house (704–633–2086). The house is notable for its remarkably intact interior, where the original wallpaper is still in perfect condition.

Leaving Salisbury, take Highway 52 South for an interesting drive that shows you the down-home, not the tourist, version of the Piedmont. In about 6 miles, almost before you've left Salisbury's environs, you come to Granite Quarry, where a big billboard on the left side of the road directs you to **Kluttz Piano Factory.** They deliver free, but probably not if you live in Cincinnati. Stop in and look around, even though you probably aren't looking to buy a piano while you're out tracking unbeaten paths. This place, which advertises more than 500 new and

End of an Era

*G*ranite Quarry lost a piece of its heart in 1999, when Carolina Maid, a company that made women's dresses, closed after sixty-four years in business. Unlike many textile mills and other manufacturing plants that have closed in North Carolina—Cone and Burlington Mills, for instance—Carolina Maid was always a strictly local, family-owned and run operation.

The redbrick building of about 6,500 square feet still stands intact by the highway. In its prime the plant produced up to 600 dresses a day, and almost everyone in the area either worked at Carolina Maid at one time or another or has kin who did.

When the plant closed, many of the workers were already well past retirement age. They had stayed on, not just for the income, but because coming to work was a social thing for them. Their coworkers were also their friends and, often, their relatives.

Sam Miller, who worked in the cutting room for forty years, remembered the time a local baker tried to hire him away from Carolina Maid, saying, "As long as there are people, they're going to be eating bread."

Sam replied, "As long as there's women, they're gonna be wearing dresses."

He told the story and shook his head, saying "Boy, was I wrong."

rebuilt pianos, is awesome. The showroom, where you try out new and reconditioned pianos, looks fairly standard, but you'll be dumbfounded by the work area, which seems roughly the size of a football field, filled with pianos—whole pianos and pieces of pianos in every make, model, and size. Ten minutes of just looking will tell you more about what's inside a piano than you've ever dreamed you could know. The people who work here talk as casually about the good and bad traits of grands, uprights, spinets, Yamahas, Wurlitzers, and Baldwins as the rest of us talk about the tomatoes in our gardens.

Outsiders sometimes get a chuckle out of the name **Kluttz,** but around here, Kluttz is just another family name, belonging not only to the owners of the piano factory but also to architects, contractors, and art shop proprietors. Everybody works hard, even the older Mr. Kluttz, who thinks nothing of being one of two men to haul a grand piano off its legs, out of a truck, and into a house. You'll notice that some of the people wear big gold belt buckles shaped like grand pianos. Ask about the buckles, and the only answer you'll get is, "It means we're special." Some workers get there as early as 4:00 A.M., but regular hours for ordinary mortals are Monday through Friday from 8:00 A.M. to 5:00 P.M. and Saturday from 8:00 A.M. to 3:00 P.M. (704–279–7237).

Continuing on Highway 52 South, which is really going east at this point, brings you to **Rockwell,** which you should pronounce *ROCK-wul,* not *RockWELL.* The town bears no relationship to Norman Rockwell, but it should: Flags fly from all the porches on Memorial Day; signs advertise BAIT, CRICKETS, AND NIGHT CRAWLERS; women still appear occasionally with their hair in curlers; neighbors stop each other in the grocery store to ask if the new "granbaby" has arrived yet; pink and blue bows on mailboxes announce when the new grans do come into the world. Stop for some good, authentic barbecue at **Darrell's Bar-BQ,** 117 East Main Street, Rockwell 28138. If you call ahead, you can even pick it up at a drive-through window, although then you'll miss the chance to mingle with the local people inside (704–279–6300). Darrell's is open Tuesday through Saturday from 10:00 A.M. to 9:00 P.M. Closed Sunday and Monday.

Back on Highway 52 and driving southeast again, you'll pass lots of modest country homes, some in dreadful disarray and some perfectly kept, with geraniums and picket fences. After about 10 miles, find the turn from Highway 52 onto Old Beatty Ford Road for an hour's diversion down a rural entrepreneurial row. Turn left onto a road that crosses the railroad tracks and runs past a large quarry operation. You'll drive about 12 miles along this road, past a Soil Conservation Service demonstration farm on the left; a home-based sewing-machine repair shop called Sew and Sew; another home business, "Why Knot Upholstery"; and Miller Farms Racing (a track around grassy fields). Among these little businesses, many yards have for-sale signs offering produce in season, a piece of used farm equipment, a boat, a camper "like new" with tow bar and a pickup (there must be a story in that one), firewood, oil paintings—it all changes with fortune and the seasons. You'll also pass a couple of uncommonly attractive older churches, the kind with their own manicured graveyards in back. Old Concord Road intersects Old Beatty Ford Road after about 12 miles. Turn left. Drive about 3 miles more, passing Roy Cline Road and Irish Potato Road, and turn right immediately onto Goldfish Road. You're at **Greendale,** 6465 Goldfish Road, Kannapolis 28083, which from the outside looks like one more sprawling roadside building. Inside you'll find wonder and the ultimate rural entrepreneurial enterprise.

Long rows of beautifully clear, brightly lighted aquariums gleam in the dim room. Here in the boonies, where if you tell your mother you're going to the fish store she assumes you're going to buy flounder, you discover gouramis and guppies, oscars, cichlids, corals, and saltwater exotics whose names you don't even know, all apparently thriving. OK, you can't keep goldfish on the road, but just looking beats watching television, and you may find the selection and prices on aquarium equipment appealing enough to tease a traveler's check out of your wallet before you leave.

Greendale started out as a goldfish farm back in 1929, when Rufus Green got laid off by Cannon Mills and decided to make his living raising goldfish in outdoor ponds to sell to dime stores. One of his first sales was to get money to buy a shirt for church. The years passed, Rufus died, and his wife maintained the business as well as she could. Rufus's son, George, returned in 1978 from another war that wasn't called one, with his wife, Gaysorn, a classical dancer from Bangkok. By now hobbyists had turned enthusiastically to exotic tropical fish, so it made sense for Greendale to develop accordingly. The whole story, in a yellowing newspaper clipping, is taped to the front wall.

It's hard to imagine there would be enough customers to keep the business going, but they come from all directions: Concord, Kannapolis, Salisbury, Albemarle. The store is closed on Tuesday, partly because new shipments of plants and fish come then. On Wednesday it's so busy that, as one employee put it, "People just come in and throw money at you." They're all there: Gay and George, Mrs. Rufus Green, and local young people who work here and often get themselves hooked on the hobby in the process. You can always find someone to chat with about the troublesome habits of live bearers and how hard it is not to disrupt a gourami's bubble nest (704–933–1798). Open Monday and Wednesday through Saturday from 10:00 A.M. to 6:00 P.M. and Sunday from 2:00 to 6:00 P.M. Closed Tuesday.

When you leave, depending on which way you turn, you may see a large block-lettered sign inside a cul-de-sac in front of a mobile home: IF YOU DON'T HAVE BUSINESS HERE, THIS IS A GOOD PLACE FOR YOU TO TURN AROUND. This may be the only guy in the county who *isn't* looking for customers at home. The best way to return to Highway 52 is the way you came in. Since everything looks different going in the opposite direction, you'll see things you missed the first time and won't feel that you're backtracking.

Coming into Misenhiemer, Highway 52 runs through the middle of the small **Pfeiffer College** campus, where all the classroom buildings, administration buildings, dormitories, and faculty houses are made of red brick. You might think that this is the kind of place a film director would like to shoot *Who's Afraid of Virginia Woolf?*, although a director would never get approval in this Bible pocket. If it did happen, people would raise a big stink in the *Stanley News and Press*.

Farm Country

From Pfeiffer College it's only a couple of miles to the intersection of Highway 52 and Highway 49 at Richfield. Go north on Highway 49 for about as long as you need to take two deep breaths and pull into the parking lot of the **Motel Restaurant.** This is the breakfast and lunch spot for many of the local farmers, the people who work in the mobile-home factories and the Perfect Fit textile plant down the road. For breakfast you get two eggs, bacon, grits or hash browns, biscuits or corn bread, and coffee for less than $5.00. Lunch is one meat (meatloaf or fried fish, maybe; the selections are written on a blackboard at the door), two vegetables, and beverage for less than $5.00. Sit at the counter and you can study the ever-lengthening row of imprinted mugs: *Old Age Ain't No Place for Sissies, If God Wanted Me to Cook and Clean My Hands Would've Been Made of Aluminum, My Parents Went to Myrtle Beach and All They Got Me Was This Dumb Mug, God Loves You and I'm Trying.*

The Motel Restaurant waitresses know all the regulars by name, ask, "You doin' OK?" as they take your order, and after the first time, remember what it is that you always have. They like a good joke. Did you hear about the prostitute who told her tax consultant that she was a chicken farmer? Well, she said . . . Country music plays in the background, and while Willie and Waylon are appreciated, one of the waitresses says she'd really like to marry Garth Brooks, even if she is already married. But Randy Travis, now, he's one of our own, coming from Monroe and all. This is the kind of place where everybody knows everybody, and the local bank manager sits next to the local welder, who calls his regular morning trip to the restaurant "going to the office." When you've had all the coffee or iced tea you can hold, leave a couple quarters on the counter, pay your bill, and when someone says, "Come back," you say, "I'll do it." Open Monday through Friday from 5:00 A.M. to 2:00 P.M. and Saturday from 5:00 to 11:00 A.M.

From here you could take Highway 49 North through the Uhwarrie Forest back up to Asheboro, or you could go south for an interesting drive to Charlotte. Expect to have to be patient. The road is only one lane in each direction, with few places to pass, and you'll probably spend some time behind a tractor or a slow-moving truck hauling logs. Even going slowly, you'll be at Mount Pleasant in ten or fifteen minutes.

Shortly before you come to the crossroads at Mount Pleasant, a sign on the right advertises **Cline's Country Antiques.** A big, rusting antique tractor marks the lane back to the seven long buildings where Don Cline manages an ever-changing stock. He buys and wholesales antiques by the truckload but attends with equal care to your $5.00 purchase of an old advertising sign or kitchen utensil. One of the most fascinating things you can do is ask for a particular kind of antique—an oak washstand or armoire, or a pie safe, for instance—and then watch Don reflect a minute before he directs you, without consulting any kind of inventory list at all, to the precise building and corner in which you'll find what you're looking for. No one's quite sure how he does it, but no matter how often or how fast his inventory changes, Don always knows where everything is.

His appearance reflects the fact that Don detests malls and spending money on glitzy new things; he prides himself on living out of his junk. His britches came from a load the pickers hauled in, his sweater was in a bin of post office surplus that he found at a dumpster, and his Sunday suit was part of the stock he got when he bought all the remaining merchandise of a department store that went out of business several years ago.

If he's not out supervising the coming and going of truckloads, Don will probably be sitting in the old barber chair by the wood stove in the barn, talking with visiting dealers or reading old issues of antiques magazines. Don collaborated with a professional writer on the book *Buying and Selling Antiques*. Across from Don's barber chair, Vichard, his assistant, nailed up a wooden box to hold copies of the book, with a sign above that reads THE BOOK and an arrow pointing down to the copies that are for sale.

The idea of Don's writing a book seems surprising when you first encounter his plain-old-country-boy demeanor, but pay attention, ask a few questions, and you'll learn that he has taught economics in a couple of area colleges, has a photographic memory, and is perfectly willing to let you think he's stupid if you're so inclined because it helps business. Not that he's dishonest; he won't sell an imperfect piece without pointing out the flaw, he won't knowingly misrepresent anything, and he charges only a modest markup on his merchandise. Don Cline may be the most scrupulously honest antiques dealer in the business, but he doesn't see any reason to rouse your jousting instincts by flaunting his brain.

Actually, in the beginning he wasn't that eager to go into business at all. It's just that he loved auctions and couldn't resist good buys. When he got married, his wife pointed out that unless he started moving stuff out at something close to the speed with which he brought it in, there wasn't going to be room for her. Then, too, there on his father's farm were all those long chicken sheds, empty since the cholesterol scare made producing eggs unprofitable. All the setup really needed was customers, so Don began to let it be known that he had some stuff to sell. The rest, as they say, is history. Cline's Country Antiques (704–436–6824) is open from sometime around 8:00 or 9:00 A.M. to sometime about dark, Wednesday through Saturday. Closed Sunday, Monday, and Tuesday.

If you get to hanging around the Cline place so late that you don't feel like driving anymore, you could stay at the *Carolina Country Inn* in Mount Pleasant. This is a simple, clean, quiet motel, with a sign out front pointing out how many long country miles you still have to travel to reach Charlotte or Raleigh and inviting you to stay there instead. A few rooms have refrigerators. Rates are modest (704–436–9616).

When you get to where Highway 601 meets Highway 49, you may decide to make a side trip on Highway 601 South to Highway 200 and follow the signs to the *Reed Gold Mine* at Stanfield, about 10 miles east of Concord (704–721–4653). This is the site of the first authenticated gold find in the United States. It seems that Conrad Reed found a gold nugget the size of a brick on his farm and after that sort of lost interest in farming. We tend to associate the gold rushes with Alaska and California, but the fever burned here in North Carolina back in the late 1820s. For a time more people worked at gold mining than any other occupation except farming. Here and there in the state you still find places such as Morning Star Explorations at Richfield, where the search for more gold continues or has begun anew. At the Reed Gold Mine State Historic Site, you can pan for gold in the spring and summer and tour the mining area year-round.

In the visitors center, exhibits and a film explain the history and mining process. Admission is free, but a modest fee is charged for panning. Open April 1 to October 31, Monday through Saturday from 9:00 A.M. to 5:00 P.M. and Sunday from 1:00 to 5:00 P.M. Open November 1 through March 31, Tuesday through Saturday from 10:00 A.M. to 4:00 P.M. and Sunday from 1:00 to 4:00 P.M. Closed Monday.

Land of the New

Charlotte's an exciting place to visit these days. It's growing so fast that you can find something new almost every day. People seem to exude civic pride. Because they're so pleased about the way things are going, they're incredibly nice to visitors. *Charlotte* has reason for pride: a National Basketball Association expansion team, the Charlotte Hornets;

the women's professional basketball team, the Charlotte Sting; the Carolina Panthers NFL football team; the Charlotte Knights professional baseball team; NASCAR racing at Charlotte Motor Speedway; Douglas International Airport, with direct flights to major cities; a Pulitzer Prize-winning newspaper, the *Charlotte Observer;* the highly rated University of North Carolina at Charlotte; a slew of smaller colleges and universities; new skyscrapers; and both a new and an old coliseum.

Until Hurricane Hugo hit in the fall of 1989, Charlotte was famous for its streets lined with huge old oak trees. People called the city "The Shady Lady." Since the 90-mile-per-hour winds, things are a lot more open—including some roofs—but even before the repairs were finished, committees were planting new trees and Charlottians were looking proudly at the neighborliness and cooperation with which they handled the days- and weeks-long power outage and the physical destruction to homes, neighborhoods, and businesses. That fighting spirit, they'll tell you, has always been part of the city's heritage.

The city was named for Queen Charlotte of Mecklenburg, wife of King George III, and it still calls itself "The Queen City," but the city rebelled against England in 1775 and earned from General Cornwallis the complaint that Charlotte was "a hornet's nest." That historical epithet figured in naming the new NBA team the Hornets.

Charlotte's growth brings traffic, unfortunately, along with the excitement, but it would be too bad to miss some of the city's special features because of traffic. The best advice for a visitor to minimize problems is to study a city map ahead of time and try to avoid the major high-traffic highways—Interstates 85 and 77 and Independence Boulevard—as much as possible. Once you're actually in the city, the traffic isn't bad, except at rush hour; it's the main arteries that clog up. Don't hesitate to ask for directions if you get confused. People seem to be used to it and are good at helping, probably because the ongoing construction everywhere has forced them to figure out new routes.

You'll find enough special places here to warrant spending a night, so perhaps you'll want to arrange for accommodations first. In addition to plenty of standard hotels and motels, Charlotte has an exceptionally pleasant and successful bed-and-breakfast inn, the Inn on Providence, 6700 Providence Road.

At *The Homeplace* (704–365–1936), Frank and Peggy Dearien bought a restored country Victorian home with the requisite heart-of-pine floors, formal parlor, and 10-foot beaded ceilings. The next thing anyone knew, they were operating a bed-and-breakfast inn, serving bountiful breakfasts, and as a bit of lagniappe, evening desserts. The house is decorated in a soothing combination of blue and rose colors. A unique aspect of the decor is the collection of primitive paintings by John Gentry, Peggy's father, with his handwritten stories on the back personalizing each one. This inn has become very popular with business travelers, so it's always busy. You will need to make a reservation well ahead of time to stay here.

The *Mint Museum of Art,* at 2730 Randolph Road, Charlotte 28207, has exhibits that celebrate both local history and world culture. The name comes from the building's having been a branch of the United States Mint in the 1800s. That made sense back when the Piedmont was producing most of the country's gold.

In 1988 the museum created a huge stir with the exhibit "Ramses the Great: the Pharaoh and His Time," which featured, among other items, a gold statue of the pharaoh so large the building had to be modified to give him extra headroom. That exhibit is gone now, but a new permanent collection, "Spanish Colonial Art," is attracting attention. Other permanent collections include American and European paintings, African artifacts, pre-Columbian art, costumes, and gold and currency of the Carolinas.

The Mint Museum Gift Shop specializes in offerings that reflect the museum exhibits. For instance, in connection with the pre-Columbian art exhibit, the shop sells replicas of pre-Columbian gold charms. Artifacts imported directly from African suppliers complement the museum's African displays. As the exhibits change, so do some of the gifts. A standard item in the shop that makes a nice gift is the miniature brass replica of Queen Charlotte's gold crown. A painting in which she wears the original crown hangs in a prominent position. The museum is open Tuesday from 10:00 A.M. to 10:00 P.M.; Wednesday through Saturday from 10:00 A.M. to 5:00 P.M.; and Sunday from 1:00 to 6:00 P.M. Closed Monday. Also closed Christmas and New Year's Day. Modest admission charged but free Tuesday from 5:00 to 10:00 P.M. and the second Sunday of each month (704–337–2000).

Another museum in the vicinity worth your attention is the *Hezekiah Alexander Homesite* and Museum of History, at 3500 Shamrock Drive. The Hezekiah Alexander house is the oldest dwelling still standing in Mecklenburg County. It was built of local quarry stone in 1774 and has been restored. Costumed guides lead tours of the house, log kitchen, barn, and gardens. The history museum displays local crafts and artifacts. Hezekiah was a delegate to the Fifth Provincial Congress and served on the committee that drafted the North Carolina State

The Hezekiah Alexander Homesite

Constitution and Bill of Rights. The site has a number of fascinating details. The house is known as "The Rockhouse." Its doors are unusually low by today's standards, a feature intended to keep heat inside when people opened the doors. In the master bedroom a rope bed dominates the room. In this kind of bed a latticework of ropes supported the mattress. Every so often the ropes had to be tightened—giving rise to the old phrase, "Sleep tight." Don't even think about the origins of the rest of the phrase, "Don't let the bedbugs bite." The boys' rooms on the back side of the house also served as an army post during the Revolutionary War. And in the re-created spring house behind the house, you can see how milk and butter were cooled in the late 1700s. Open Tuesday from 10:00 A.M. to 9:00 P.M., Wednesday through Saturday from 10:00 A.M. to 5:00 P.M., and Sunday from 1:00 to 5:00 P.M. Moderate admission fees. For rates and tour hours, call (704) 568–1774.

In uptown Charlotte at 301 North Tryon Street, Charlotte 28202, the kids will enjoy *Discovery Place,* a hands-on science and technology museum where they can enjoy some close-up experiences with fish and birds, the natural sciences, and computers (704–372–6261). One of the most impressive exhibits is the tropical rain forest, which fills three stories with plants, rocks, waterfalls, and appropriate wildlife. The exhibits related to the human body are interesting, too. One description claims that you learn about characteristics of the human body in a "hands-on manner," which could make you nervous if you didn't know about models and machines. Open weekdays from 9:00

A.M. to 5:00 P.M., Saturday from 9:00 A.M. to 6:00 P.M., and Sunday from 1:00 to 6:00 P.M. Admission is $6.50 for adults; $5.00 for children ages six to twelve and seniors; $2.75 for children ages three to five.

When you need nourishment, you have a surprisingly varied choice, especially when you consider that only a decade or so ago your choices were Southern homestyle and Southern homestyle plus a Greek restaurant with food remarkably similar to Southern homestyle. A recent local magazine noted that virtually every national cuisine is represented in Charlotte now, sometimes by several different restaurants. People actually travel to Charlotte just to eat. In the uptown area, *Carpe Diem,* 431 South Tryon Street, offers a variety of "new American" entrees, including vegetarian dishes, reflecting some Middle Eastern and Caribbean influences. The restaurant serves lunch and dinner. Phone (704) 377–7976. *The Pewter Rose,* at 1820 South Boulevard, Charlotte 28203 is close to the southeast edge of town and not difficult to reach (704–332–8149). Helen Scruggs had a small luncheon restaurant of the same name at Spirit Square in uptown Charlotte. Before opening the new and improved restaurant, she studied the culinary arts in France and then duplicated the feel with a cozy French country decor in the new Pewter Rose, in a renovated textile mill. You'll feel comfortable here in either informal or business dress, and you'll find menu items ranging from fancy burgers to some outstanding salads and platters. The smoked turkey with béarnaise mayonnaise on orange nut bread is worth several trips across town. All the desserts, which you can order for lunch or dinner or in the bar, are homemade.

Charlotte has a brewpub, *Southend Brewery and Smokehouse,* at 2100 South Boulevard, Charlotte 28203, in the Atherton Mill Complex. This is a large establishment with the brewing vessels, enclosed in a glassed-in room, serving as the visual centerpiece of the space. The kitchen is also fully visible. The food is California style but also includes a number of smoked specialties, including ribs and sausages. They serve astonishingly large portions. One of the principals in this operation is said to have "invented" Bud Lite. Phone (704) 358–4677.

Olé Olé, 709 Kings Drive, Charlotte 28204, serves tasty Spanish food in a pleasant environment. They do an especially good job with pork and veal, served with black beans and saffron rice or garlic mashed potatoes. Open for lunch Monday through Friday, dinner nightly. Phone (704) 358–1102. Web site: www.oleole.com.

On the north side of Charlotte, on Highway 49, the botanical gardens at the University of North Carolina at Charlotte deserve a lot more attention than they receive. The *UNC Charlotte Botanical Gardens* have three parts: the McMillan Greenhouse, the VanLandingham Glen, and the Susie Harwood Garden. The greenhouse has one of the best collections of tropical orchids in the south, with something like 800 species. The tropical rain forest conservatory is a convincing simulation of a real rain forest. Other greenhouse rooms include a cactus room and a cool room. A great variety of carniverous plants grow in a protected outside area by the greenhouses. The VanLandingham Glen started as a rhododendron garden in 1966 and has expanded to include more than 4,000 rhododendrons, mostly hybrids. Another interesting feature is the 1,000 species of Carolina-native plants growing in the gardens. The Hardwood garden, with gravel paths, is more formal and includes exotic plants from around the world. The collection of Japanese maples is noteworthy, as is the winter garden. The greenhouse is open during normal business hours, but you can visit the gardens any time. The best way to find the gardens is to go onto campus through the main gate on Highway 49 and follow the signs to the visitor parking garage and ask for directions from there. For more information call the university's main switchboard at (704) 547–2000.

About 20 miles west of Charlotte, in Gastonia, which you can reach quickly on Interstate 85, the *Schiele Museum of Natural History and Planetarium* at 1500 East Garrison Boulevard, Gastonia 28053, attracts large numbers of visitors, especially schoolchildren, with its collection of North American mammals in habitat settings, a 100-seat planetarium, a restored pioneer site of the 1700s, and a reconstructed Catawba Indian village. Other exhibits deal with everything from forestry to archaeology. A brochure maps out several self-guided tour suggestions for the outside grounds. Don't skip this one because it's popular; it has good reason for being so. Open Monday through Saturday from 9:00 A.M. to 5:00 P.M. and Sunday from 1:00 to 5:00 P.M. Planetarium shows offered only Saturday and Sunday afternoons. Modest admission fee. Call (704) 866–6908 for details.

PLACES TO STAY IN
THE LOWER PIEDMONT

CHARLOTTE
Comfort Inn–UNCC
I–85 Service Road
Charlotte 28269
(704) 598–0007
(800) 882–3835

Fairfield Inn by Marriott
7920 Arrowridge Boulevard
Charlotte 28273
(704) 319–5100

Holiday Inn–Independence
3501 East Independence
Boulevard
Charlotte 28205
(704) 537–1010

La Quinta Inn
3100 South I–85
Service Road
Charlotte 28208
(704) 393–5306

Red Roof Inn Coliseum
131 Red Roof Drive
Charlotte 28217
(704) 529–1020

MT. AIRY
Comfort Inn
2136 Rockford Street
Mt. Airy 27030
(336) 789–2000
(800) 672–1667

Hampton Inn
2029 Rockford Street
Mt. Airy 27030
(336) 789–5999
(800) 565–5249

Mayberry Motor Inn
U.S. Bypass 52 North
Mt. Airy 27030
(336) 786–4109

SALISBURY
Days Inn
1810 Lutheran Synod Drive
Salisbury 28144
(704) 633–4211

Holiday Inn
520 South Jake Alexander
Boulevard
Salisbury 28144
(704) 637–3100

Hampton Inn
1001 Klumac Road
Salisbury 28144
(704) 637–8000
(800) 426–7866

Rodeway Inn
321 Bendix Drive
Salisbury 28144
(704) 633–5961
(800) 753–3746

STATESVILLE
Fairfield Inn by Marriott
1505 East Broad Street
Statesville 28625
(704) 878–2091

Hampton Inn
715 Sullivan Road
Statesville 28677
(704) 878–2721
(800) 426–7866

Holiday Inn I–77
1215 Garner Bagnal
Boulevard
Statesville 28677
(704) 873–6927

PLACES TO EAT IN
THE LOWER PIEDMONT

CHARLOTTE
Providence Cafe
110 Perrin Place
Charlotte 28207
(704) 376–2008

Rheinland Haus
2418 Park Road
Charlotte 28203
(704) 376–3836

Thai Taste
324 East Boulevard
Charlotte 28203
(704) 332–0001

Amalfi's Pasta and Pizza
8542 University City
Boulevard
Charlotte 28213
(704) 547–8651

Gus' Sir Beef
4101 Monroe Street
(704) 377–3210
and 324 South Tryon
Charlotte 28205
(704) 347–5741

The Lower Piedmont Web Sites:

Charlotte
www.charlotteub.org

Salisbury and Spencer
www.visitsalisburync.com

MT. AIRY

Bluebird Diner
206 North Main Street
Mt. Airy 27030
(336) 789–1644

Leon's Burger Express
407 North Main Street
Mt. Airy 27030
(336) 789–0849

Panda Garden
864 Highway 52 North
Mt. Airy 27030
(336) 789–0266

Wagon Wheel Family
Restaurant
845 West Pine Street
Mt. Airy 27030
(336) 789–4653

SALISBURY

The Bagel and Deli Shop
127 North Main Street
Salisbury 28144
(704) 642–1154

Checkered Flag Barbecue
1530 South Main Street
Salisbury 28144
(704) 636–2628

City View Restaurant
1518 East Innes Street
Salisbury 28144
(704) 636–1761

El Cancun Mexican
Restaurant
1007 East Innes Street
Salisbury 28144
(704) 637–1155

Farmhouse Restaurant
1602 Jake Alexander
Boulevard
Salisbury 28144
(704) 633–3276

Light House Family Style
Seafood Restaurant
1517 East Innes Street
Salisbury 28144
(704) 636–5005

STATESVILLE

Sagebrush Steak House
and Saloon
117 Turnersburg Road
Statesville 28625
(704) 873–2466

Carolina Bar-B-Q
213 Salisbury Road
Statesville 28677
(704) 873–5585

Mayo's Italian Restaurant
123 North Center Street
Statesville 28625
(704) 872–5557

The Black Angus Grille
125 North Center Street
Statesville 28625
(704) 872–4200

Gluttons
1539 East Broad Street
Statesville 28625
(704) 872–6951

The Mountains

The Western Mountains

hatever you plan in the North Carolina mountains, allow about twice as much travel time as usual. Narrow roads wind through woodland and countryside, up hills so steep you sometimes feel as though your car will peel off the road backward, from hairpin turns into switchbacks followed by more curves. The squiggles don't all show on the maps, and the maps can't allow for the time it takes if you get behind a big truck with no place to pass for 50 miles. Decide ahead of time not to hurry; relax and absorb the peerless scenery.

One way to enjoy the panoramic views of mountains and valleys is by driving some part of the ***Blue Ridge Parkway.*** It stretches from Shenandoah National Park in Virginia along the Blue Ridge Mountains into the southern part of the Black Mountains, through the Craggies, the Pisgahs, the Balsams, and into the Great Smokies, a total of 469 miles. The maximum speed limit along the parkway is 45 miles per hour, but in reality, traffic is often slower. It doesn't take much arithmetic to figure that it would take a long time to cover the entire length of the parkway at 30 or 40 miles per hour. The best way to plan a trip is to alternate stretches of the parkway with drives on the roads you can reach by turning off along the way. Crossovers from the parkway are marked with mileposts that are numbered and named.

Before you get on the parkway, spend some time enjoying the Nantahala National Forest, Nantahala Gorge, and Bryson City in the mountains. ***Randolph House,*** 223 Freymont Road, Bryson City 28713, built in 1895 by Amos Frye, is run today by his niece, Ruth Adams, and her husband, Bill, as a homey country inn. As Ruth tells it, Amos once had owned all the timber around, but when the government decided to declare most of the area national forestland, Amos had to sell. He kept the right to lumber out the sold acreage for a limited time; to get his money's worth, he set to building, using wood, of course, as fast as he could. Randolph House was one of the results.

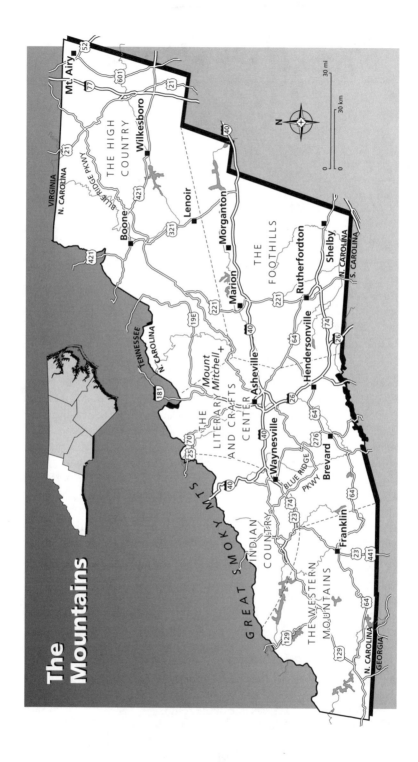

The
Mountains

THE MOUNTAINS

ANNUAL EVENTS IN THE MOUNTAINS

Asheville
**Annual Spring Wildflower
and Bird Pilgrimage**
(early May)
(828) 251–6444

**Biltmore Estate's Annual
Festival of Flowers**
(early May)
(828) 274–6333
or (800) 543–2961

**Black Mountain
Sourwood Festival**
(mid August)
(828) 669–2300
(800) 669–2301

**Blowing Rock
Independence Day Festival**
July 4
(828) 295–7851

Boone
Firefly Festival
(early June)
(828) 264–2225

Annual Apple Festival
(late October)
(828) 264–2120

Because the house is furnished with family antiques that have always been there, things don't all match, leaving you with the feeling that if you blink hard you'll see old Amos there in the worn leather chair. The inn's dinners are strictly by reservation because Ruth hates waste, and when you make the reservation, you choose from a list of entrees planned for that night. The cuisine might be called "Southern Gourmet," featuring choices such as Cornish hen in orange sauce and trout in pecan sauce, served perhaps with a classic Southern squash casserole and a dessert of Three Hundred Dollar Chocolate Cake or Mile High Lemon Pie. Bill maintains a nice wine list. The inn is open April through October (828–488–3472 or 800–480–3472).

From Bryson City drive 9 miles southwest on Highway 19 to **Nantahala Outdoor Center** at the Nantahala Gorge. The outdoor center attracts the outdoors crowd, especially rafters and hikers. This is a congenial place to hire a guide and all the equipment you need for a white-water rafting trip down the Nantahala River. It's also great for fishing, picnicking, and hiking. Part of the fun is watching the serious rafters, who, as one observer put it, seem to have a continuing contest to see who can show up in the most worn, mismatched, clothes-don't-matter outfit. The Nantahala Outdoor Center Restaurant, right by the river, has been a popular eating place with hikers and rafters for years. Some of the most popular recipes have been bound into a cookbook, *River Runners Special,* with each recipe listed for difficulty (Class I, II, III, and so on) like the rapids on the river. Vegetarian lentil mushroom soup is Class II; amaretto cream pie is Class IV. Some years ago the restaurant's name became River's End, to note the addition of another restaurant, Relia's Garden, at the center.

At **River's End** you'll feel perfectly comfortable in your mismatched hiking clothes and down vest, sitting at a rustic table looking out over the river while you gobble a hearty serving of spicy beef stew with the restaurant's special herb bread. Relia's Garden is also casual but a bit more upscale in its atmosphere and offerings. With a view of the mountains rather than the river, this restaurant sits in a field on the hill across

It Was Inevitable

*I*n his younger years a good friend of mine spent most of his free time at the Nantahala Outdoor Center (they call it NOC). Several of his brothers were river guides over the years, and they finally convinced their mother, a good–natured Pittsburgh lady, to venture onto the river on a raft. She listened to the lecture about keeping her feet pointed downstream if she fell off, but she didn't take it very seriously. And she buckled into her life vest without protest but didn't take it very seriously either. She listened to the paddling instructions without getting especially serious. But she did know what to do if the raft dumped her off.

It did. And that nice lady ended up floating rapidly in icy water, with her feet pointed downsteam, bouyed by her flotation vest, shouting to her sons at the top of her lungs, "I'll never forgive you for this."

the garden, landscaped with terraced gardens of herbs, unusual vegetables, and exotic plants. A walk through the gardens crushes fragrant bits of mint and thyme underfoot, so that no matter how hungry you were to begin with, your appetite's whetted even more by the time you go inside. Entrees range from fettuccine to prime rib. The county is dry, but brown-bagging beer and wine is permitted.

Staff members of the Nantahala Outdoor Center, from guides to cooks, tend to return year after year, as do visitors. Moreover, the presence of the family that started the center is still much in evidence. Relia's Garden, for instance, is named for Arelia, wife of the founder and for many years director of food service. Her plants fill the terrace gardens. Spending time here feels like being part of an extended family or a close community. It is special. The center and restaurants operate from roughly mid-March to November 1, depending on the weather. River's End is open daily from 7:00 A.M. to 9:00 P.M. Relia's Garden serves breakfast daily from 8:00 to 10:30 A.M., lunch from 11:00 A.M. to 2:00 P.M., and dinner from 5:00 to 9:00 P.M. (10:00 P.M. Saturday). In the colder months, hours may be cut back. For information about the time you plan to be here, phone (704) 488–2175.

Just a few miles (a long walk or a short ride) beyond the outdoor center on Highway 19, **Nantahala Village** offers a less strenuous and very agreeable alternative approach to the river, the gorge, and the forest. Built before the white-water craze as a rustic resort in the woods, Nantahala Village has simple rooms in the inn and a variety of cozy cabins built of logs or native stone, with knotty-pine interiors. The cabins have kitchens; some have fireplaces. The original inn burned

AUTHOR'S FAVORITE PLACES IN THE MOUNTAINS

Nantahala Outdoor Center

Folk Art Center

New River State Park

Hot Springs

Carl Sandburg Home
  National Historic Site

Mt. Mitchell State Park

North Carolina
  Mining Museum

Lake Lure

Chimney Rock Park

Black Mountain

Carrigan Farms

down in 1997, but it has been replaced by a new structure with classic architecture.

The dining room in the inn serves an interesting combination of traditional foods—chicken, beef, and so on—popular entrees lower in fat and emphasizing the flavors of fresh herbs. John Burton and Jan Letendre, the owners, are committed to keeping the original atmosphere and setting but wanted to update the dining room menu to include vegetarian and lighter fare. They offer these options along with the traditional southern mountain favorites. They're also committed to getting people into appropriate accommodations. For instance, they wouldn't put a family with tiny children into a cabin that has a deck jutting out over a cliff or an elderly person into a room that requires a lot of walking to reach. Nantahala Village is usually open from mid-March to January 1, but weather could change this. It's a good idea to call ahead (828–488–2826, or outside North Carolina 800–438–1507). Web site: www.nvmc.com.

Indier Country

*P*icking up the Blue Ridge Parkway at Cherokee brings you to some decisions about the kind of tourist you mean to be. The town, in the **Qualla Boundary Cherokee Indian Reservation** where Highways 441 and 19 meet, maintains several features dedicated to preserving and explaining the history of the Cherokee nation, which was nearly wiped out by the infamous "Trail of Tears" forced walk in 1838, when the U.S. government tried to relocate all Indians to west of the Mississippi River. Some of the Cherokees escaped the march by hiding in the hills.

Eventually they were able to return to this area, where they were once the powerful Cherokee nation. Their story is told in **Unto These Hills,** an outdoor drama played by a cast of 130 people, beginning between 8:00 and 9:00 P.M. nightly, except Sunday, from mid-June through late August, in an outdoor theater that seats 2,800 people. The program is presented by the Cherokee Historical Association with support from the Theatre Arts Section of the North Carolina Arts Council and funds appropriated by the North Carolina General Assembly. The story begins with Spanish explorer Hernando DeSoto's arrival in 1540 and climaxes with the Trail of Tears exodus. Many of the players are descendants of the Cherokee who lived the story. Moderately high admission fee. Box office (828–497–2111) open from 9:00 A.M. to 10:00 P.M. during the summer season and from 9:00 A.M. to 4:30 P.M. in the off-season. The story and performances are frankly moving; it's not uncommon to see people in the audience cry. Web site: www.dnet.net/~cheratt.

Unfortunately, activities of this caliber are surrounded by the tourist-tacky pseudo-Indian concessions that seem to plague the areas around Indian populations across the country. Trying to sort out the authentic and the merely exploitative can be depressing. You can count on quality at the *Oconaluftee Indian Village,* sponsored by the Cherokee Historical Association. It is a living replication of a 1750s Cherokee village and shows you Indians practicing their historical crafts of basket making, pottery, canoe building, food preparations, and weaponry, and perhaps even more important, explains the culture within which these activities proceeded. Hour-long tours begin every five minutes, but you are not locked into them, and there is plenty of time for exploring, photographing, and questioning. Open from 9:00 A.M. to 5:30 P.M., May through October. Moderately high admission charge (828–497–2111).

Qualla Arts and Crafts Mutual, Inc., the most successful Indian-owned and -operated craft cooperative in the country, at the entrance of the *Unto These Hills* theater on Highway 441, offers you an opportunity to buy genuine Indian beadwork, baskets, wood carvings, pots, masks, and the like. Cherokee work is displayed in separate rooms from that of other tribes. Open daily, 8:00 A.M. to 4:30 P.M. These hours may vary slightly seasonally. It's a good idea to call ahead (828–497–3103).

Finally, the *Museum of the Cherokee Indian* displays traditional arts and crafts and offers a video on the history of the nation, along with displays of tools and various accounts of the Trail of Tears journey. Computer-generated images and holographic imaging bring scenes to life. Open daily from 9:00 A.M. to 5:30 P.M., later during the summer. Modest admission charged. Closed Thanksgiving, Christmas, and New Year's Day. For full information about attractions call (282) 497–3481.

Cherokee is considered the gateway to the Great Smoky Mountains, and it seems important to mention, however briefly, the *Great Smoky Mountains National Park,* established in 1934 partly with money donated by John D. Rockefeller. The park merits a full book in itself: Elevations climb as you move along the northeast; plant life, wildlife, and scenery invite superlatives; the bears and the weather are unpredictable. About half the park falls in Tennessee, but North Carolinians, figuring there's plenty for all, forgive that. Staying on the North Carolina side, you'll find enough hiking, fishing, and camping to last most of your life without being repetitious. There are several visitors centers in the park. For information, call (616) 436–5615. It's a Tennessee number, but it's also park headquarters and the best place to start when you need advance information. The park is said to have attracted more than ten million visitors annually in recent years, mostly in the summer, although with about 500,000 acres to explore, there'd seem to be enough room for everyone. You'll probably enjoy your visit more if you avoid the peak summer season.

Your next major stop should probably be Asheville, altitude 2,250 feet, population about 62,000. You can amble along the Blue Ridge Parkway to get there, or go more directly along Highway 19. You'll go through Maggie Valley, and you might detour onto Highway 23 to stop in *Waynesville* (you are now at an altitude of 3,000 feet), a little town of Scotch-Irish and English founding where travelers like to stop to get away from the obvious tourist attractions and enjoy some real people. Waynesville is the home of the annual *Ramps Festival.* The ramp is a rank, onionlike, wild plant of no particular virtue, except that every summer the American Legion throws a big party to cook it all the ways they can think of: steamed ramps, braised ramps, ramps à la king, ramps fritters. Presumably, folks eats the results, but that is not as conspicuous as the cooking, which leaves a garlicky odor heavy on the town all day. For some reason it's a popular time and place for politicians to appear. The festival is always held on the first Sunday in May, at the American Legion Park, 171 Legion Drive, Waynesville 28786. A ramp-eating contest is the high point of the day, unless you're one of the contestants, in which case it may be the beginning of a big belly ache for the rest of the day. For more information call (828) 456–8691. Other ramp festivals are held in nearby counties, but an American Legion representative says, "Ours was the first one, and it's the real one. The others aren't like ours." If you'd like to spend a night and have dinner in congenial, rustic surroundings here, try *Grandview Lodge,* owned and operated by Stanley and Linda Arnold (828–456–5212). The Arnolds are relative newcomers, escapees from corporate Chicago. The inn has been operating for the past fifty-plus years; the Arnolds took it over as part of a longtime dream in 1986. Linda's cooking, which emphasizes fresh produce and herbs, whole-grain flours, and homemade desserts, has been so popular that she published a cookbook, *The Grandview Lodge Cookbook,* for guests who hope to duplicate some of her meals at home. Stanley loves to play bridge: If you were to show up as a threesome looking for a fourth, you'd win his heart forever. Stan has another talent that fits interestingly into the Waynesville scene: He speaks Polish, Russian, German, and Hebrew. In recent years Waynesville has become known for international folk-dance festivals—which gives Stan a chance to try every language he knows.

Here's a place to stay and dine that you probably wouldn't find unless you were specifically looking for it. The **Old Stone Inn** (828–456–3333 or 800–432–8499), owned and operated by Cindy and Robert Zinser, was known in earlier years as Heath Lodge. It's a larger operation, technically an inn rather than a bed-and-breakfast, tucked under lots of shady foliage and rhododendron on top of a hill at the edge of Waynesville.

The Zinsers have upgraded the inn in many ways since they bought it, improving the rooms, making the dining room more attractive and, best of all, moving from old-style Southern all-you-can-eat meals served at huge round tables to more sophisticated and very good food served at tables appropriate for the size of your party.

The shady site, comfortable rooms, and good food (with wine and beer available) make this a great rejuvenating spot. A game room has a television and a piano, and upstairs in the main building is a reading lounge where people won't try to strike up a conversation if what you're there for is to read.

Another place to eat in Waynesville is **Maggie's Galley III** (828–456–8945) at 22 Howell Mill Road, Waynesville 28786. The building housing the restaurant was made from primitive log cabins. An earlier owner had an antiques business here, and as his need for space grew, he just kept tacking on additional old cabins. He used five cabins to make the building as it is today. Each of the cabins has a story and a bit of history attached. The restaurant has a flier with all the information. The food at the restaurant includes fresh seafood, steaks, and a good selection of sandwiches. The atmosphere is zany and a meal here, in addition to being good, is a lot of fun. Open daily from 11:30 A.M. to 9:30 P.M., Maggie's Galley is usually busy; reservations are a good idea.

Lomo Grill, 44 Church Street, Waynesville 28786, has earned a reputation for serving interesting and unusual Italian Mediterranean food, with more specialties coming from its Argentine grill. The restaurant has a nice wine list, too. For dinner reservations call (828) 452–5222. Although the restaurant is open only from April through December, its bakery and cafe, known as **Lomo's** (828–452–1515), has an entrance around the corner on Montgomery Street, and you can stop here for sandwiches, pastries, soups, and salads from 11:00 A.M. to 3:00 P.M. daily. The entire building is red brick, inside and out, which makes for great atmosphere.

One spot in the area that has a Waynesville address, but is actually out of town and 5,000 feet up, offers fine food, rustic lodging, hiking trails, and an entry to the Great Smoky Mountains National Park. *The Swag,* 2300 Swag Road, Waynesville 28786, comprises a collection of pioneer buildings that were hauled up the mountain about thirty years ago. Innkeeper Deener Matthews has managed to combine rustic elements such as the rough wood interior walls of the rooms with luxurious amenities, including handmade covers on the beds, coffee grinders, coffeemakers, hair dryers, and terry-cloth robes in the rooms. She's managed something similar in the dining room, where guests sit around handmade tables to enjoy first-rate food professionally prepared and served.

And although the other recreational facilities are tucked unobtrusively into the property, you can find everything from a racquetball court and sauna to a library. For more details call (828) 926–0430 or (800) 789–7672. Web site: www.theswag.com.

All that is up on the mountain. Down in the valley you'll find some other interesting attractions. *Maggie Valley* is a year-round resort

Let's Get Lost

*B*eing able to walk through the backyard of The Swag and right into the forest of the Great Smoky Mountain National Park was an opportunity too good to ignore. The hiking trails were all there, well marked and shown on a large map on the grounds. Sorry to say, I forgot to look at it. But figuring that all the trails would loop, I just got onto one and started walking. After walking a couple of hours, I was on a road I had never heard of, with no money in my pocket and no place to spend it anyway.

I asked an old man in a pickup truck where I was. He told me, but I was still disoriented. He gave me a ride to a campground where he introduced me to some friends with a trailer. Within minutes, I was sitting at a picnic table, digging into hot roast beef sandwiches, sliced fresh tomatoes, and mashed potatoes. We were all laughing and chatting so much, it was like a party.

Eventually, the idea of getting back where I belonged came up. Everyone knew right where The Swag was, because a swag is a dip in the mountains. It was about 30 miles away by road, a substantial drive for a stranger to make for another stranger.

The old man not only drove me, he had fun doing it, telling me all about his family, life in this area, secrets you can learn on back roads, and who lives on them. When we got back to The Swag, he got out of the truck to look around. "Always wanted to see the view from up here," he said. Then we hugged and he was gone.

That's why I love North Carolina.

town between Cherokee and Waynesville. On both sides of U.S. Highway 19, or Soco Road, which runs through the valley, you'll see one motel after another, every kind of eating place, and souvenir shops galore—generally not the kind of places an off-the-beaten-path traveler wants to visit at all. But you'll also find a couple of attractions unusual enough to be worth the short drive if you've spent a night in Waynesville. What these two attractions have in common is that each began as a labor of love.

Little House, Big Story

It must have been some conversation the day more than ten years ago when Jim Lindsey asked Bill Thomas if he'd like to build doll houses instead of real houses. They both grin when they remember it, but neither of them will tell you a word of what they said.

Thomas brings his real house-building craftsmanship to building houses on the inch-to-the-foot scale. Sometimes he even uses the same house plans.

The Stomping Ground is a huge building on Highway 19 with a massive dance floor and seating for 2,000 people. Kyle Edwards hopes to make it the world center for clogging. The Edwards are a clogging family, but they've always thought of it as "mountain dancing." Kyle thinks the word *clogging* came into use in 1935, in Chattanooga, Tennessee. His mother and his uncle performed with a Maggie Valley team in the 1920s that performed in the White House for President Franklin D. Roosevelt and the Queen of England. Kyle and his wife, Mary Sue, also danced on teams. Their son, Burton, was a world champion clogger in 1981, when he was eighteen. And their daugher, Becky, had won two championships by the time she was thirteen. It doesn't take a rocket scientist to figure out that if you go to The Stomping Ground, you're either going to clog or watch clogging. Dances and shows are held every night from April through November. A number of large display cases related to clogging give you a lot of information about the history, contests, and fun of the dance. Call (828) 926–1288 for details about times, shows, and admission fees. Don't hang up if you get what sounds like a private home instead of a business, with a recorded message telling you that you've reached 926–1288. The telephone rings at the Stomping Ground, in Mary Sue's beauty shop, and in the family's residence. Just leave a message. They'll get back to you.

Lindsey Miniature Village, also on Highway 19, 1110 Soco Road, Maggie Valley 28751, is the only miniature village in the United States built on the 1:12 or inch-to-the-foot scale. Jim and Marjorie Lindsey developed an interest in miniatures in 1982, when they were on a business trip to Canada and stumbled on a miniature village named Cullin Gardens, on the inch-to-the-foot scale.

They came home and began to do likewise. Some of the earliest buildings in the village represent North Pack Square in Asheville, but when the Lindseys decided to set up in Maggie Valley rather than Asheville, they began to focus on local history and buildings. Some of the better-known houses include the Carl Sandburg Home and the Thomas Wolfe boyhood home. The Stomping Ground is there, too.

Lights and sound effects add realism to the displays. You'll see a bonfire and hear Cherokees whooping at the Indian village. Kids scream and yell in the old school. One house is on fire. Not only do you hear the sounds of fire fighters, you even smell the smoke. Figures in emergency vehicles struggle to put out the fire.

The enterprise is a family affair, so every time someone in the family builds a new home, it gets miniaturized for the display, too. The village may be closed during the winter months. Call (828) 926–6277 or (800) 390–9422 for details.

The Literary and Crafts Center

It's only 25 miles from Waynesville to Asheville. **Asheville** is crammed with arts, crafts, antiques, literary and musical people, and a healthy assortment of free spirits deeply involved in the unique Appalachian culture. The best place to see and buy a variety of area crafts is the **Folk Art Center,** just east of town at milepost 382 on the Blue Ridge Parkway, about a half mile north of Highway 70. It has been operated by the Southern Highland Handicraft Guild since 1980 and houses permanent and traveling exhibits and the Allanstand Craft Shop, where you can buy items similar to those in the exhibits. Crafts represented include weaving, pottery, basketry, quilting, jewelry, wood carving, stitchery, and musical instruments. Admission is free; donations are welcome. Open every day except Thanksgiving, Christmas, and New Year's Day from 9:00 A.M. to 5:00 P.M. Closed occasionally for inventory and changing exhibitions (828–298–7928).

At the edge of town, two well-known attractions have become almost obligatory stops for anyone who wants to claim to have seen the area: Grove Park Inn and Biltmore Estate. Both nearly defy description. As newspaper writer Jean Thwaite once said of **Grove Park Inn,** 290 Macon Avenue, Asheville 28804, "It would almost be ugly, were it not so interesting." The building, of a size that seems to dwarf pyramids, is built of red boulders hauled from Sunset Mountain, on which it's located, in 1913. William Grove did well, to understate matters, in pharmaceuticals in St. Louis. He liked Asheville, so he bought a lot of it, including Sunset

Mountain. Then, eschewing architects, who didn't understand him, he got his son-in-law to design and build (without a contractor) the massive hotel. The inn is 500 feet long, with a flagstone-floored lobby 80 feet wide and almost half the length of a football field. The fireplaces at each end are so big they burn 12-foot logs, and when there's no fire, children can walk into them upright to play.

George Washington didn't sleep here, but practically everyone else of importance did: Thomas Edison, Henry Ford, Enrico Caruso, the Roosevelts, Dwight Eisenhower, even F. Scott Fitzgerald. Today the inn is popular with people looking for a place to celebrate a special occasion and with companies and organizations that want somewhere extra nice to gather their members.

After recent additions the inn has more than 500 rooms. Facilities include five restaurants, four cocktail lounges, indoor and outdoor swimming pools, golf, tennis, racquetball, and a fitness center with an aerobics room, weight room, Nautilus equipment, whirlpools, and saunas. The accommodations are luxurious; rates are correspondingly high, although they drop considerably in the off-season, when a variety of special packages are available (828–252–2711 or 800–438–5800).

Many of the packages include a tour of the *Biltmore Estate,* which seems appropriate because it operates on the same grand scale. Like Mr. Grove, George Vanderbilt liked Asheville, and he, too, had a little money. He bought a lot of Asheville, too, about 125,000 acres, and had a 250-room private home built on the property. (Today only 7,500 acres belong to the estate. The rest is part of the Blue Ridge Parkway or Mount Pisgah National Forest.) The home was famous from the beginning for the beauty of its design and workmanship. The master builders were brought from Europe. The home was also famous for being ahead of its time in its modern conveniences, having early forerunners of washing machines and driers. Art in the mansion includes originals by Boldini, Ming dynasty china, and antiques that belonged to Napoleon.

It will take you the better part of a day to see the place properly, especially if you go beyond the mansion to explore the gardens and visit the winery. Although the *Biltmore Estate Winery* is still relatively young, some oenophiles say the wines—red, white, rosé, and champagne—are developing nicely. They are for sale, priced in the moderate range. Admission fees to the Biltmore Estate are high. The estate is open daily from 9:00 A.M. to 5:00 P.M. (828–274–6333 or 800–299–4730).

If you're not overwhelmed by the grandeur of Biltmore Estate, you're a

Biltmore Estate

rare bird. A nice way to decompress and get things back in perspective again is to spend a night at *Cedar Crest,* 674 Biltmore Avenue, Asheville 28803 (828–252–1389 or 800–252–0310). This bed-and-breakfast inn has ten rooms in the main house and a guest cottage. There is a two-bedroom suite with a parlor and fireplace and a single-bedroom suite with a parlor. This is an 1890 Queen Anne–style Victorian mansion in which the work was purportedly done by the same craftsmen who worked on the Biltmore mansion. Apparently, once they were in this country and established in the little village built for them to work on Biltmore, they decided to hang around afterward and pick up a few odd jobs. Like the Biltmore Estate, Cedar Crest is so full of wonderful features that you can't take them all in at once, but the scale is more human and easier to relate to. The elaborate, first-generation oak woodwork differs in every room, with such subtle distinctions as being heavy and masculine in the library, but delicate and ornate in the dining room, which was considered ladies' territory. Other special features in the house include a corner fireplace with fluted columns, a gilded cherub, and splendid stained-glass windows. There's a secret closet where silverware used to be hidden in troubled times. And the house has what may be the longest (6 feet) and smallest (4 feet) bathtubs in North Carolina. Jack McEwan will guide you through the splendors of the place with infectious enthusiasm. Then, to hone in on the down-to-earth, creature-comfort level, you need to know about Barbara McEwan's "Victorian hanging garden," as she calls it. At Cedar Crest the bed sheets, after they are washed, are hung out on the clothesline to dry in the sun. If you've never slept inhaling the fragrance of line-dried sheets, you'll have to trust the word of those who have. It's the ultimate sensual delight. Web site: www.cedarcrestvictorianinn.com.

Another place in Asheville worth a stop is the **Richmond Hill Inn** (87 Richmond Hill Drive, Asheville 28006; 828–252–7313 or 888–742–4565), even if you aren't looking for overnight lodging. This is a luxurious inn with a heroic saved-from-the-wrecking-ball story. The century-old mansion was the home of a former congressman and diplomat, Richmond Pearson, and his wife, Gabrielle. It was one of the most innovative and elegant homes of its time. But it outlasted the people who wanted to live that way and could afford it. Toward the end, the Pearson's daughter, Marjorie, then an elderly woman, lived there alone, using just one room.

In subsequent sales and maneuvering, the building was scheduled to be torn down and then reprieved several times. Many community organizations, including the Preservation Society, campaigned and raised money to try to save the mansion. They also found the Michel family, which was willing to buy and restore it. It was moved, *all in one piece,* to its current spot on the hill. You can begin your stay here by watching a videotape showing the tense moving process.

The building was preserved where possible and restored or re-created where necessary, with fidelity to the mansion's original state. Much work was done by hand as it would originally have been, rather than with electric tools. Now listed on the National Register of Historic Places, it is considered one of the best examples of a Queen Anne–style mansion in North Carolina. It's a must-see if you are interested in architecture and preservation.

Because of the fine woodwork, soaring ceilings, and generously sized rooms, the mansion makes a fine inn. Some guest rooms are named for Pearson family members who once lived in them, others for important guests, and, on the third floor, for Asheville-connected writers, such as Carl Sandburg. Each writer's room has a picture of the writer and a collection of his or her books.

Also re-creating the past, several hundred of Mr. Pearson's own books have been recovered and placed in the inn library along with books about North Carolina and those by North Carolina authors.

The restaurant is open to the public for dinner. It reflects the mansion's history in being named "Gabrielle's," after Mrs. Pearson. The food, however, is clearly a product of modern times. Considered American and nouvelle cuisine, it features lighter sauces and more healthful preparation than earlier haute cuisine.

Finding the place is tricky the first time. From Interstate 240 take the 19/23 Weaverville exit. Continue on 19/23 and take exit 251 (UNC–

Asheville). Turn left at the bottom of the ramp. At the first stoplight, turn left again onto Riverside Drive. Turn right on Pearson Bridge Road and cross the bridge. At the sharp curve, turn right on Richmond Hill Drive. The mansion is at the top of the hill.

On a more modest scale, **Albemarle Inn,** 86 Edgemont Road, Asheville 28801, in a quiet residential area on three quarters of an acre within walking distance of many of Asheville's attractions, is gracious place to stay. The inn is a large white 1909 Greek Revival mansion. The front porch extends the full length of the house, braced with four 30-foot pillars. Béla Bartók wrote his *Third Piano Concerto* here, reportedly inspired by the natural quiet and birdsong of the place. The innkeepers emphasize service, helping guests plan special weekends and catering to dietary preferences.

An evening social hour with wine or cider and snacks is a time for studying the Albemarle's collection of menus and choosing a restaurant for dinner. Call (828) 255–0027 or (800) 621–7435. Web site: www.albe-marleinn.com.

One thing you might not expect to find in a mountain city is **The Botanical Gardens at Asheville,** located on a ten-acre site next to the campus of the University of North Carolina at Asheville. The gardens were begun in 1960 by the Asheville Garden Club and designed by Doan Ogden, a landscape architect of repute. The gardens are open all year, and no matter when you visit, you'll find something in bloom, bud, or fruit.

The Botany Center is open from March to December. Other parts of the gardens include a library and gift shop. You can arrange for garden tours or use a map to explore on your own. Special places in the property include a spring house, a garden for the blind, a rock garden, an azalea garden, and an herb garden. For more detailed information about the gardens, call the Botany Center at (828) 252–5190.

Here's the unexpected kind of place you can find in Asheville. **Blue Moon Bakery,** 60 Biltmore Avenue, Asheville 28801 (828–252–6063), operated by Chris and Margaret Kobler, specializes in European-style breads and a variety of specialty breads. Chris was a program manager for the Small Business Administration in Washington, D.C., when, at the age of forty-five, he says, "I woke up and realized I was a baker." A village baker, no less. They settled in North Carolina because Margaret has family here and settled on Asheville for its sophistication and cultural activities. It was just the kind of place they thought would support a baker. Chris bought an expensive French oven and in the process got himself in touch with Dan Leider, author of *Bread Alone,* who operates one of the world's best-known bakeries in France.

Your choices here range from old-fashioned European–style baguettes, slow-rising sourdoughs, and such specialties as raisin-pecan bread and an assortment of pastries. The bakery also has a cafe that seats about eighty in an informal atmosphere dominated by a mural depicting bakers and bread. European prints on the walls add to the French feel.

Another enterprise run by "transplants" to the area is the ***Mountain Smoke House,*** River Ridge Business Center, 802 Fairview Road 28803 (828–298–8121). Catherine Mitchell Proctor used to be a lawyer. Calling themselves "semiretired," she and her husband, Marshall, left New York City to open a small lunch bistro. It was so popular they ended up buying the Mountain Smoke House, where they specialize in barbecue and a variety of smoked meats, prime rib, chicken and turkey breast, and mountain trout. Catherine also uses recipes she and her famiy loved growing up in Birmingham—Hoppin' John, sweet-potato chips, collards, okra, sweet-potato pie, fruit cobblers, and the like.

Evening entertainment includes clog dancers, fiddle players, banjo pickers, and a dance caller. Most evenings the action gets so lively the crowd dances or sings along. Open beginning at 11:45 A.M. for lunch and dinner Tuesday through Saturday.

An integral part of Asheville's intellectual and musical activity is ***Malaprops Bookstore/Cafe,*** 55 Haywood Street, Asheville 28801, where the ambience resembles what one imagines for Paris of the 1950s. Emoke Bracz, the owner, writes poetry. Other staff members produce fiction, nonfiction, and cartoons. North Carolina writers, of whom there are an astonishing number, stop in to browse or autograph, depending on their current state of productivity. In the background, music progresses through selections of jazz, New Age, and folk, all of which you can buy in the downstairs cafe, where people sit around sipping coffee concoctions, nibbling desserts, and, presumably, talking either about their own writing or about the books upstairs. The offerings include many titles in poetry, feminist and women's books, and American Indian, travel, and North Carolina selections.

The unusual book stock and the unique atmosphere here have made Malaprops something of a tourist attraction as well as a local center of the literati. Interestingly, the store is admired by many other bookstore proprietors and staff in the state. And although Malaprops likes paying customers as much as the next store, old school desks scattered about the place make for comfortable browsing, too (828–254–6734). Open

THE MOUNTAINS

BETTER KNOWN ATTRACTIONS IN THE MOUNTAINS

ASHEVILLE
Biltmore Estate
(828) 274–6333
(800) 543–2961

Blue Ridge Parkway
(828) 298–0398

BLOWING ROCK
The Blowing Rock
(828) 295–7111

CHEROKEE
Cherokee Indian Reservation
(828) 497–9195
(800) 438–1601

Harrah's Cherokee Casino
(800) 438–1601

CHIMNEY ROCK
Chimney Rock Park
(828) 625–9611
(800) 277–9611

Monday through Thursday from 9:00 A.M. to 9:00 P.M.; Friday and Saturday from 9:00 A.M. to 11:00 P.M.; Sunday from 9:00 A.M. to 6:00 P.M.

While you're feeling literary, visit the *Thomas Wolfe Memorial,* 48 Spring Street. This is the novelist's boyhood home, described in his novel, *Look Homeward, Angel,* as "Dixieland." In real life it was called "The Old Kentucky Home." Wolfe's mother, Julia, ran a boardinghouse in the rambling Victorian house, and its various rooms and furnishings, along with local people, were all incorporated into Wolfe's novel, mostly in unflattering terms. The people of Asheville didn't like that one bit, which led to Wolfe's second novel, *You Can't Go Home Again.* After Wolfe died, the townspeople relented, as they often do when a troublesome celebrity stops being troublesome and remains merely famous, and bought the house to turn into a memorial for him. It is now a North Carolina State Historic Site. Visiting the house, which has been kept the same as it was when the Wolfes lived in it and has descriptions from Wolfe's writing in appropriate places so you can compare the words with the reality, goes a long way toward explaining the often gloomy tone of his writing. Nominal admission fee. The Wolfe house was damaged by fire a few years ago. Restoration is in process. Call (828) 253–8304 for schedule and rate details. Web site: www.home. att.net~wolfememorial.

Just about 10 miles outside Asheville, near Weaverville on Reems Creek Road off Highway 25 North, is another state historic site, the *Zebulon B. Vance Birthplace.* Vance was a Civil War officer, a U.S. senator, and governor of North Carolina. In fascinating contrast to the splendor of the Biltmore Estate, this restored pioneer farmstead has only a five-room log house and some outbuildings. The log house was reconstructed around the original chimneys. The outbuildings, including a loom house, springhouse, toolshed, smokehouse, corncrib, and slave cabin, are furnished as they would have been between 1795 and 1840. Displays instruct you further in life of the times. Admission is free. Open April through October, Monday through Saturday from 9:00 A.M. to 5:00 P.M. and Sunday from 1:00 to 5:00 P.M. November through March, closed Monday and open shorter hours other days (828–645–6706).

Also outside the city, *The North Carolina Arboretum,* at milepost 393 (off Highway 191), features southern Appalacian landscape plants on a 426-acre site, as well as hiking and nature trails. Call (828) 665–2492. Web site: www.ncarboretum.org. The arboretum also has a state-of-the-art greenhouse complex.

Asheville makes a good center from which to go in several different directions. Following the parkway takes you to *New River State Park.* A drive of about 20 miles down Interstate 26 takes you into the southern mountains, where Flat Rock, Hendersonville, and Saluda offer many rural pleasures and some interesting crafts and antiques shops. Driving northeast from Asheville along the Blue Ridge Parkway takes you higher into the mountains to Blowing Rock and environs. And a scenic ride east along Interstate 40 and Highway 226 to Polkville brings you back into the lower elevations of the Piedmont.

If you follow the parkway almost to the Virginia border, getting off to drive north on Highway 221, you come to the oldest river in North America and the second oldest (the Nile is older) in the world. It's the only major river in the country that runs south to north. Paradoxically called New River, it meanders peacefully through more than 100 miles of northwestern North Carolina. The name was the result of surveyors' surprise when they finally chanced upon the river they hadn't known about in this remote part of the state in 1749.

You'll enjoy good access to the river from New River State Park (336–982–2587), an area of breathtakingly lovely mountains, valleys, woods, and fields, 8 miles southeast of Jefferson off Highway 88 on State Road 1588. Compared to other state parks, New River shows up infrequently in travel books and articles, probably because it is in a remote part of the state and because the facilities are primitive. This is the river to find if you like placid canoeing rather than wild races through white water and want fishing spots not bothered by heavy powerboat traffic. There are canoe landings and campgrounds. The woods are great for hiking and are full of spots that cry out for a simple picnic.

Behind the peaceful scene lies the story of a dramatic struggle that isn't anywhere near being over. It started in the 1960s, when the Appalachian Power Company planned to build a dam there, eliciting tremendous public objection. In protective response Congress designated the area a National Wild and Scenic River in 1976, effectively stopping the power company.

But little funding was ever forthcoming to actually buy and protect the land, and gradually a new force is changing the scene along the river:

subdivision and development. New houses, roads, and lots are begin-ning to appear on what was farmland or woodland. There's even a golf course in the works. Although none of it is in the state park, of course, people who like their countryside bucolic and unspoiled are getting nervous, whereas those who value economic development for the area are digging in their heels and sending out the bulldozers.

Given the usual inclination of those who can afford to build in the pret-tiest places—high on mountain summits, on beaches and islands, and along rivers—it's hard to say what will happen along the New River in the coming decade. The good news is that the state park is, as locals like to call the river, "a national treasure" and should remain a special place to visit for a long time to come.

About thirty-five minutes north of Asheville, in Madison County, you'll find an interesting cluster of places near the **French Broad River.** This river is a step above the Nantahala River in difficulty for white-water rafting, but the water is warmer and far fewer users come into the area, so your experience will be considerably more off-the-beaten-path than it is on the Nantahala. The greater part of Madison County is part of Pisgah National Forest, and the Appalachian Trail passes through the county, offering short segments of trail for day hikers. In the little town of **Hot Springs,** you can soak in outdoor tubs along the banks of the river. Hot mineral water, flowing constantly from natural springs at a temperature of about 100 degrees, has often been considered therapeutic and is certainly relaxing, the more so if you indulge in a massage while you are there. Spa rates are figured by the hour and vary from $12 to $25, depending on the time of day. Massage rates are calculated by the half-hour and become proportionately slightly less expensive per half hour the longer the time you reserve. For information about the hot springs and massages, phone (828) 622–7676 or (800) 462–0933. For information about white-water raft-ing tours, phone Carolina Wilderness (800–872–7437) in Hot Springs. For information about hiking, contact the Visitors Information Center at the Forest Supervisor's Office, P.O. Box 2750, Asheville 28802.

On the drive down Interstate 26, one of the most interesting stops is the **Carl Sandburg Home National Historic Site,** a 240-acre farm called **Connemara,** a bit south of Hendersonville in Flat Rock. Sandburg spent the last twenty-two years of his life here, mostly writing, while his wife and daughter managed the place as a goat farm. His collection of poems, *Honey and Salt,* was written here when he was eighty-five. The poems contrast with such earlier works as "Chicago," reflecting not only the work of an older man, but also of one living in different surroundings.

For instance, in the poem "Cahokia," Sandburg writes about an Indian watching a butterfly rise from a cocoon, flowers sprouting in spring, and the sun moving. The Indian, Sandburg writes, doesn't worship the sun but dances and sings to the "makers and movers of the sun." It takes on added significance when you know that Flat Rock was named for a large granite plateau that had once been a Cherokee sacred ground. Sandburg's life here was influenced not only by the early cycles of nature but also by Cherokee Indian lore. Similarly, looking across the mountains, it's easy to understand how Sandburg might have arrived at his poem "Shadows Fall Blue on the Mountains."

When you visit Sandburg's study at Connemara, both the man and his poetry seem alive. The study is said to be exactly as he left it, with a shawl tossed over the back of his desk chair, a clunky manual typewriter standing on an upended crate, and stacks of paper and disorderly piles of books everywhere. A fascinating aspect of the entire home is the simplicity of its furnishings. To say the interior is plain puts it mildly. The furniture resembles what you find in a summer camp, functional but not decorative. Also fascinating is the fact that every room is crammed with books, all of which appear to have been well used. Similarly, the rooms where Helga kept records about breeding her goats are functional and were apparently furnished with no thought to decoration. What you find outside seems more carefully designed. You may also walk along trails on the grounds, where you'll see the kinds of plants and wildlife from which Sandburg must have drawn many of his images. Nominal admission is charged. Open daily except Christmas from 9:00 A.M. to 5:00 P.M. Inquire about some special seasonal activities (828–693–4178).

The town's *Historic Flat Rock District* is on the National Register of Historic Places. It began about 150 years ago as summer estates for wealthy people from Charleston, South Carolina. Web site: www.historic flatrock.org. Flat Rock has a wonderful place to enjoy a good dinner and spend the night. *Highland Lake Inn,* on Highland Lake Drive, is a complex with a lodge, cabins, and cottages scattered on a wooded property that also has a lake, an olympic-size swimming pool, and 100 acres of walking trails. The Lindsey family dream was to create a self-sufficient compound, and although they haven't managed that entirely yet, they've come close. The restaurant serves vegetables and herbs organically grown on the property, bread baked from organic wheat stone-ground in the inn's kitchen, and eggs from free-range chickens. The food is simply wonderful. Offerings range from something as simple as a chicken pot pie with a puff pastry crust to some elaborate pasta and seafood dishes and lamb with lime sauce. Every bite you take bursts with flavor. If you are traveling with children, this is a place where you can take them to find out how to take an egg out of a chicken nest, see vegetables growing in a garden, and watch a goat being milked. Phone (828) 693–6812 or (800) 762–1276. Web site: www.highlandlake.com.

From Flat Rock you can head over onto Highway 176, driving about 12 miles to *Saluda,* a little town of less than 1,000 people, with a notable concentration of antiques and artisans. Walking around in the little town itself, you'll find several shops selling local crafts and antiques and a general store run by a pair of women reminiscent of the sisters on *The Waltons* television show, except, of course, they aren't offering Mason jars full of the "recipe"—as far as anyone knows.

The town is at the crest of the steepest mainline railroad in the country. The business district is on the National Register of Historic Places.

Saluda has two overnight possibilities, quite different from each other. At the top of a steep hill, overlooking Saluda's main street, Dottie Eargle's *Woods House,* at Henderson and Church Streets, Saluda 28773, has six rooms, including one in a separate cottage. The place is furnished throughout with late Victorian and turn-of-the-century antiques, highlighted by an outstanding collection of old needlework displayed throughout the inn. Dorothy has run an antiques shop for many years, and she has the ability to put together a room as only those intimate with antiques and their earlier uses can. (She cooks breakfast in a real country kitchen that has a wood-burning stove.) The inn (828–749–9562) is open April through October. In the center of town, Dorothy has a real estate office, now grown to three rooms, entirely furnished with antique oak office furniture. If you admire those old, functional oak file cabinets, bookcases, and desks and chairs, it's worth a trip to Saluda just to see the office.

Like Asheville, Saluda has a bakery that comes as a surprise. Debi Thomas started out catering for *Mother Earth News,* whose facilities are in the country nearby. In her own *Wildflour Bakery* (21 Main Street, 828–252–6063), Thomas still concentrates on flavor and nutrition. She and her friends have created all the recipes, including a variety of vegetarian soups, salads, and sandwiches. All her recipes use stone-ground flour, ground fresh as needed from untreated wheat. Ingredients are measured and mixed mostly by hand.

Wildflour offers a variety of loaves, ranging from the regular oatmeal bread and the nutritious Boobie Bread (seven grains) to gourmet choices such as roasted walnut and English cheddar bread. In addition to earning a living, Thomas says her reward is older people who say, "I remember good bread like this."

A few miles into the country, in a totally different mood, **The Orchard Inn** (800–581–3800), on Highway 176, Saluda 28773, sits atop the Saluda rise on eighteen wooded acres at an elevation of 2,500 feet. This place is filled with beautifully arranged antiques, art, and books and, of course, has a spectacular view from every side. The inn has an excellent chefs who does magical things with trout and beef, and so on, emphasizing flavor and presentation without relying on heavy, fatty sauces. The breads and desserts that have guests raving. All this food is served on a glassed-in porch that overlooks the Warrior Mountain Range. Web site: www.orchardinn.com.

When you call these Saluda telephone numbers, be patient. Sometimes the little local phone company has problems; always through the ringing you hear burbles and rasps like something out of the days of hand-cranked phones, and you feel that a very young Aunt Bee should answer.

The High Country

The next drive you might make from Asheville continues north on the Blue Ridge Parkway to **Mount Mitchell State Park,** elevation 6,684 feet, the highest point in the eastern United States. You'll leave the parkway at milepost 355.4 to take Highway 128 to the 1,500-acre wilderness park. It's a 5-mile drive to the peak, but it will feel a lot longer. The park has hiking trails, picnic areas, a visitors center with maps, camping areas, and a lookout tower from which you can see what must be the most stunning mountain views east of the Mississippi. There are also a restaurant and a refreshment stand. Be careful while you're here. Mount Mitchell is named for Dr. Elisha Mitchell, who fell off the summit and died. Your falling off too probably wouldn't lead to getting the mountain renamed in your honor. The park is closed in winter (828–675–4611).

The next step you might try along the parkway is at milepost 331, where Highway 226 and State Road 1100 take you to Emerald Village near Little Switzerland. At Emerald Village, established on the site of the Old McKinney and Bon Ami mines, you can visit the **North Carolina Mining Museum,** which displays the tools used at the height of gem mining in the area. Outdoor displays and a printed trail guide explain the entire mining process, and you'll have the opportunity to look for your own emeralds, rubies, aquamarines, and the like. More vigorous all-day tours through mines not previously open to the public, complete with hard hats, rock hammers, and a chuck-wagon lunch, are available at scheduled times. If your gem hunting doesn't go well, you can pick up something at the shop or have a rough gem cut, polished, and set into a piece of jewelry. Other attractions include a fluorescent mineral display, railroad items, and a craft shop. Open from 9:00 A.M. to 5:00 P.M., May 1 through October 31. Open an hour longer in the evening from Memorial Day to Labor Day (828–765–6463). Web site: evwhole@m-y.net.

From here you could return to the parkway or go north on Highway 221 to get to *Linville Caverns* and *Linville Falls,* just beyond the caverns. If you're back on the parkway, exit at milepost 317.4 and turn left on Highway 221. Linville Caverns lie under Humpback Mountain and were believed to be have been forgotten by the white race until about one hundred years ago, when fish that seemed to be swimming out of the mountains caught the attention of explorers. During the Civil War, deserters from troops on both sides hid in the caverns. Today the caverns are lit electrically, showing stalactites and stalagmites and trout that, having always swum in the dark, can't see. Guides lead the tours 2,000 feet underground, pointing out important features and answering questions. A modest admission fee is charged. Open June 1 through Labor Day from 9:00 A.M. to 6:00 P.M. Closed at 5:00 P.M. in April, May, September, and October and 4:30 P.M. in March and November. Open weekends only in December, January, and February; closed Thanksgiving and Christmas (828–756–4171).

Linville Falls comprises two waterfalls at Linville Gorge and a primeval canyon in the sizable wilderness area given to the Blue Ridge Parkway by John D. Rockefeller. The gorge is the deepest cut east of the Grand Canyon. There are hiking trails and picnic spots.

Still moving north along the parkway, you'll come to *Grandfather Mountain,* where, if you've got the nerve for it, you can walk across the *Mile-High Swinging Bridge,* a 218-foot suspension bridge between two peaks that sways in the wind. Should you quite sensibly prefer to put your feet on something more solid, Grandfather Mountain has lots of hiking trails. You'll need to pick up a moderately priced permit and a trail map at the entrance. This is the area where the *Scottish Highland Games,* open to the public, are held the second weekend in July every year. It is also a spot that attracts hang gliders. Open from 8:00 A.M. to dusk summers; closed at 4:30 P.M., sometimes earlier, in winter. Admission is $10.00 for adults, $5.00 for children aged four to twelve. Phone (828) 733–4337 or (800) 468–7325. Web site: www.grandfather.com.

A few minutes farther on Highway 221 brings you to the **Blowing Rock,** a cliff 4,090 feet above sea level that overhangs Johns River Gorge, 3,000 feet below, at the town of Blowing Rock. Because of the way the gorge is shaped and overhung, air blows upward, making snow appear to fall upside down and throwing upward light objects tossed over the edge. According to the legend of Blowing Rock, a Cherokee brave leaped to his death here to keep his tribe from making him return to the plains, leaving his Chickasaw wife behind. She prayed to the Great Spirit until the sky turned red and the wind blew her brave back up onto the rock. A wind has blown up from the valley ever since. A moderate admission is charged. Hours vary with the season and the weather. For details call (828) 295–7111.

By the time you get to Blowing Rock, the children will probably have heard of **Tweetsie Railroad,** a family theme park that has been operating in North Carolina since 1956. It's touristy but kind of fun. Coal-fired steam engines pull the train of open cars through 3 miles of staged events: a train robbery, an Indian raid, and so on. Also, a chairlift carries you up to Mouse Mountain, where you can pan for gold and walk through the petting farm. Another section of the park duplicates a country fair of the early 1900s, right down to the cotton candy. Among other features are an ice-cream parlor, a jail, and a firehouse. Moderately high admission is charged. Open daily from Memorial Day through October from 9:00 A.M. to 6:00 P.M., with shorter hours and some features closed weekdays after Labor Day. The days and hours of operation here can, as one employee put it, "change at any time," so do call ahead (828–264–9061 or 800–526–5740). Web site: www.tweetsie-railroad.com.

Blowing Rock has several places to spend the night, including the long-popular **Green Park Inn** (828–295–3141) and the newer **Meadowbrook Inn** (828–295–4300). Meadowbrook Inn has forty-six rooms and serves continental breakfast, lunch, and dinner. Web site: www.meadowbrook-inn.com. You are also just 8 miles south of Boone, a commercial resort area where you'll find lots of motels, which, though out of spirit with the off-the-beaten-path traveler, are easy and comfortable when you're tired and just need to sleep. A more romantic place, **Gideon Ridge Inn** (828–295–3644), a small inn with ten guest rooms and a fireplace, is becoming known for its cozy rustic interior and good breakfasts.

When you have more energy, save it to drive on up into **Valle Crucis,** close to Boone but totally unlike it in nature. Although the little town sees hundreds and hundreds of visitors, it manages to continue operating and looking like a small town. Its history dates back to 1780, when Samuel

Tweetsie Railroad

Hix, the first known white settler in Valle Crucis, staked a claim to 1,000 acres. Later he traded the land for a gun, a dog, and a sheepskin. Eventually it became an Episcopal mission, named Valle Crucis because three creeks came together in the shape of a cross. Today the mission serves as a retreat for many church denominations.

People stop most often at the **Mast Store,** an authentic general store listed on the National Register of Historic Places, which still sells penny candy, seeds, leather boots, Woolrich sweaters, flannel shirts, long johns, and about everything else you can think of, mostly stacked, not too neatly, along wooden shelves. The store sends out a mail-order catalog reminiscent of early L. L. Bean. The Mast General Store has a couple of other locatoins, but this is the original 1883 landmark, listed on the National Register of Historic Places as one of the best remaining examples of an old country store. Web site: www.mastgeneralstore.com.

The **Mast Farm Inn,** not associated with the store, is just outside the village on State Road 1112 (828–963–5857). It's one of the most pleasant places in the area to stay, and a night's accommodation includes breakfast. Dinner is served at small tables suited to the size of your party, and the menu is à la carte, by reservation. The owners call the food "southern gourmet." It includes sautéed shrimp, trout prepared in various ways, and such favorites as grits with sautéed shrimp and white cheddar. Of the desserts, fruit cobblers are the most popular. Mast Farm is also on the National Register of Historic Places as a restored, self-contained mountain homestead, comprising a springhouse, icehouse, washhouse, barn, blacksmith shop, gazebo, and cabin, in addition to the inn. Sleeping here is quiet and comfortable. The antiques are sparingly arranged to avoid a sense of clutter.

The Foothills

nstead of heading north from Asheville, you may choose to start east toward the foothills and the Piedmont. A drive of about forty minutes on Highway 74, heading southeast from Asheville, takes you to the little vacation community of **Lake Lure.** Everything centers on the 1,500-acre lake, which has 27 miles of shoreline. The area is surrounded by the Blue Ridge Mountains. It's in the heart of the thermal belt, where the climate is almost always a bit milder than the extremes of heat and cold in the rest of North Carolina. The temperate climate makes Lake Lure excellent for boating, fishing, hiking, and horseback riding year-round.

Sterling Stables (828–625–9009) at nearby Gerton offers rides that pass waterfalls and streams and a 25-mile view of Strawberry Gap. On weekends they also offer riding lessons and often have cookouts. The people here are known for their good humor and entertaining rides.

For hiking you have your choice of hundreds of trails. Organized hikes leave from **Chimney Rock Park** (828–625–9611 or 800–277–9611), located on U.S. Highway 64/74 in Chimney Rock, a private park with hiking trails, easier paths, and even an elevator to the top. From the top you can look down and see Lake Lure and mountains in all directions. Hickory Nut Falls, one of the highest waterfalls in the East, is on the grounds. The park is open daily from 8:30 A.M. to 7:00 P.M. from mid-April through October and from 8:30 A.M. to 6:00 P.M. November to mid-April. In bad weather the park closes. Rates vary seasonally. For simpler hiking you can ask almost any local person to recommend a favorite trail. These personal favorites are loosely kept secrets because no one wants them to become overrun with lookey-loos and littered with aluminum cans, but locals gladly share the information with anyone who cares enough to ask personally. Many climactic scenes of the film the *Last of the Mohicans,* starring Daniel Day-Lewis, were filmed at Chimney Rock. Web site: www.chimneyrockpark.com.

Bob's Marina, open every day of the week year-round, rents boats and tosses in information about the best fishing spots for free (828–625–4522).

For a more gossipy, less strenuous ride, 28-foot pontoon showboats leave every half-hour from the pier beside the beach in the center of town. The tour follows the shoreline, and the guide shows you where *Dirty Dancing* and several other movies were filmed, talks about the history of the lake, and tells stories of some strange local lore (828– 625–9323).

For total relaxation, in comfortable lodgings with good company and a spectacular view, try the *Lodge on Lake Lure* (828–625–2789 or 800–733–2785), the only lodge directly on the lake. The massive stone fireplace and lakefront dining room and porch create a quintessential country-inn atmosphere where rocking and reading seem like the most appropriate activities of the day. The lodge was originally built as a hideaway for the North Carolina Highway Patrol in the 1930s. Stories of the shenanigans of those years add to the fun of the place, as do Jack and Robin Stanier, the good-humored innkeepers. Robin's expansive breakfasts are good enough to have earned a place in several cookbooks and make you full enough to skip lunch. Web site: www.lodgeonlakelure.com.

For dinner, try the *Point of View Restaurant* (828–625–4380), which takes its name from its location on a stony point overlooking the lake. It's less than half a mile from the lodge, so you can walk to it easily. In this rustic setting the service is casual and friendly. The menu includes mountain trout, a rack of lamb specialty, seafood, and Continental-style entrees. All spirits are served. The restaurant's hours vary and the place is popular, so it's a good idea to make a reservation before you go.

From here it's an easy drive up either Highway 74A or State Road 9 to Interstate 40, where you'll find *Black Mountain,* an interesting village that was once a Cherokee Indian center and now is a thriving community specializing in all kinds of top-quality arts and crafts. The town has taken to calling itself "the front porch of western North Carolina," a name that seems to suit the peaceful but interesting atmosphere of the community.

In May and October Black Mountain sponsors the Mountain Music Festival, during which musicians play the old mountain music on dulcimers, fiddles, bagpipes, and mandolins. In August the Sourwood Festival features more music and dancing and a large arts and crafts show. These events are fun; they're also well attended, so if you have any notion of being in Black Mountain when they occur, you will need to arrange for lodging well ahead of time. The *Black Mountain Inn* (828–669–6528) is a small place at 718 Old Highway 70, Black Mountain 28711, with six guest rooms. The building was once a studio and retreat where artists and writers such as Norman Rockwell and John Steinbeck spent time. The decor is casual country, the breakfasts are buffet-style, with home-baked breads and homemade granola. Web site: www.blackmountaininn.com. The *Monte Vista Hotel* (828–669–2119 or 800–441–5400), 308 West State Street, Black Mountain 28711, has both food and lodging in a cozy environment typified by antiques, a stone fireplace, and old-time southern cooking. The hotel has thirty-six guest rooms, with hardwood floors, antiques, and chintz. The dining room serves three meals a day, featuring everything from biscuits to southern fried chicken to ambrosia.

Visiting the **Song of the Wood,** at 203 West State Street, Black Mountain 28711, a workshop and salesroom devoted to dulcimers and unusual string instruments and their music, leaves you feeling exhilarated and refreshed. Jerry Read Smith makes hammered dulcimers and the even more unusual bowed psaltery, a small triangular instrument played with a violin-type bow, similar to a medieval bowed harp. JoAnn, Jerry's sister, manages the showroom. Everything about the shop is devoted to keeping the old music alive, producing fine-quality handmade instruments and surrounding you with music.

You'll first be attracted by the music coming through outside speakers. When you get inside, they'll play lots more music for you. You may hear the music from their independent record albums, *The Strayaway Child* and *Heartdance.* The shop sells a highly personal selection of other tapes and albums, mainly hammered dulcimer music, piano music, and Celtic music. The shop is light and airy, with instruments on the walls, a fuel-efficient wood-burning stove, and a mountain rocker. You're invited to sit down and try any of the instruments or listen to the recorded music. If you're interested and ask, you can almost always manage to be shown through the workshop area and have the whole process explained to you. Open from 10:00 A.M. to 5:00 P.M. Monday through Saturday (828–669–7675).

As for shopping, the streets are lined with crafts shops, antiques shops and antiques malls, and a craft co-op. For instance, on Cherry Street, **The Seven Sisters Gallery and Shop** (828–669–5107) is notable for its fine selection of pottery, jewelry, fiber art, wood crafts, and glass art. This shop is open from 10:00 A.M. to 5:00 P.M. Monday through Saturday, 1:00 to 5:00 P.M. Sunday. On State Street, **Catawba Sunrise Gallery** (828–669–4045) has a colorful assortment of blown glass, stained glass, fused glass, jewelry, and pottery. Hours vary with days of the week. You may want to call ahead. And on Sutton Avenue the **Old Depot** (828–669–6583), a nonprofit arts and crafts center of the Swannanoa Valley, is located in the old Southern Railway Depot. The building, constructed in 1893, was turned into a crafts center in 1976. Classes, demonstrations, and crafts sales are all held here. The center is not open in winter, and hours in spring, summer, and fall may vary, so call ahead.

Sometime during your visit to Black Mountain, stop at **Mountain Bar-B-Que Restaurant** (828–669–7078) for barbecue and iced tea or one of their other items. This is a simple little place, almost incongruous in its distinctiveness, surrounded by fast-food chain eateries. In this eatery, with its red-and-white checked tablecloths, where most of the customers seem to know each other, the people who work behind the counter are friendly, and the barbecue is really good. The restaurant is open from 11:00 A.M. to 9:00 P.M. Monday through Saturday and 11:00 A.M. to 4:00 P.M. Sunday. Closed Sunday in November.

Immediately after Black Mountain, you come to *Old Fort,* an area that was still considered Cherokee Indian land for some time after white pioneers began pushing in during the mid-1770s. At the beginning of the American Revolution, General Griffith Rutherford assembled 2,500 troops to attack the Cherokees, who seemed to be siding with the British. Afterward the Indians conceded a huge portion of land, a pattern that was repeated often up to the time of the Trail of Tears in 1838. In subsequent years the Western North Carolina Railroad became important here. The *Mountain Gateway Museum* tells the story, as do the Stepp and Morgan cabins that were moved here later. The site is a branch of the North Carolina Museum of History. It's not a big, splashy place and deserves your attention for that very reason. Admission is free. Open daily from 9:00 A.M. to 5:00 P.M. and Sunday from 2:00 to 5:00 P.M. (828–668–9259). Web site: gateway@wnclink.com.

An outdoor treat in the same area is the *Catawba Falls Trail,* a special place that Eleanor Brawler wrote about for the *Charlotte Observer.* The main falls are the headwaters of the Catawba River. You'll find Catawba River Road at the Old Fort exit off Interstate 40. Follow the road through 3 miles of farmland, where you'll come to a small bridge and a private road at a tree farm. Cross the street to the right bank, walk past an old dam about a mile on, and when the path ends, cross the stream again, to the left bank. Here you should be able to hear the falls, and you'll come to a trail and then a clearing, where you'll find the waterfalls, falling from 220 feet above you. If you're hesitant about hiking into unfamiliar territory, ask in town for advice. Local people know the area.

Brawler suggests a second, shorter hike in the Falls Branch area, to see falls so little known they aren't even named. At Marion go north from Interstate 40 on Highway 221/226, crossing the Catawba River and passing the River Breeze Restaurant. Drive 5½ miles after crossing the river. Turn left at the Woodlawn Motel and continue on 0.8 mile. The paved road ends. Bear left at the fork on a dirt road far enough to park. At the little bridge you'll find a trail to the right that wanders through the rhododendrons beside a mountain stream. At the next fork bear left again to see the falls. The area is also rich in wildflowers.

After these adventures return to Interstate 40 and drive on to where Highway 226 intersects Interstate 40 at Glenwood. From here, you can enjoy a beautifully scenic drive to Polkville while you also enjoy a good brisk sit. This is one of the prettiest drives in the state.

From Polkville you might want to take a quick drive north on Highway 10 into the little village of **Casar**—pronounced *KAYser,* population about 340. It's a place you'd never know about unless someone told you. Elizabeth Sturgeon, a woman well under fifty who was raised here, remembers every quaint detail. The people who founded the town meant to call it "Caesar," but somehow they got the spelling wrong, and it's been Casar ever since. Until recently, all the major roads were dirt; even today they are not all paved. When the roads came into the center of this little spot, a stop sign stood—most of the time. Every Saturday night one old gentleman who didn't navigate too well when he was in his cups (homemade 'shine—it was a dry area) ran into it and knocked it down. Every Monday morning, someone put it up again.

Even into our high-tech age, Casar has been a place where electricity, telephones, and indoor plumbing were frills, luxuries nobody wanted. Hamburgers and hot dogs were unknown. Today, Elizabeth estimates, 95 percent of the people have power and plumbing. You still could have trouble over the hamburgers and hot dogs with the older folks.

In the center of town you can see what used to be Tom Hoyle's grocery store, where he accepted eggs and chickens in payment for flour and other merchandise.

The school used to serve grades one through twelve and have a phenomenal basketball team. School started early in the season and closed for six weeks during cotton-picking time because all the children, generally ten to twelve to a family, were needed to work in the fields you see around the school. Elizabeth still has her cotton-picking sack. If you look behind the school, you can find the place on the bank where the kids ran down to the store to buy penny suckers with coconut in them.

Elizabeth doesn't live in Casar any more, but she goes back often and finds it only a little changed—more modern in its technology, but the same warm little place as far as its people go. Park your car and walk around awhile. Elizabeth says, "You might get looked at, but somebody will come to see if you need help."

Somehow, Art Linkletter found out about this area and started a golf resort called **Pine Mountain Lake** about 7 miles on toward Morganton.

Certainly you could get a hamburger in the restaurant there, but the resort hasn't tainted Casar one bit.

When you return to **Polkville,** pick up Highway 182 to Lincolnton and then Highway 150 on to Mooresville, a town of about 9,000 people, where you can find the necessities of traveling in a congenial environment. Shortly after you pass through Mooresville, still on Highway 150, you'll come to **Carrigan Farms,** a place worth visiting any time of year. By the road in front of rows of greenhouses in a large shelter, you can buy asparagus and hanging baskets in April, strawberries in May and June, fresh vegetables all summer, cider and pumpkins in October, and poinsettias in November and December. Growing produce and plants, with twenty-five people employed, this farm is the effort of Doug and Susan Carrigan, Doug's parents, and his grandparents. Yet this is more than a family farm; it's a farm involved in the community in ways that make you feel good, even though you live somewhere else. For instance, the walls are covered with letters and drawings from school kids who've visited the farm.

> Dear Susan and Doug,
>
> Susan, we liked the hayride.
>
> We also liked the way the cow thought your finger was a bottle.
>
> Doug, we liked the way you showed us the honey bees.
>
> We had fun.
>
> Love,
>
> Matthew
>
> Adam
>
> Karen
>
> Michael

Hang around to talk with the people, breathe the clear country air, and pick up whatever is in season. If you call ahead at the right time of year, you can probably even arrange a hayride (828–664–1450).

PLACES TO STAY IN THE MOUNTAINS

ASHEVILLE

Best Western
Asheville Central
22 Woodfin Street
Asheville 28805
(828) 253–1851

Comfort Inn
800 Fairview Road
Asheville 28803
(828) 298–9141

Courtyard by Marriott
1 Buckstone Place
Asheville 28805
(828) 281–0041

Days Inn North
3 Reynolds
Mountain Boulevard
Asheville 28804
(828) 645–9191

Flint Street Inns
116 Flint Street
Asheville 28801
(828) 253–6723

Grove Park Inn Resort
290 Macon Avenue
Asheville 28804
(828) 252–2711

Richmond Hill Inn
87 Richmond Hill Drive
Asheville 28806
(828) 252–7313
(888) 742–4553

BLACK MOUNTAIN

Comfort Inn
585 Highway 9
Black Mountain 28711
(828) 669–9950

BLOWING ROCK

Blowing Rock Inn
788 North Main Street
Blowing Rock 28605
(828) 295–7921

Brookside Inn
U.S. Highway 321 Bypass
Blowing Rock 28605
(828) 295–3380

Days Inn
U.S. Highway 321 Bypass
Blowing Rock 28605
(828) 295–4422

BOONE

Hampton Inn
1075 Highway 105
Boone 28607
(828) 264–0077
(800) 888–6867

High Country Inn
1785 Highway 105
Boone 28607
(828) 264–1000
(800) 334–5605

Lovill House Inn
404 Old Bristol Road
Boone 28607
(828) 264–4204
(800) 849–9466

The Mountains Web Sites:

Asheville:
Biltmore Estate
www.biltmore.com

Bryson City
www.greatsmokies.com

Cherokee City
www.cherokeecountycc©grove.com

Nantahala Outdoor Center
www.nocweb.com

Oconaluftee Indian Village
www.inet.net/-cheratt

Smoky Mountain Host of North Carolina
www.smokymtnhost.com

Waynesville
www.smokymountains.com

BRYSON CITY
Hemlock Inn
Off U.S. Highway 19
Bryson City 28713
(828) 488–2886

CHEROKEE
Best Western
Great Smokies Inn
Acquonia Road
Cherokee 28719
(828) 497–2020

Comfort Inn
Junction of
Highways 19 and 441
Cherokee 28719
(828) 497–2411

FLAT ROCK
Highland Lake Inn
Highland Lake Drive
Flat Rock 28731
(828) 693–6812
(800) 762–1376

LAKE LURE
Lake Lure Inn
Highway 74/64A
Lake Lure 28746
(828) 625–2525
(800) 277–5873

WAYNESVILLE
Best Western
Smoky Mountain Inn
330 Hyatt Road
Waynesville 28786
(828) 456–4402

Grandview Lodge
466 Lickstone Road
Waynesville 28786
(828) 456–5212
(800) 255–7826

**PLACES TO EAT IN
THE MOUNTAINS**

ASHEVILLE
Tassels Tea Room
25 Rankin Avenue
Asheville 28802
(828) 252–6082

Mountain Smoke House
802 Fairview Road
Asheville 28803
(828) 298–8121

Blue Moon Bakery
60 Biltmore Avenue
Asheville 28801
(828) 252–6063

Gabrielle's at
Richmond Hill
87 Richmond Hill Drive
Asheville 28806
(828) 252–7313

BLOWING ROCK
Blowing Rock Cafe
Highway 321 at
Sunset Drive
Blowing Rock 28605
(828) 295–9474

Woodlands BBQ
Highway 321 Bypass
from Sunset Drive
Blowing Rock 28605
(828) 295–3651

BOONE
Mel's Diner
1286 Highway 102
Boone 28607
(828) 265–1344

PICCADELI
2161 Blowing Rock Road
Boone 28607
(828) 262–3500

BRYSON CITY
Randolph House
Bryson City 28713
(828) 488–3472

Hemlock Inn
1 mile east of Bryson City,
off Highway 19
Bryson City 28713
(828) 488–2885

Nantahala Village
9400 Highway 19 West
Bryson City 28713
(828) 488–2826
(800) 438–1507

FLAT ROCK
Highland Lake Inn
Highland Lake Drive
Flat Rock 28731
(828) 639–6812
(800) 762–1376

LAKE LURE
Jimmy's Original
Bay Tavern
Highway 64/74A
Lake Lure 28746
(828) 625–4075

Point of View Restaurant
Highway 64/74A
Lake Lure 28746
(828) 625–4380

Lake Lure Inn
Highway 64/74A
Lake Lure 28746
(828) 625–2525
(800) 277–5873

SALUDA
Wildflour Bakery
21 Main Street
Saluda 28773
(828) 749–9224

TRYON
Pine Crest Inn
Dining Room
200 Pine Crest Lane
Tryon 28782
(828) 859–9135

WAYNESVILLE
Grandview Lodge
466 Lickstone Road
Waynesville 28786
(828) 456–5212

Maggie's Galley III
22 Howell Mill Road
Waynesville 28786
(828) 456–8945

Old Stone Inn
900 Dolan Road
Waynesville 28786
(800) 432–8499

General Index

Entries for Inns, Bed and Breakfasts, and Potteries will appear in the special indexes beginning on page 172.

A

A.E. Stevens House, 11
African-American Cultural
    Complex, 63
Alan Holden Realty, 10
Alligator River Refuge, 53
American Classic Motorcycle
    Company and Museum, 79
Andy Griffith Museum, 109
Angela Peterson Doll and
    Miniature Museum, 98
Arts and Crafts Center, 107
Artspace, 64
Asheboro, 79
Asheville, 143
Atlantic, 31
Atrium Cafe, 101
Attmore-Oliver House Museum, 36
Aurora Fossil Museum, 39
Ava Gardner Museum, 69

B

Back Porch, 43
Baker Furniture Factory Clearance
    Store, 117
Baker's Dozen, 117
Bank of the Arts, 37
Bath, 46
Becks, 3
Beaufort, 25
Beaufort Historic Site Tours, 27
Belhaven, 88
B. Everett Jordan Lake, 74
Biltmore Estate, 144
Biltmore Estate Winery, 144
Biltmore-Greensboro Hotel, 89
Bird Island, 8

Blackbeard, 42, 53
Black Mountain, 159
Blowing Rock, 156
Blue Moon Bakery, 147
Blue Ridge Parkway, 133
Bob's Bar-B-Que, 67
Bob's Marina, 158
Bob Timberlake Gallery, 96
Bodie Island Lighthouse, 49
Botanical Gardens at Asheville, 147
Broad Street Restaurant & Pub, 55
Brunches Restaurant, 40
Brunswick Town State Historic
    Site, 13
Burwell School Historic Site, 77

C

Calabash, 1
Camp Lejeune Marine Base, 22
Cannon Village at Kannapolis, 115
Cannon Village Visitor Center
    and Museum, 117
Cape Fear Coast Convention
    and Visitors Bureau, 20
Cape Fear River, 11
Cape Hatteras Lighthouse, 49
Cape Lookout Tours, 29
Captain Ben's Restaurant, 43
Captain Jim's Marina, 4
Captain Nance's Seafood
    Restaurant, 3
Captain Perry Barrow's
    Ferry Service, 29
Carl Sandburg Home National
    Historic Site, 151
Carolina Interiors, 117
Carolina Maid, 119

INDEX

Inns, Bed-and-Breakfasts

Potteries

About the Author

Sara Pitzer has been writing about people, places, and food in North Carolina and the South for fifteen years. She lives in a house in the woods in the central Piedmont area and works as a reporter for a local newspaper.